3RD
FLOOR
Science
Computer
Lab.

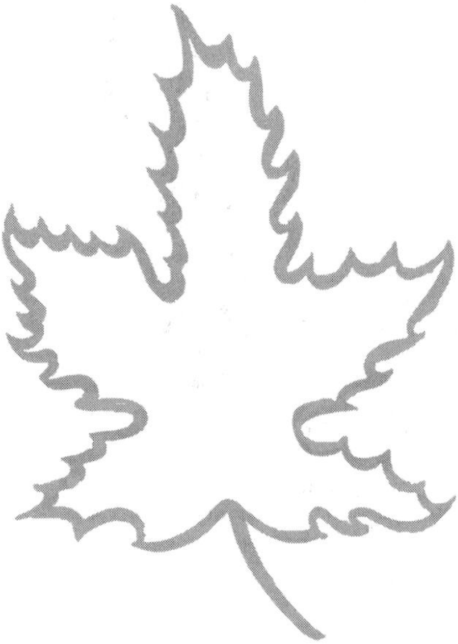

Other books by Jeff Lemire

Essex County Vol. 1: Tales From The Farm
Essex County Vol. 2: Ghost Stories
Lost Dogs

ISBN 978-1-891830-95-2
1. Farm Life
2. Graphic Novels

Essex County Volume 3: The Country Nurse © 2008 Jeff Lemire. Edited by Chris Staros. Published by Top Shelf Productions, PO Box 1282, Marietta, GA 30061-1282, USA. Publishers: Brett Warnock and Chris Staros. Top Shelf Productions® and the Top Shelf logo are registered trademarks of Top Shelf Productions, Inc. Visit our online catalog at www.topshelfcomix.com.

Visit Jeff Lemire at www.jefflemire.com/.

First Printing, October 2008. Printed in Canada.

ESSEX COUNTY VOL.3:
THE COUNTRY NURSE

BY JEFF LEMIRE

Top Shelf Productions
Atlanta / Portland

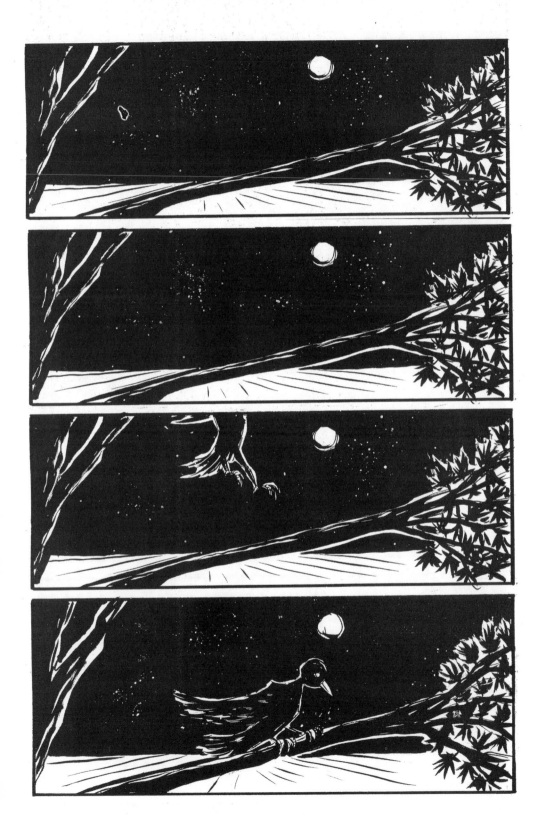

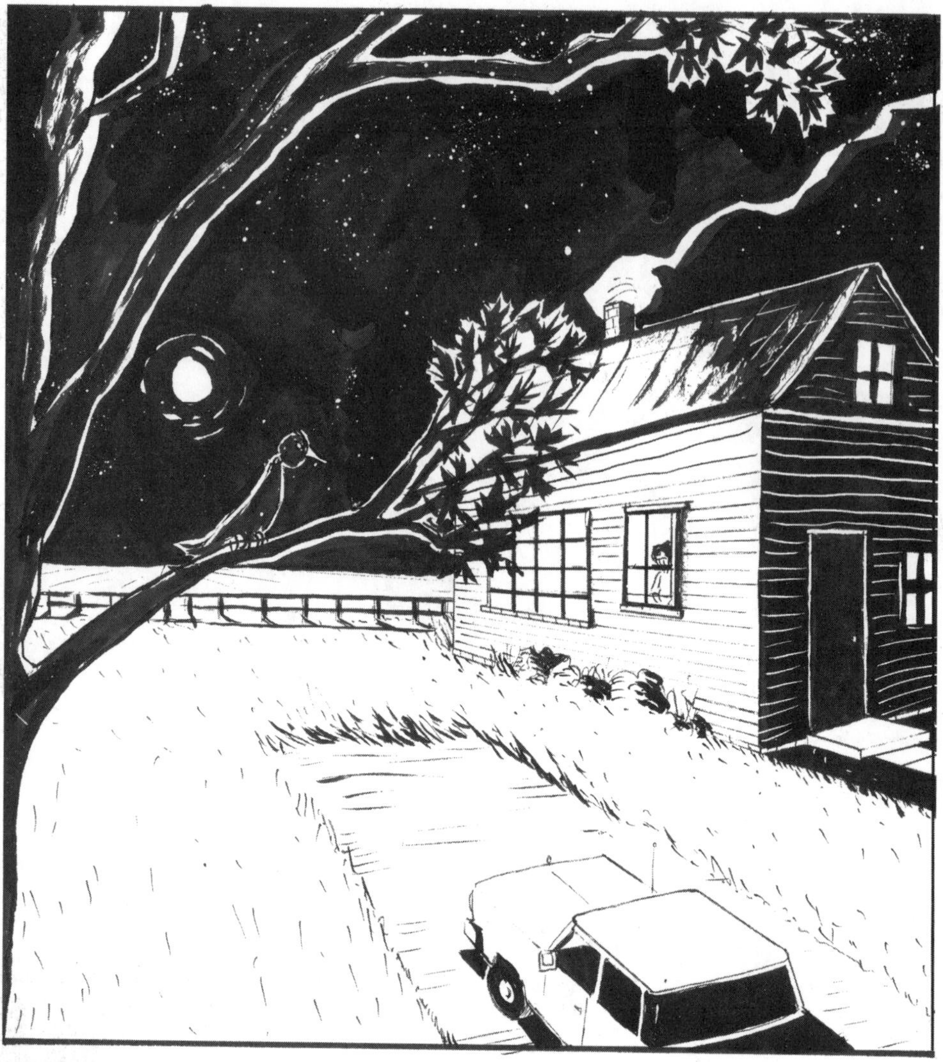

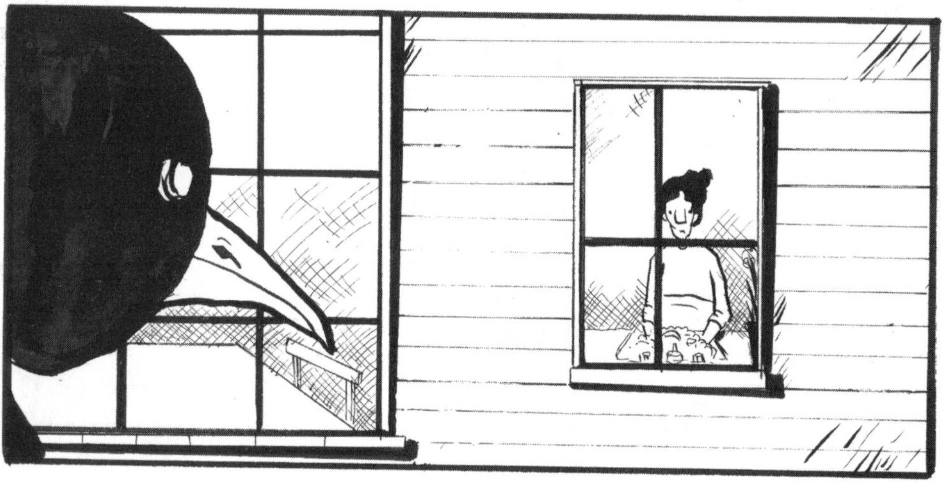

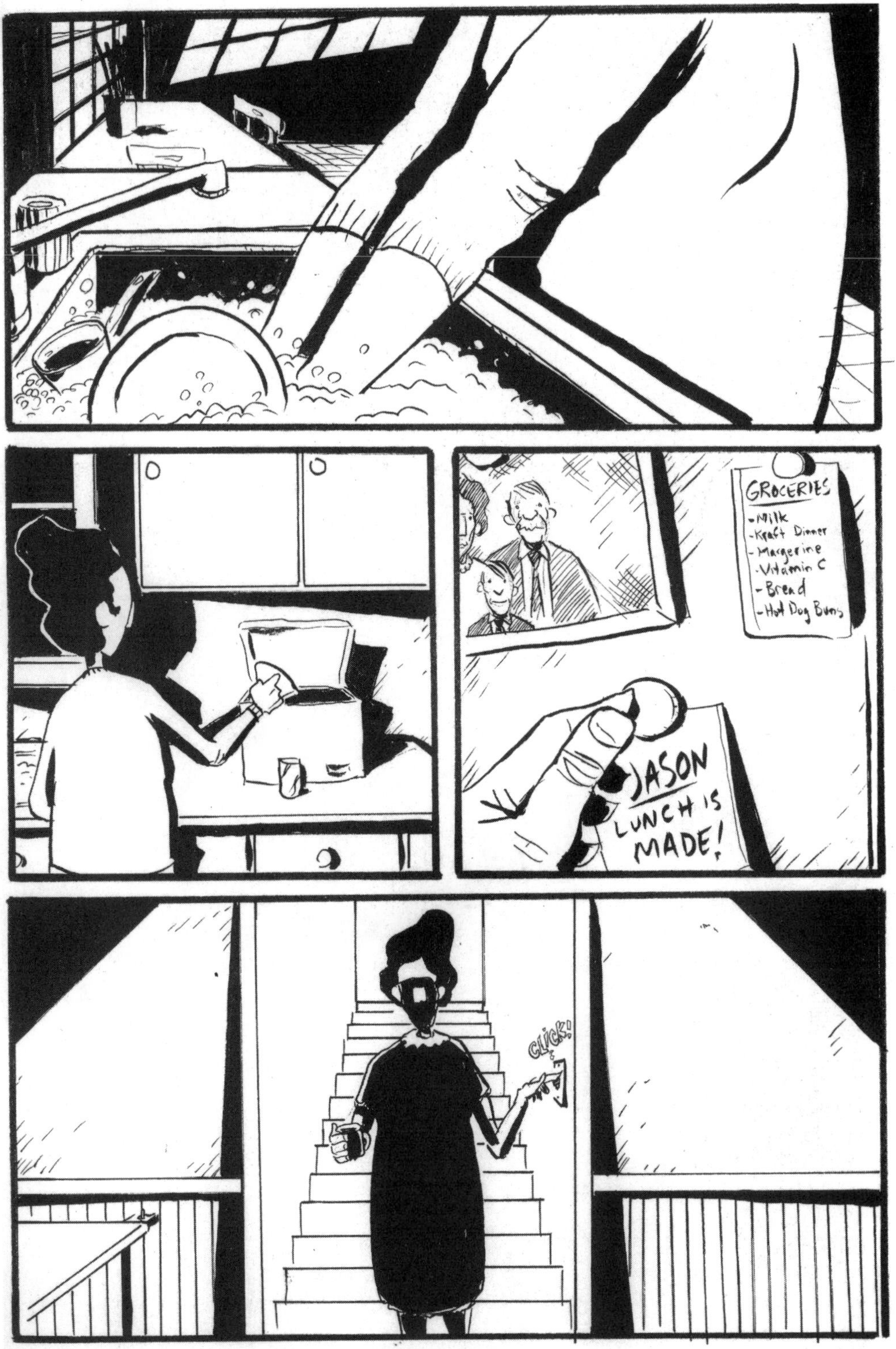
GROCERIES
-Milk
-Kraft Dinner
-Margerine
-Vitamin C
-Bread
-Hot Dog Buns
JASON
LUNCH IS
MADE!
CLICK!

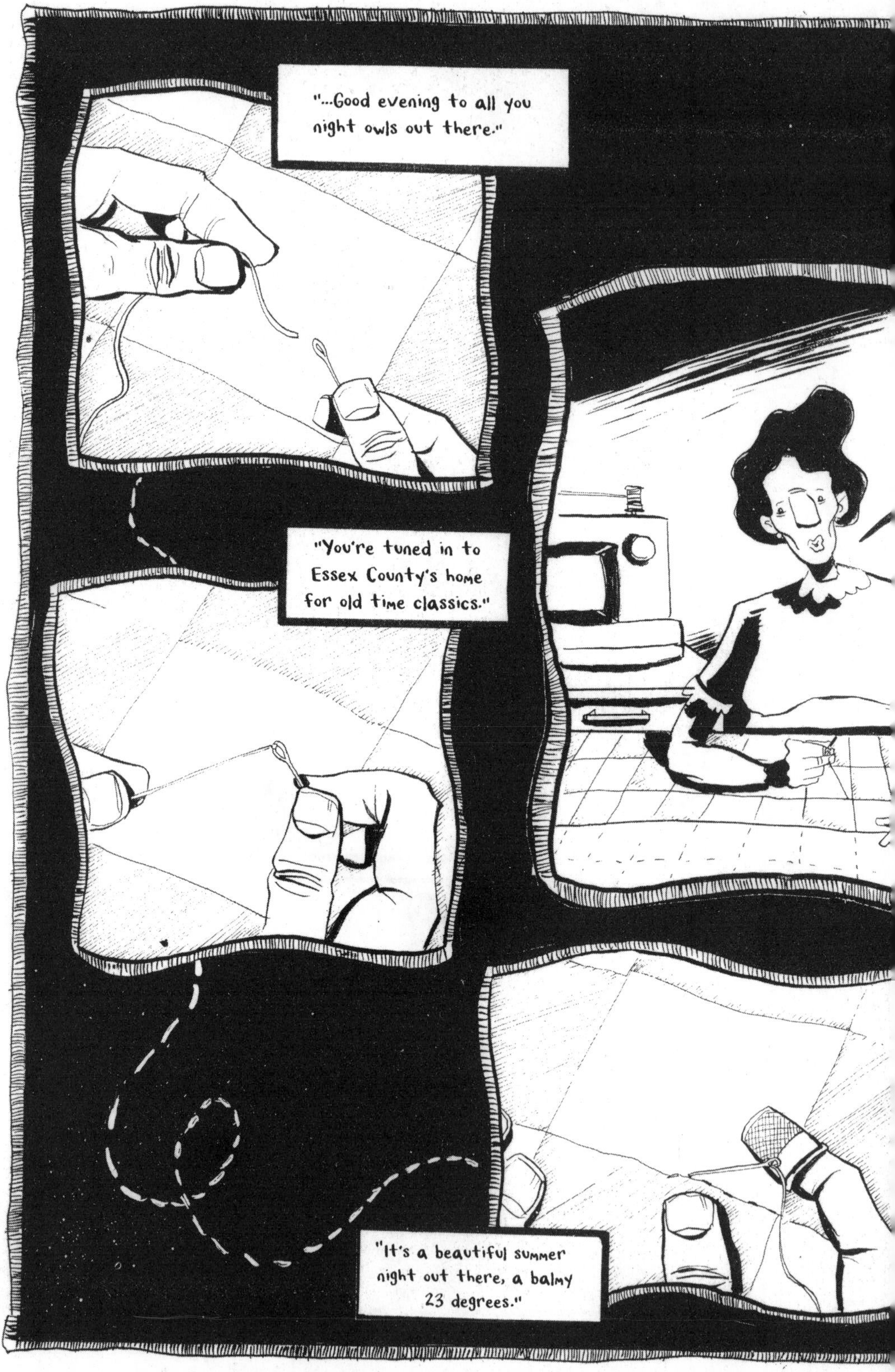
"...Good evening to all you night owls out there."
"You're tuned in to Essex County's home for old time classics."
"It's a beautiful summer night out there, a balmy 23 degrees."

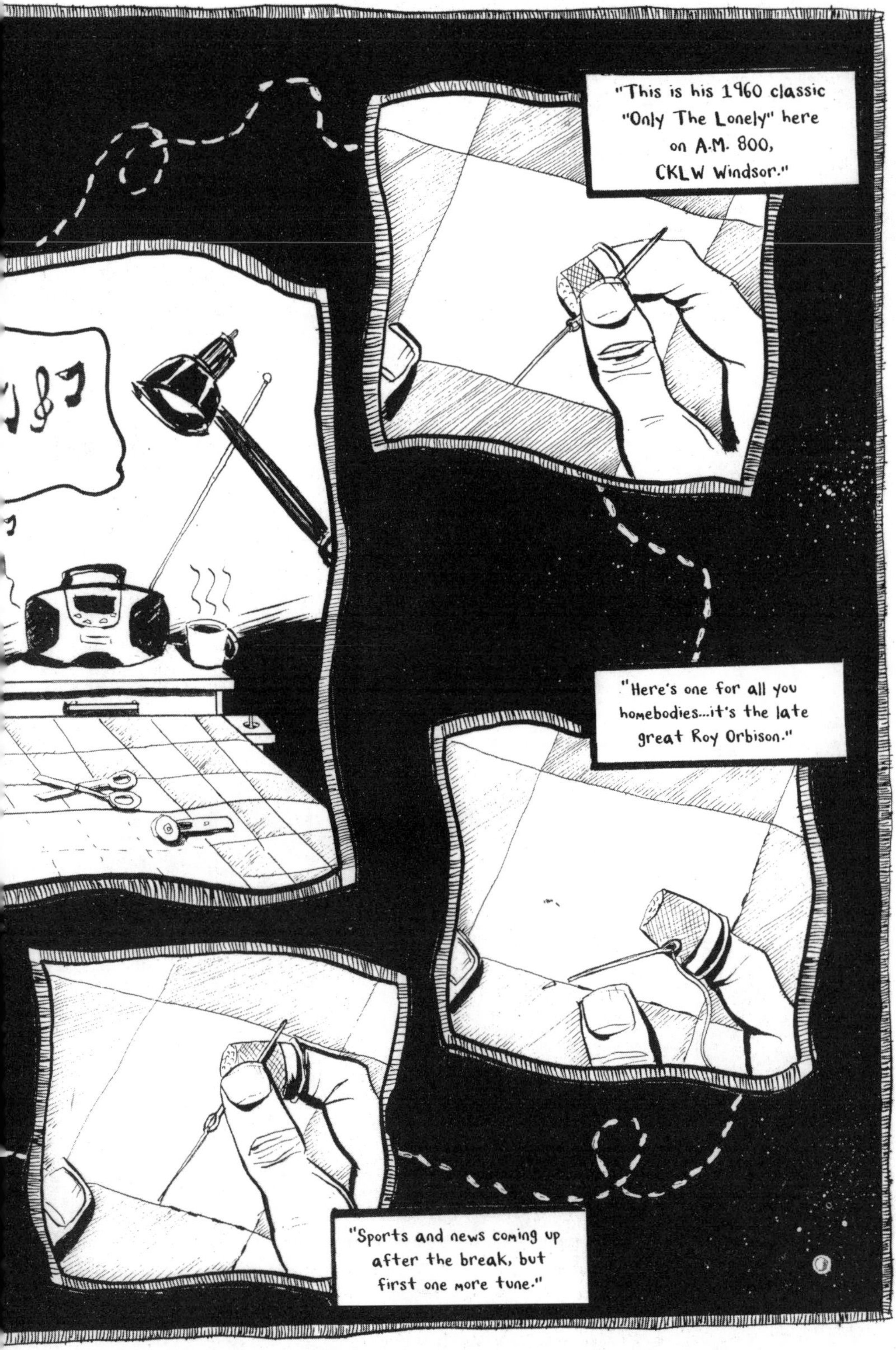
"This is his 1960 classic "Only The Lonely" here on A.M. 800, CKLW Windsor."
"Here's one for all you homebodies...it's the late great Roy Orbison."
"Sports and news coming up after the break, but first one more tune."

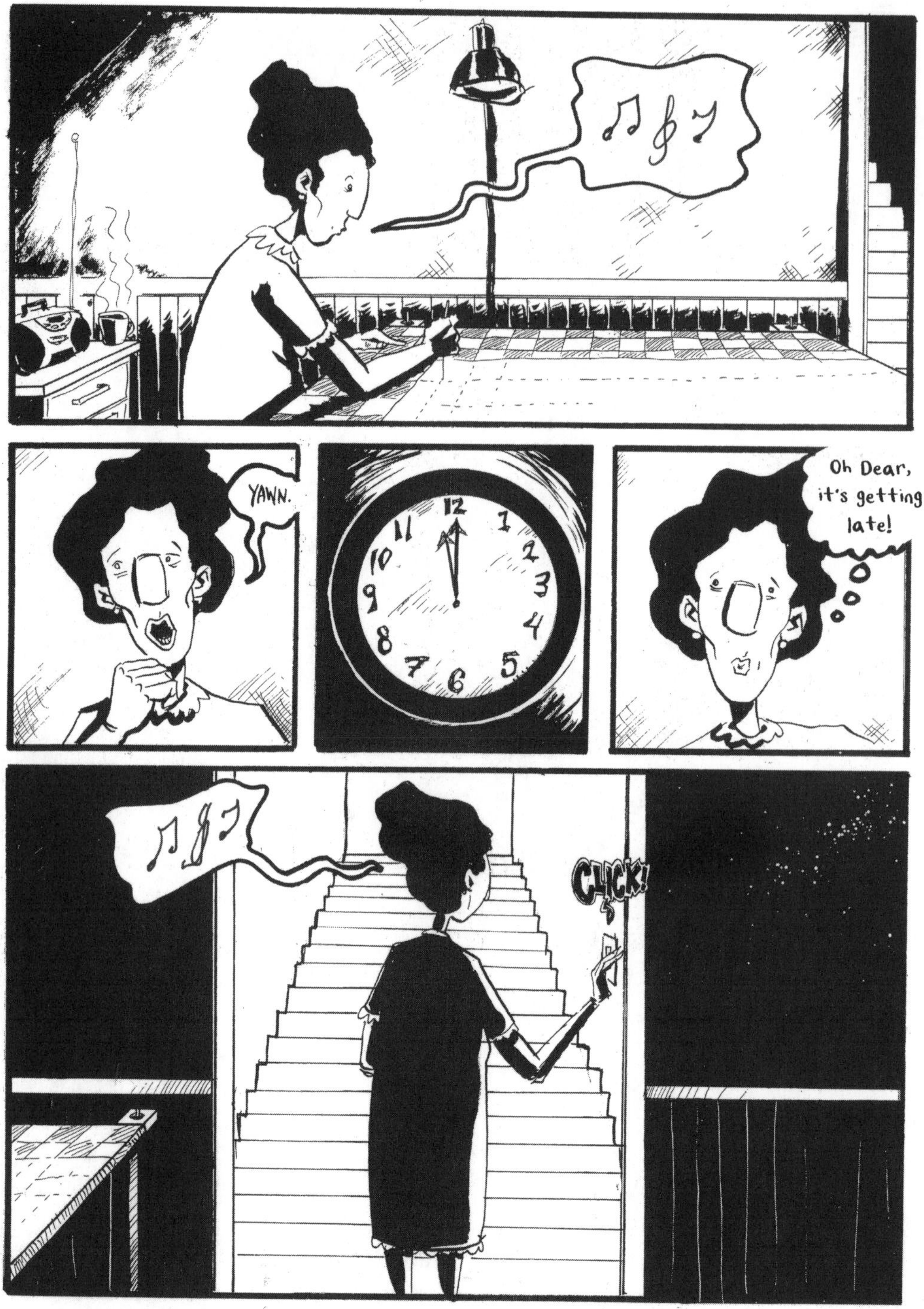
YAWN.
Oh Dear, it's getting late!
CLICK!

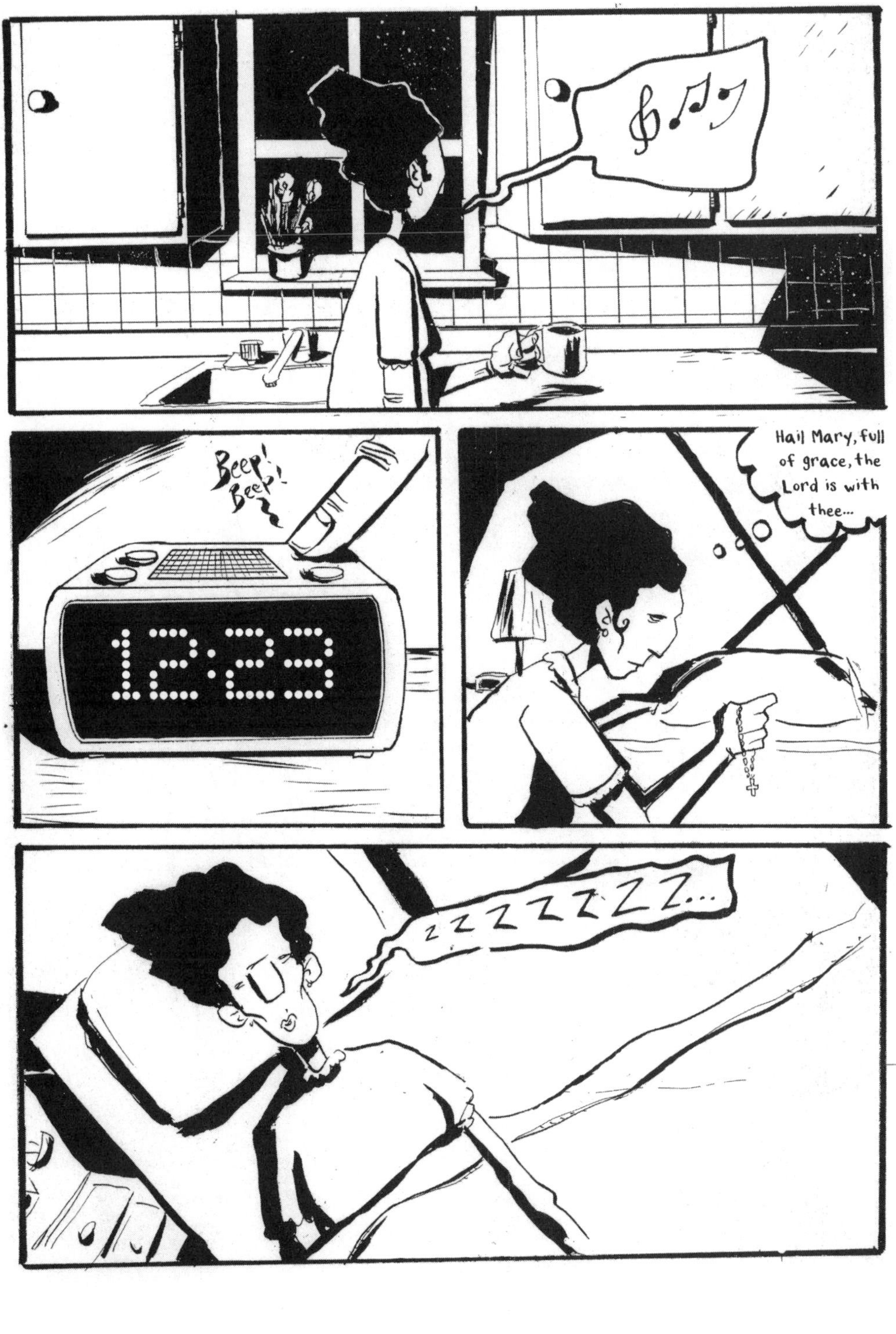
Beep! Beep!
12:23
Hail Mary, full of grace, the Lord is with thee...
zzzzzzzZZ...

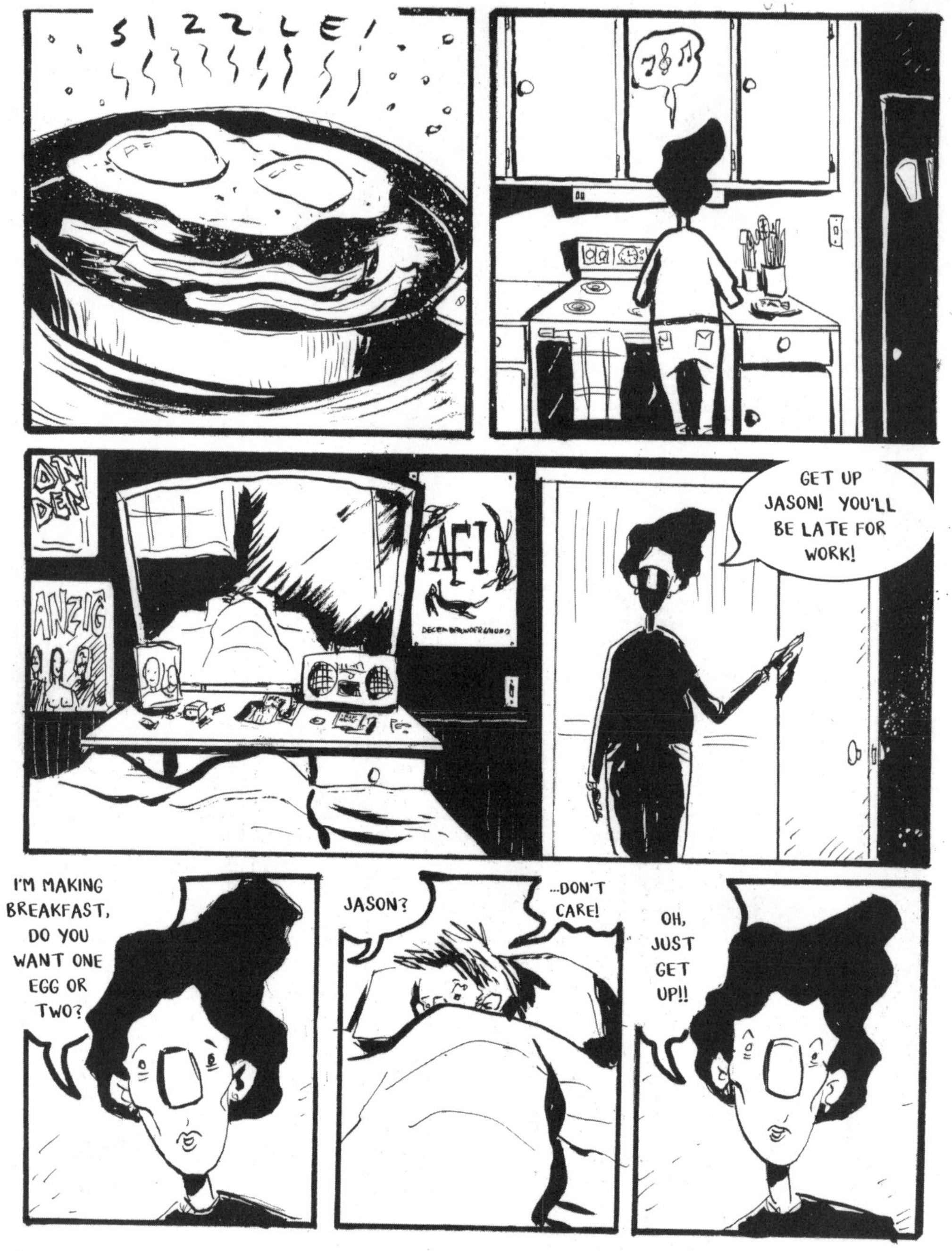
SIZZLE!
GET UP JASON! YOU'LL BE LATE FOR WORK!
I'M MAKING BREAKFAST, DO YOU WANT ONE EGG OR TWO?
JASON?
...DON'T CARE!
OH, JUST GET UP!!

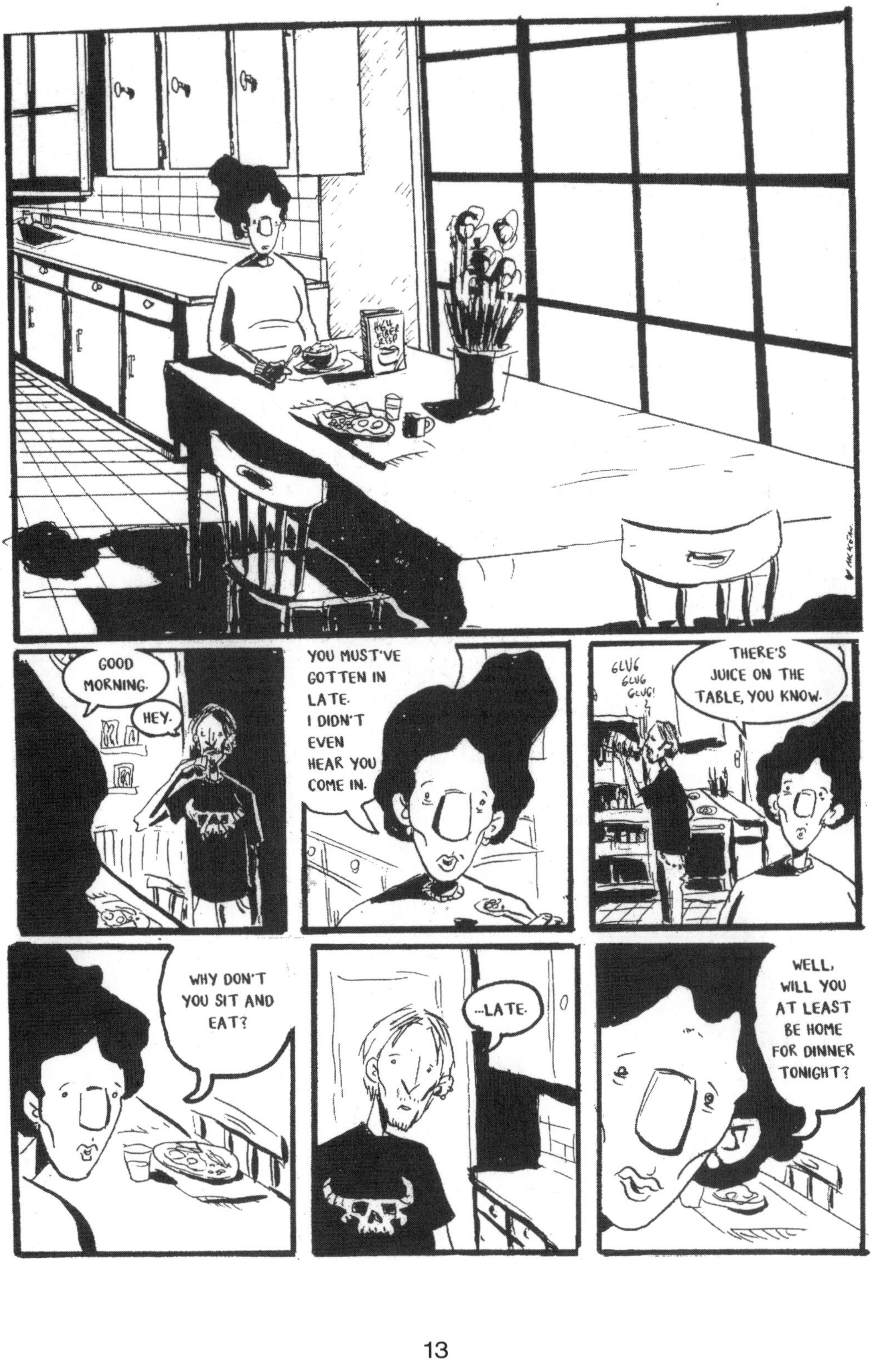
GOOD MORNING.
HEY.
YOU MUST'VE GOTTEN IN LATE. I DIDN'T EVEN HEAR YOU COME IN.
GLUG GLUG GLUG!
THERE'S JUICE ON THE TABLE, YOU KNOW.
WHY DON'T YOU SIT AND EAT?
...LATE.
WELL, WILL YOU AT LEAST BE HOME FOR DINNER TONIGHT?

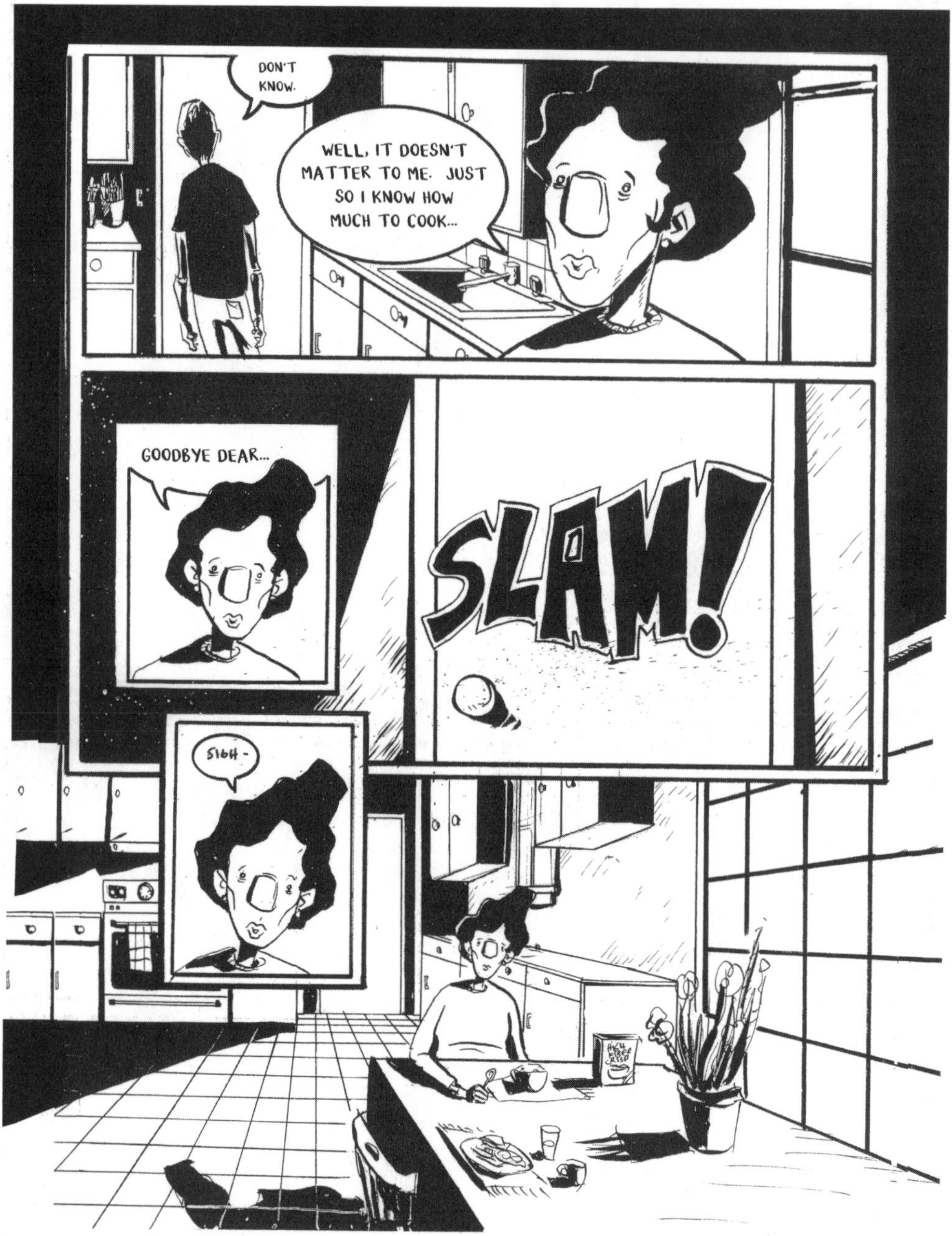
DON'T KNOW.
WELL, IT DOESN'T MATTER TO ME. JUST SO I KNOW HOW MUCH TO COOK...
GOODBYE DEAR...
SLAM!
SIGH -

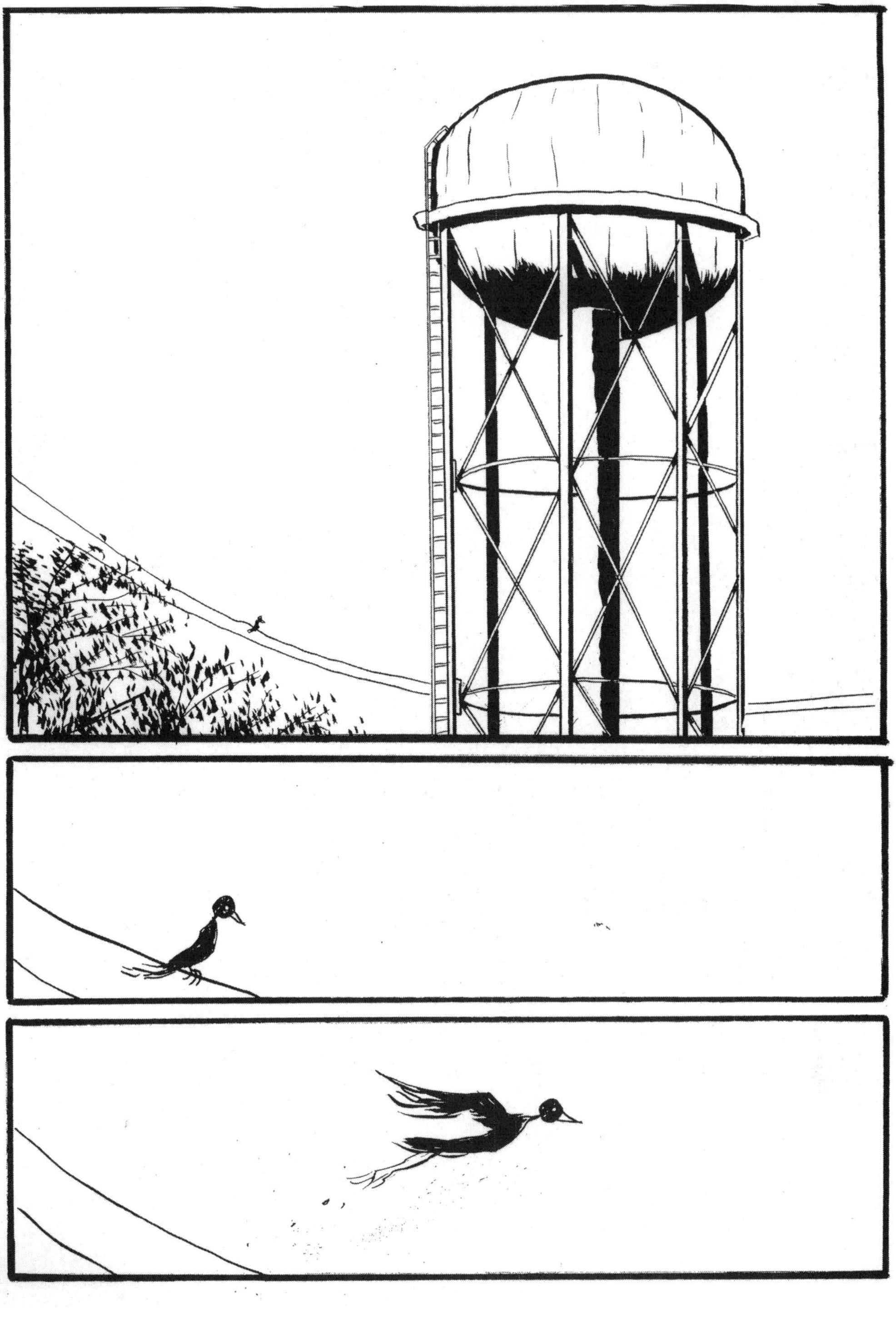

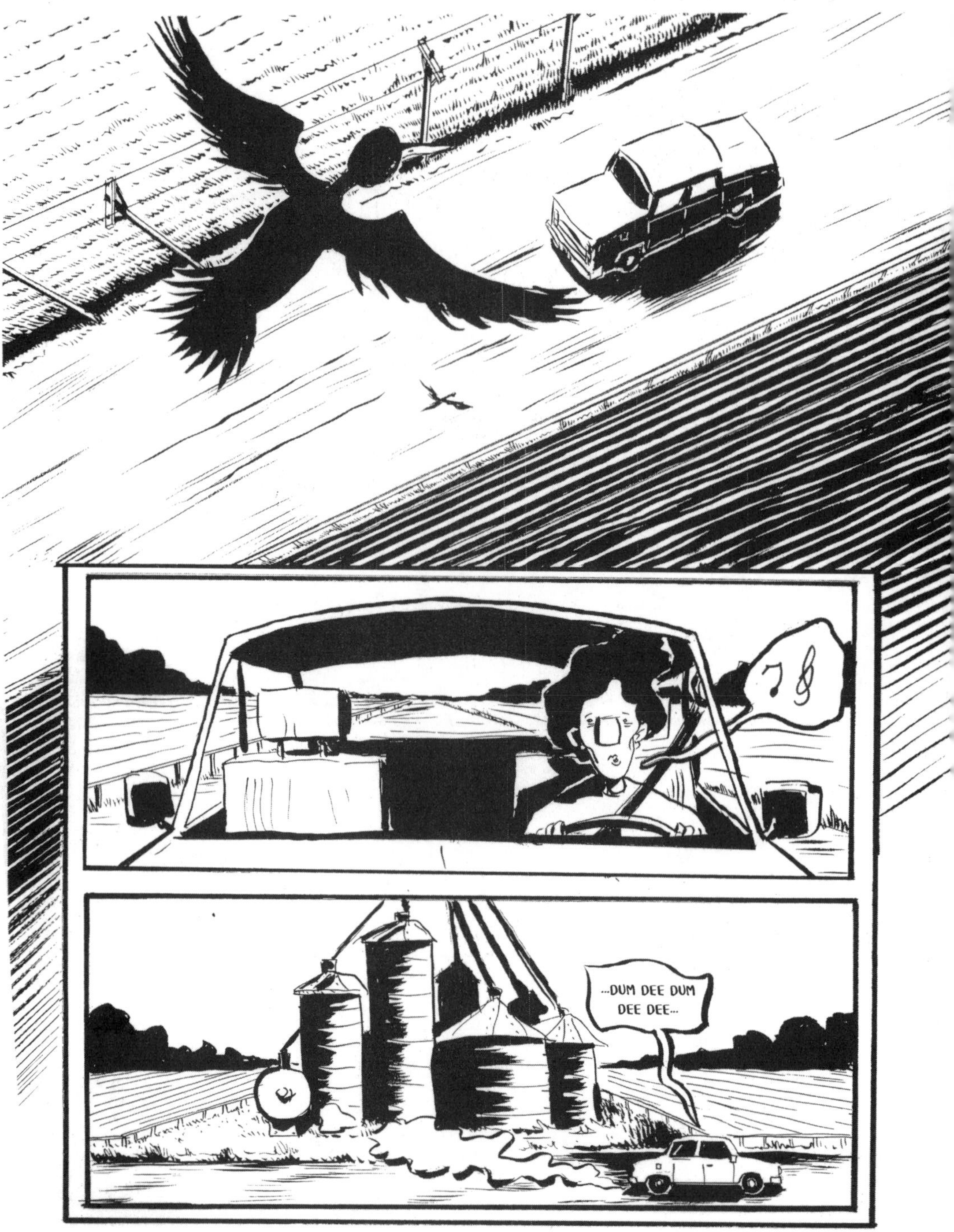
...DUM DEE DUM DEE DEE...

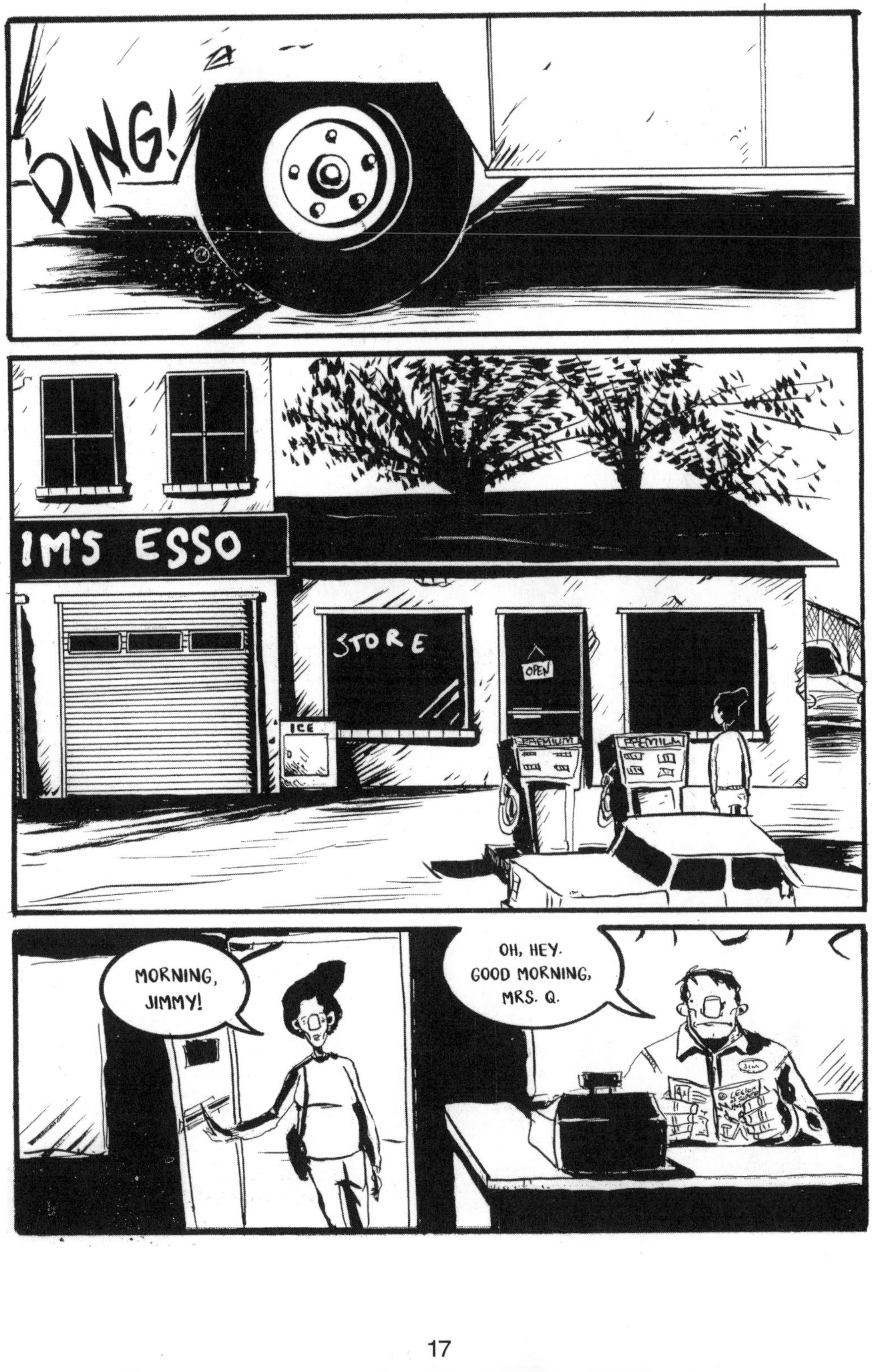
DING!
IM'S ESSO
STORE
OPEN
ICE
PREMIUM
PREMIUM
MORNING, JIMMY!
OH, HEY. GOOD MORNING, MRS. Q.
JIM

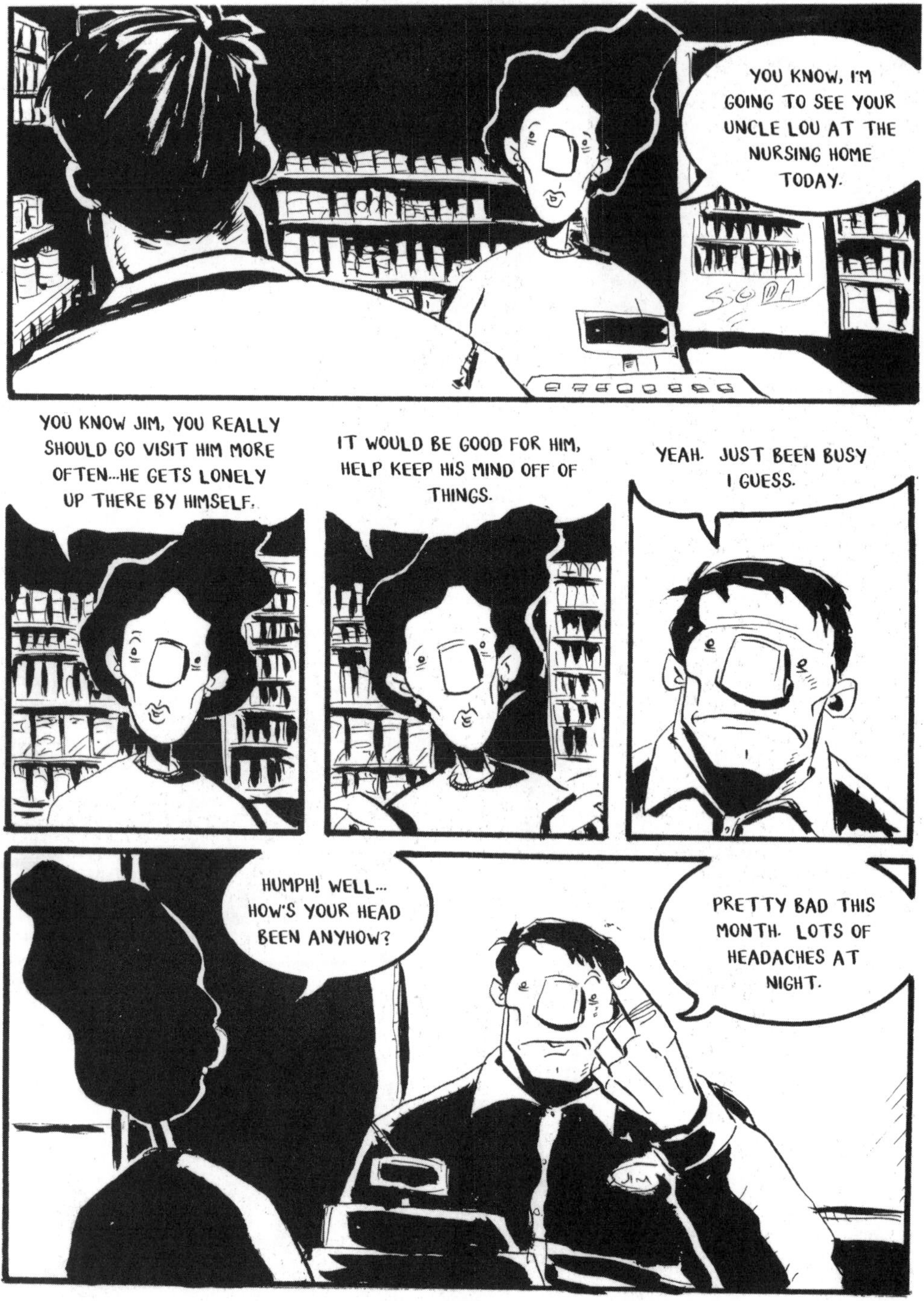
YOU KNOW, I'M GOING TO SEE YOUR UNCLE LOU AT THE NURSING HOME TODAY.
SODA
YOU KNOW JIM, YOU REALLY SHOULD GO VISIT HIM MORE OFTEN...HE GETS LONELY UP THERE BY HIMSELF.
IT WOULD BE GOOD FOR HIM, HELP KEEP HIS MIND OFF OF THINGS.
YEAH. JUST BEEN BUSY I GUESS.
HUMPH! WELL... HOW'S YOUR HEAD BEEN ANYHOW?
PRETTY BAD THIS MONTH. LOTS OF HEADACHES AT NIGHT.
JIM

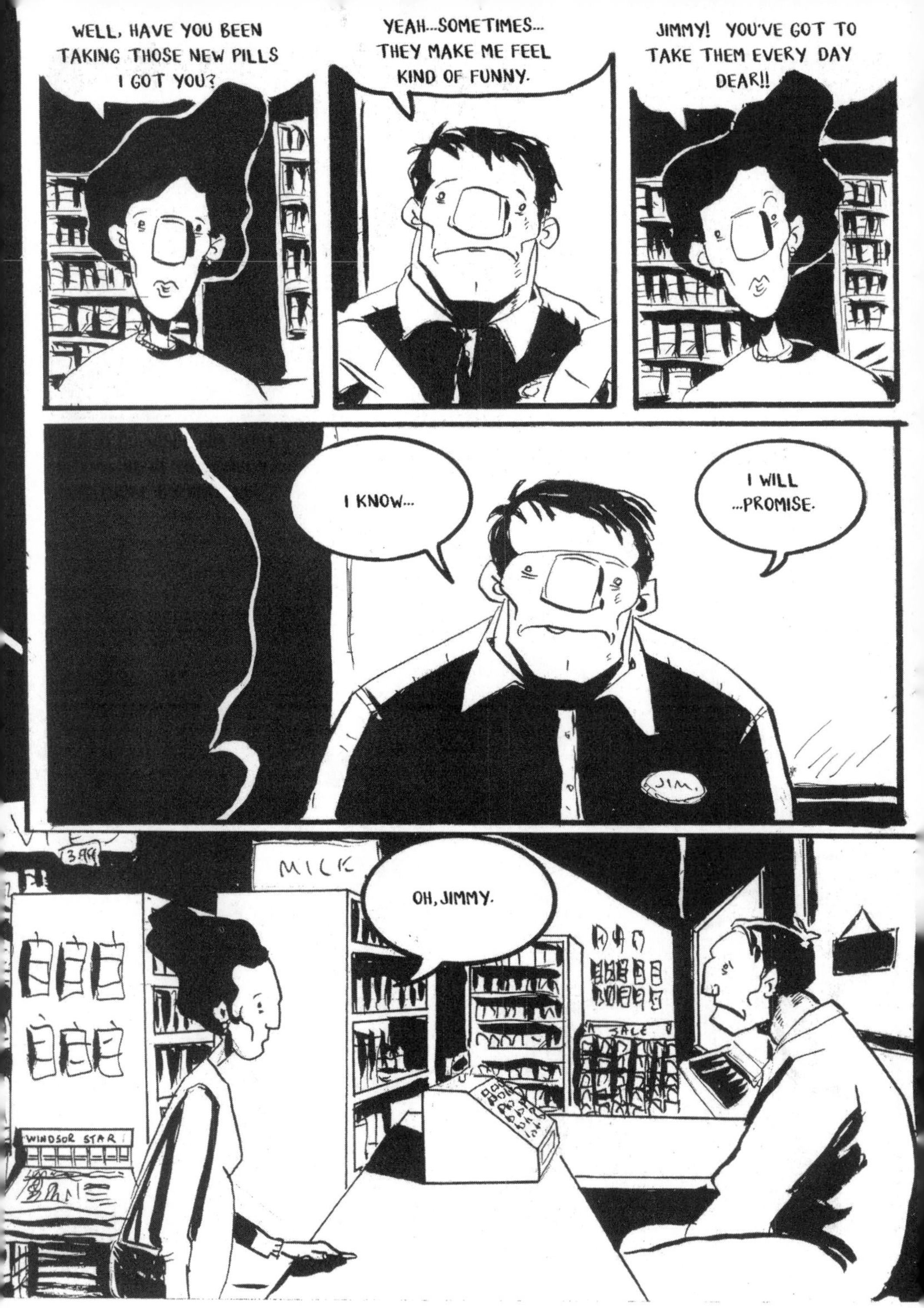
WELL, HAVE YOU BEEN TAKING THOSE NEW PILLS I GOT YOU?
YEAH...SOMETIMES... THEY MAKE ME FEEL KIND OF FUNNY.
JIMMY! YOU'VE GOT TO TAKE THEM EVERY DAY DEAR!!
I KNOW...
I WILL ...PROMISE.
JIM.
MILK
OH, JIMMY.
SALE
WINDSOR STAR

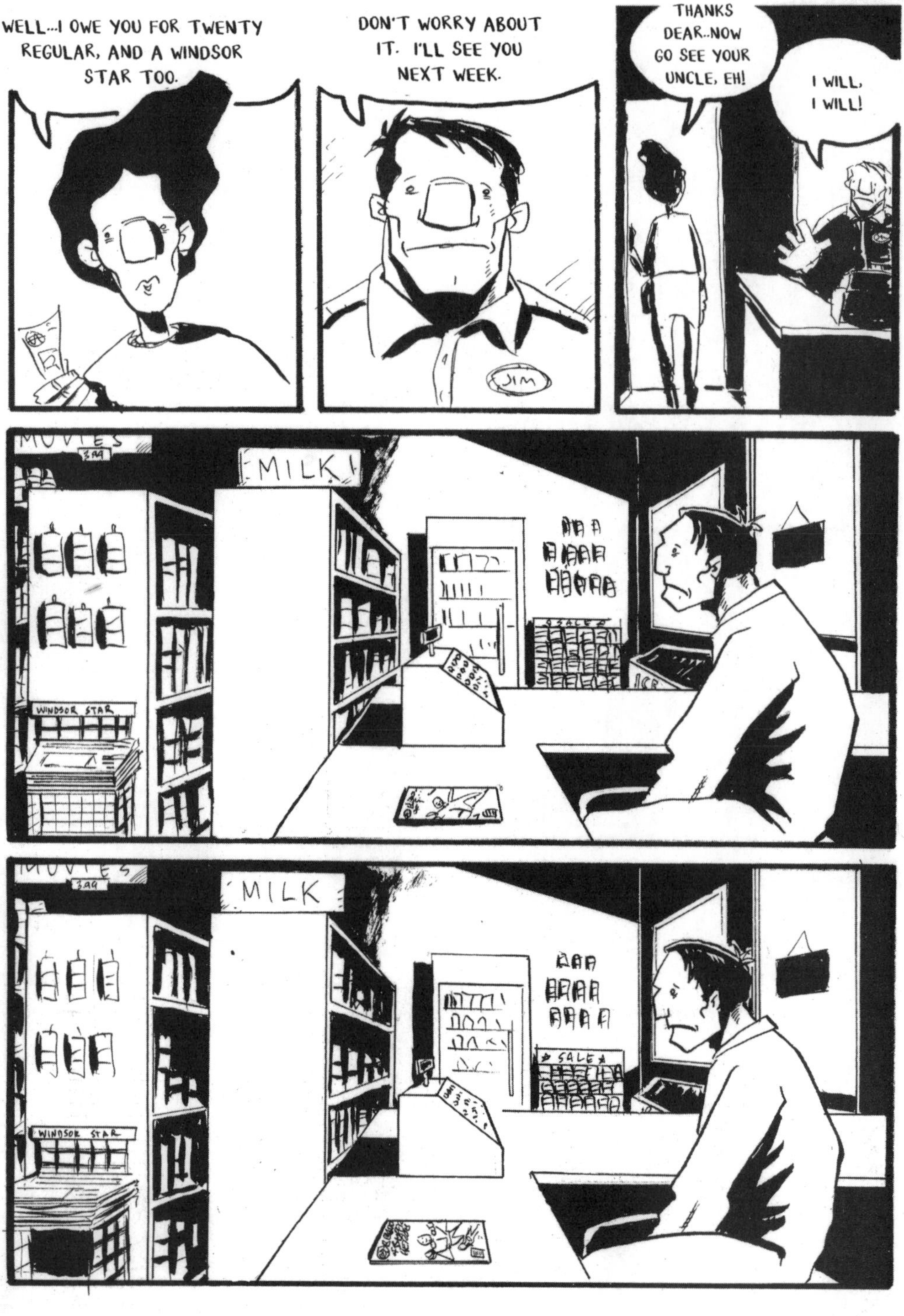
WELL...I OWE YOU FOR TWENTY REGULAR, AND A WINDSOR STAR TOO.
DON'T WORRY ABOUT IT. I'LL SEE YOU NEXT WEEK.
JIM
THANKS DEAR..NOW GO SEE YOUR UNCLE, EH!
I WILL, I WILL!
MOVIES
MILK
WINDSOR STAR
SALE
MOVIES
MILK
WINDSOR STAR
SALE

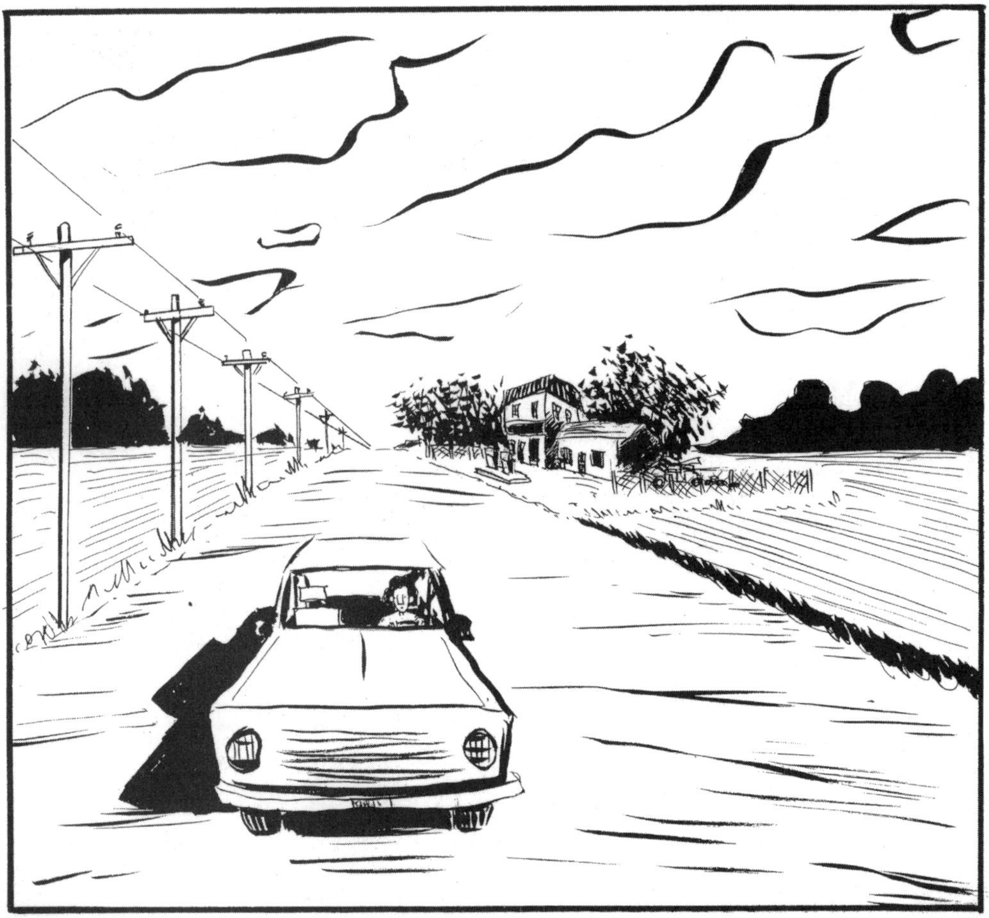

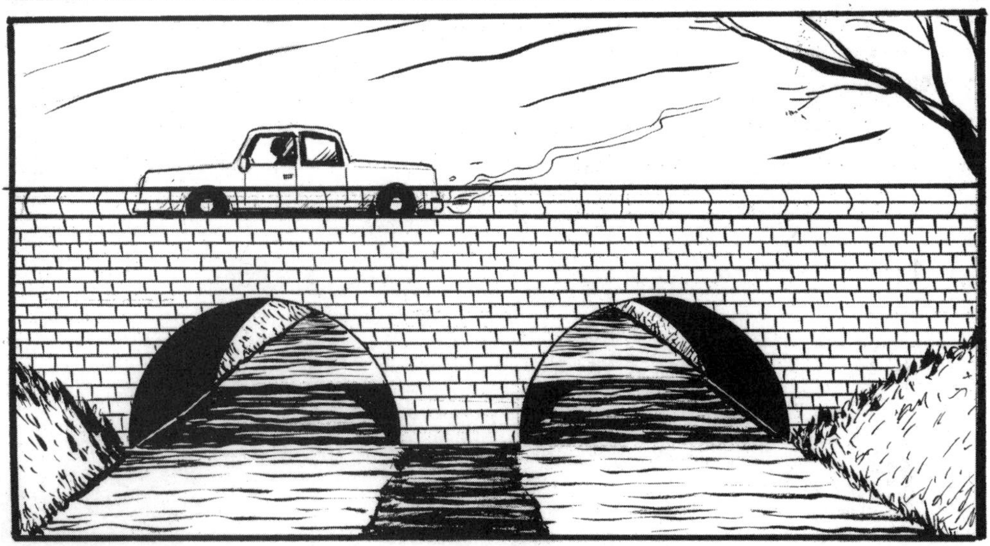

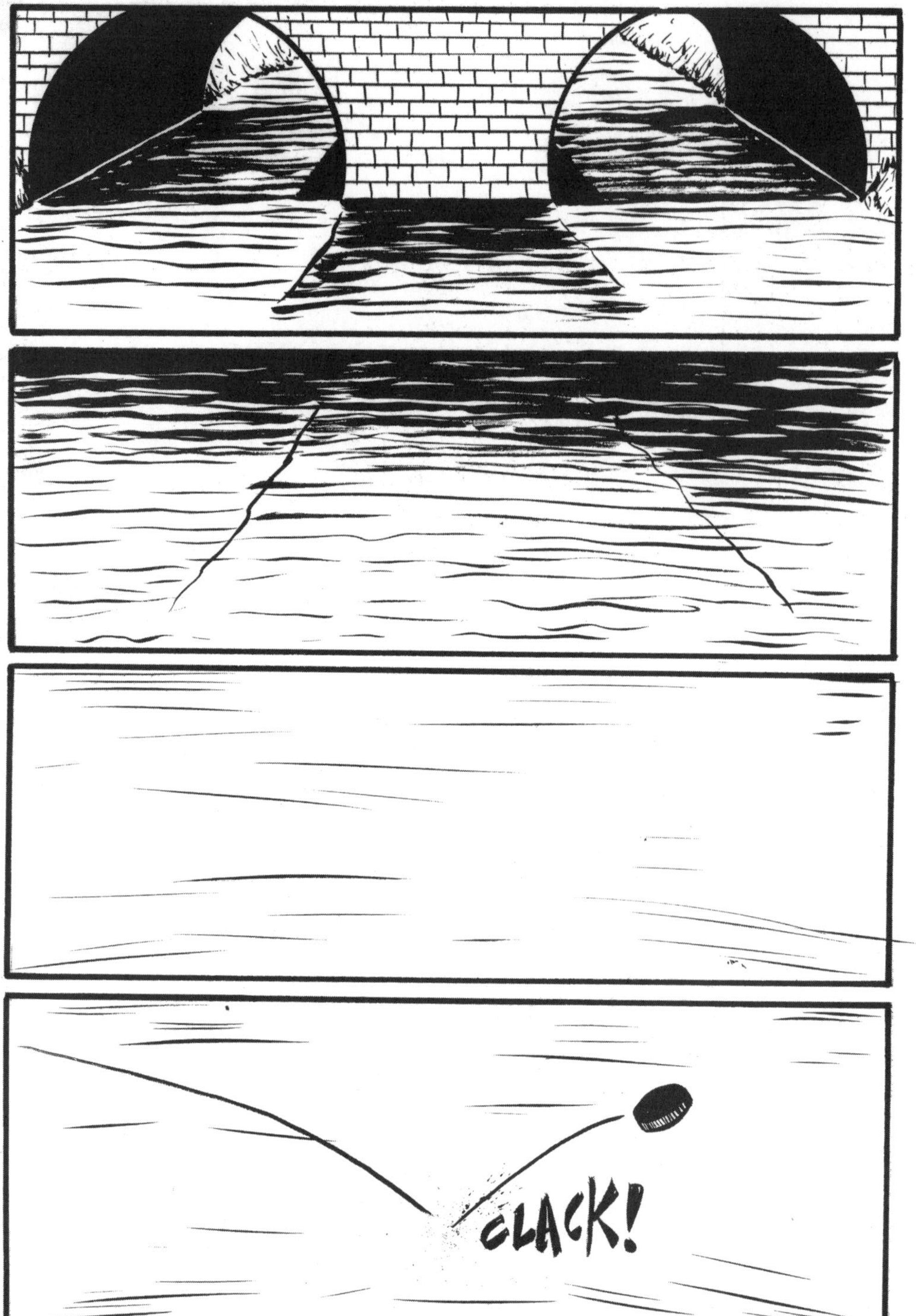
CLACK!

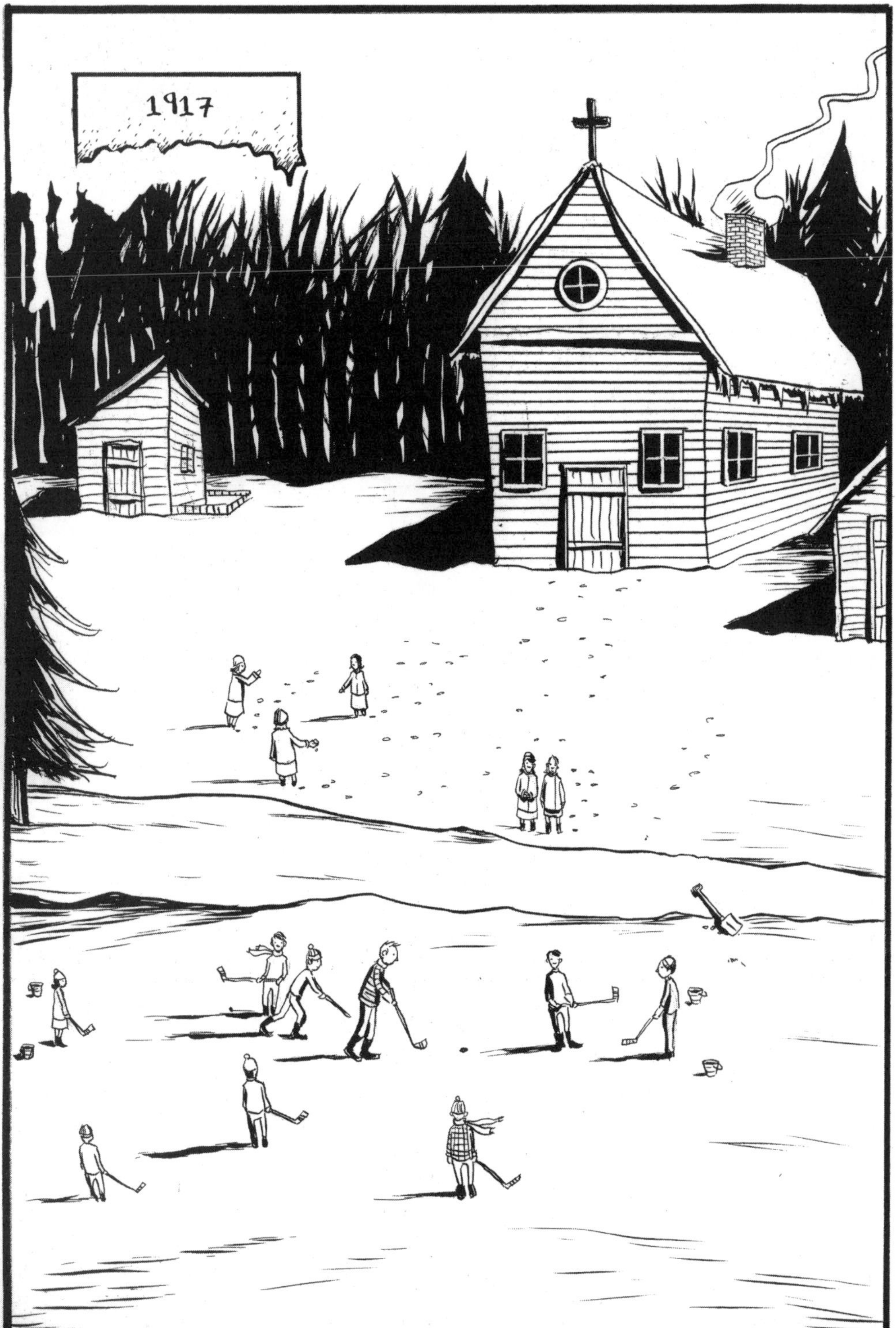
1917

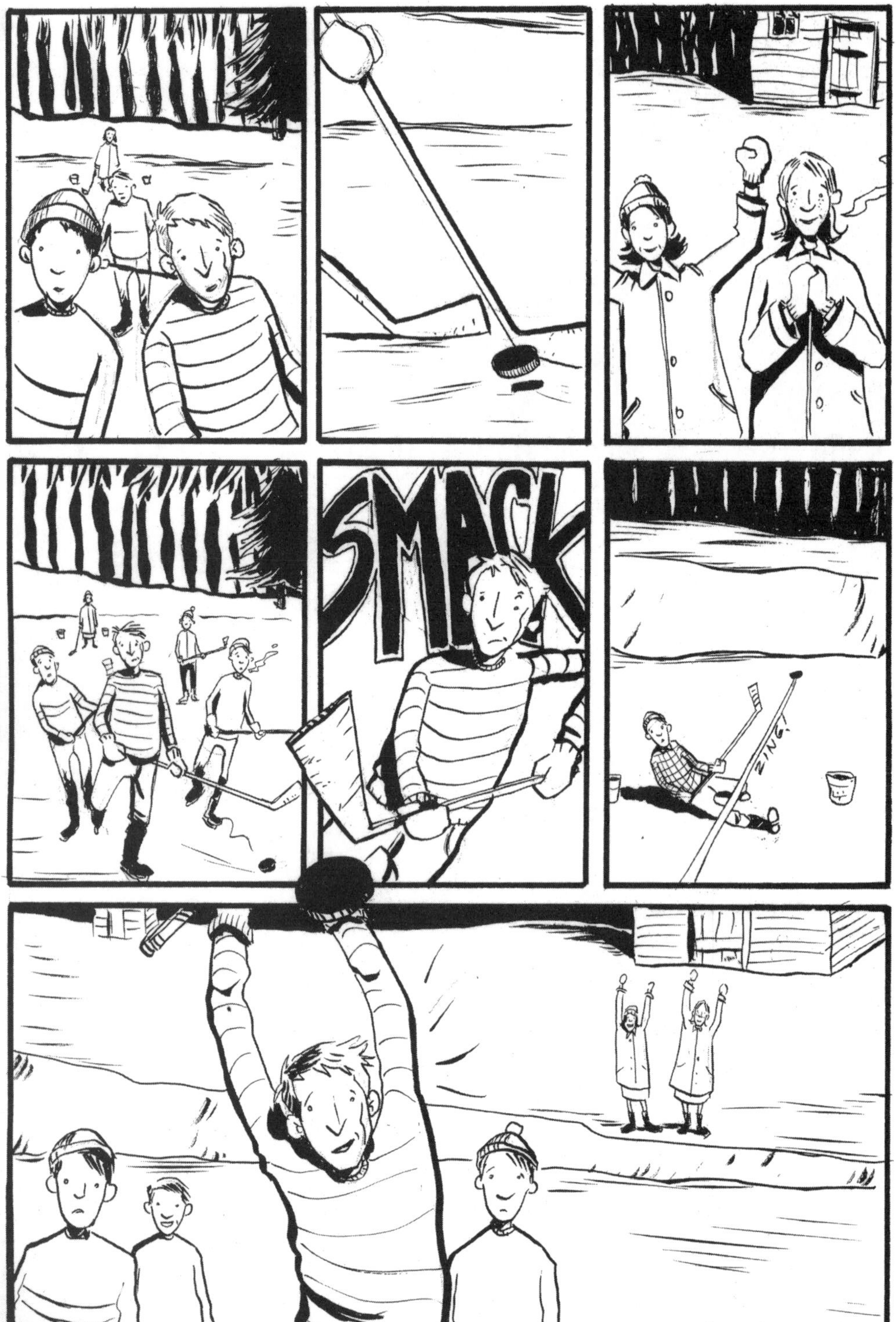
SMACK
ZING!

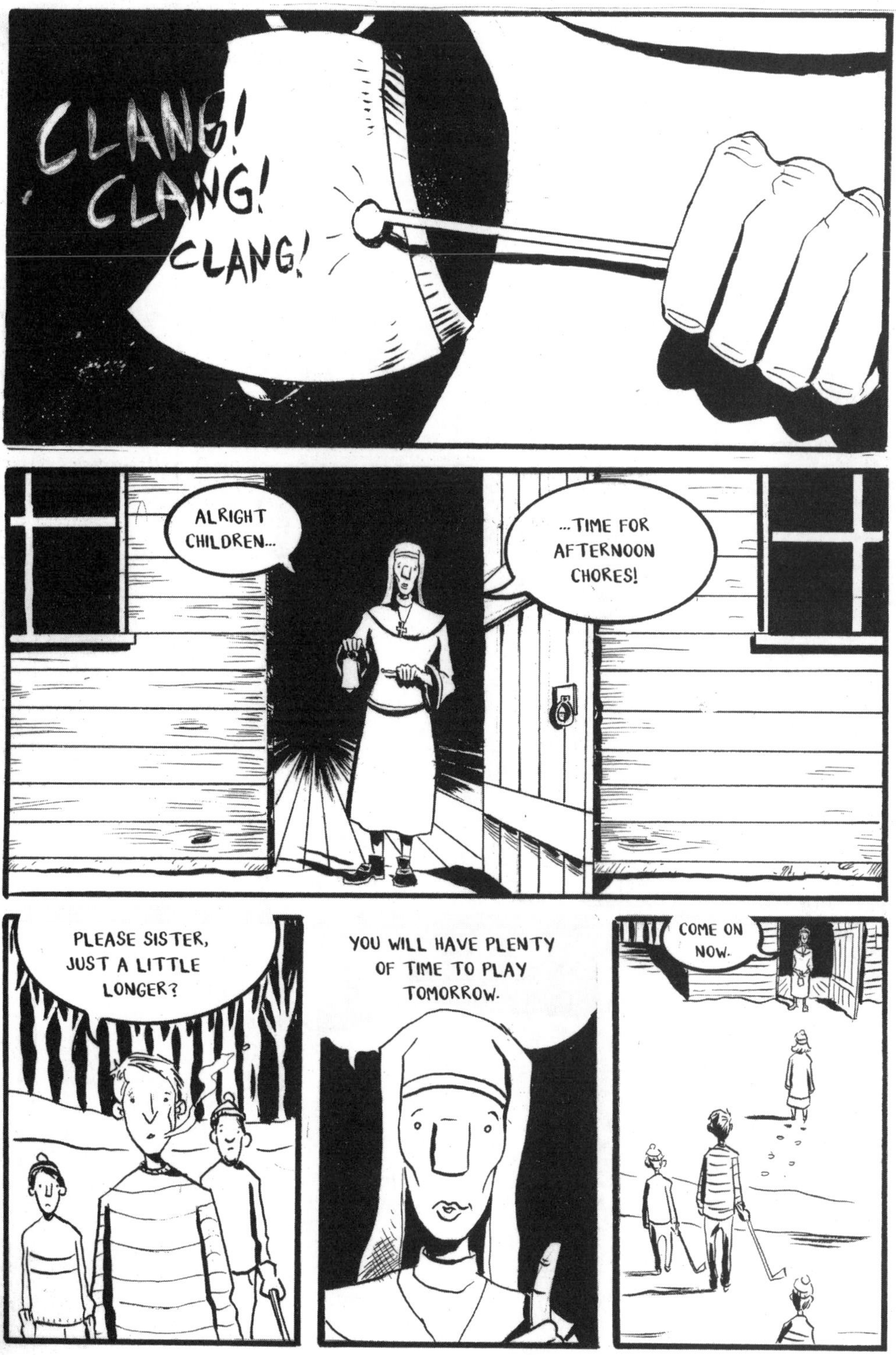
CLANG!
CLANG!
CLANG!
ALRIGHT CHILDREN...
...TIME FOR AFTERNOON CHORES!
PLEASE SISTER, JUST A LITTLE LONGER?
YOU WILL HAVE PLENTY OF TIME TO PLAY TOMORROW.
COME ON NOW.

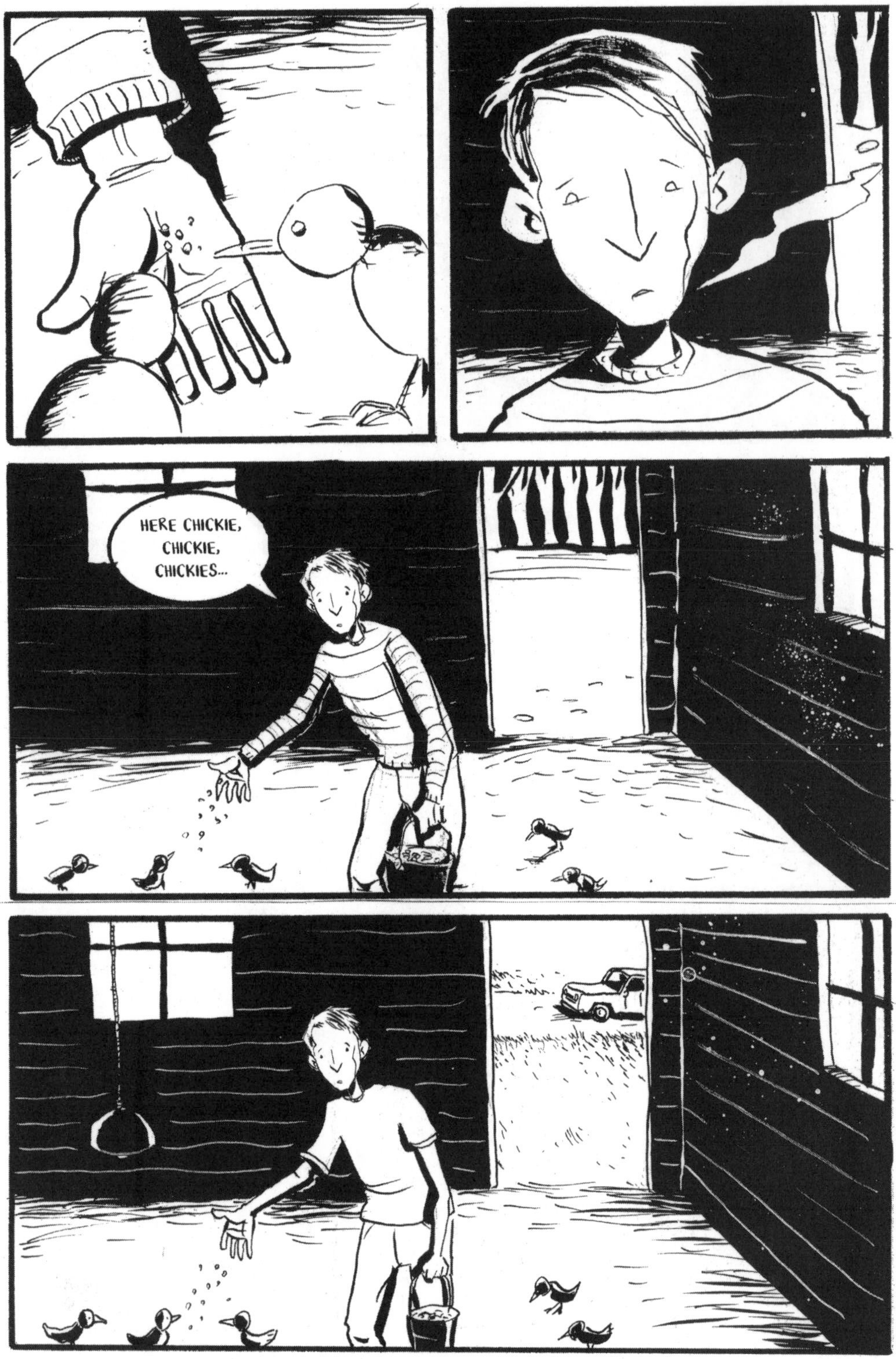
HERE CHICKIE,
CHICKIE,
CHICKIES...

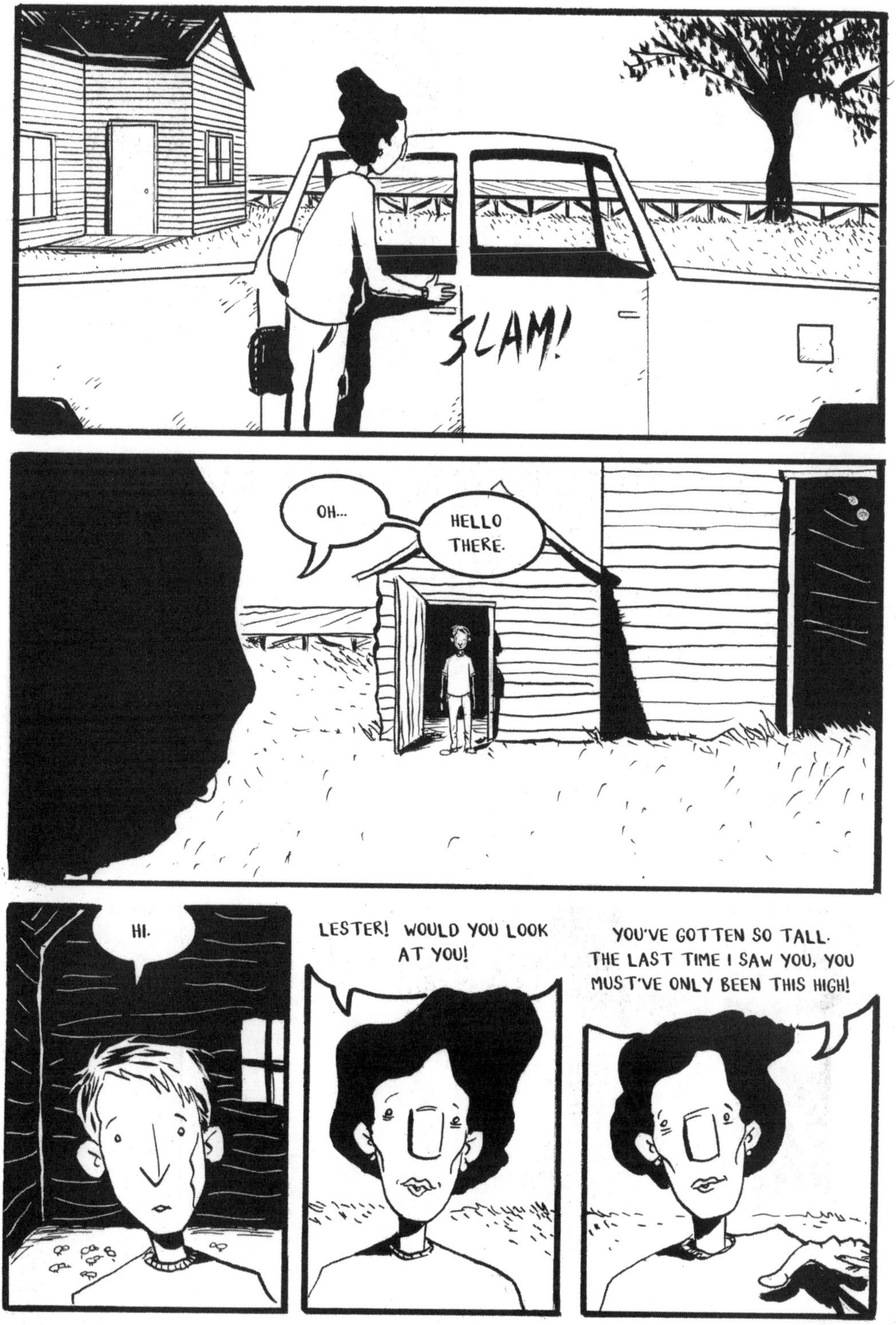
SLAM!
OH...
HELLO THERE.
HI.
LESTER! WOULD YOU LOOK AT YOU!
YOU'VE GOTTEN SO TALL. THE LAST TIME I SAW YOU, YOU MUST'VE ONLY BEEN THIS HIGH!

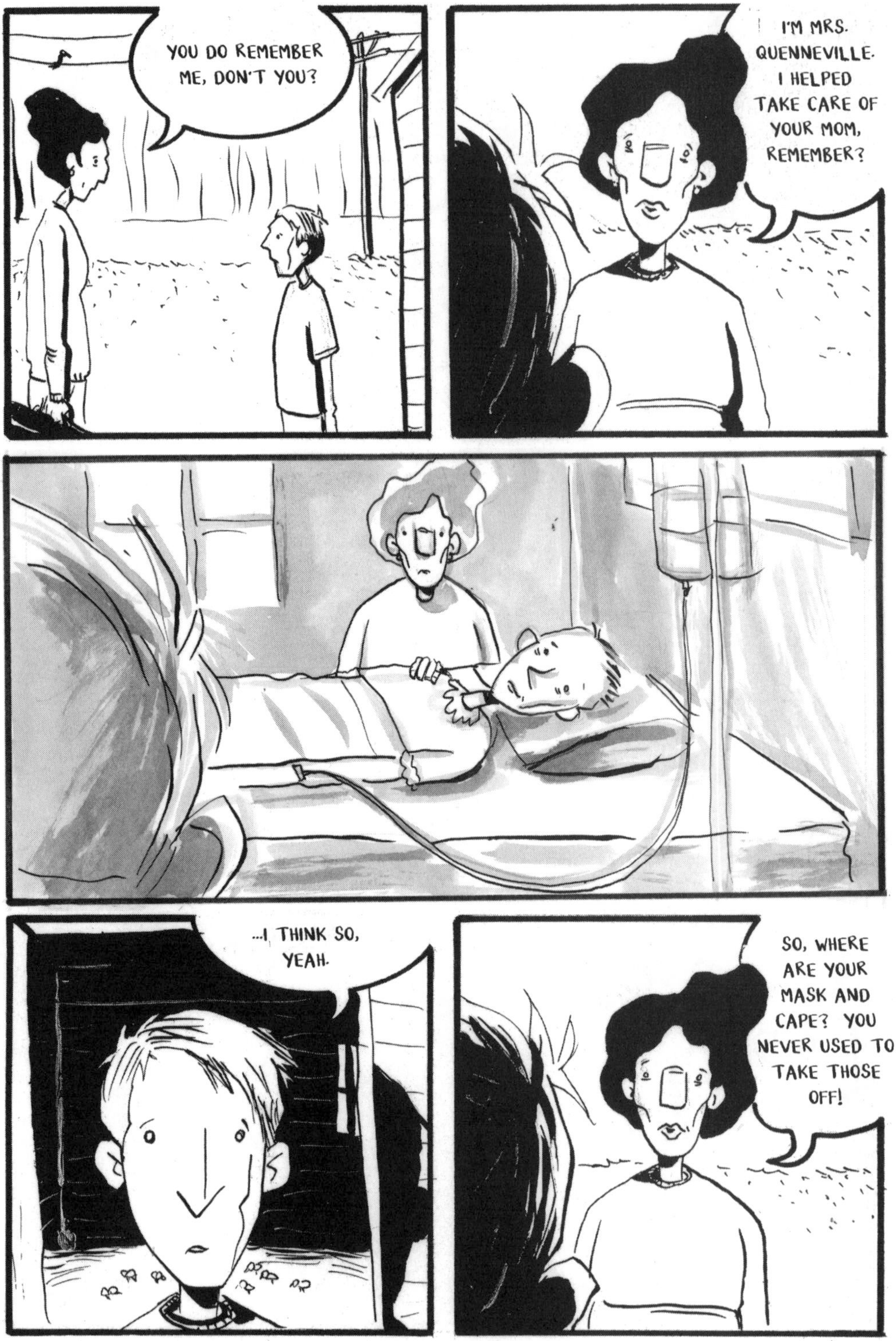
YOU DO REMEMBER ME, DON'T YOU?
I'M MRS. QUENNEVILLE. I HELPED TAKE CARE OF YOUR MOM, REMEMBER?
...I THINK SO, YEAH.
SO, WHERE ARE YOUR MASK AND CAPE? YOU NEVER USED TO TAKE THOSE OFF!

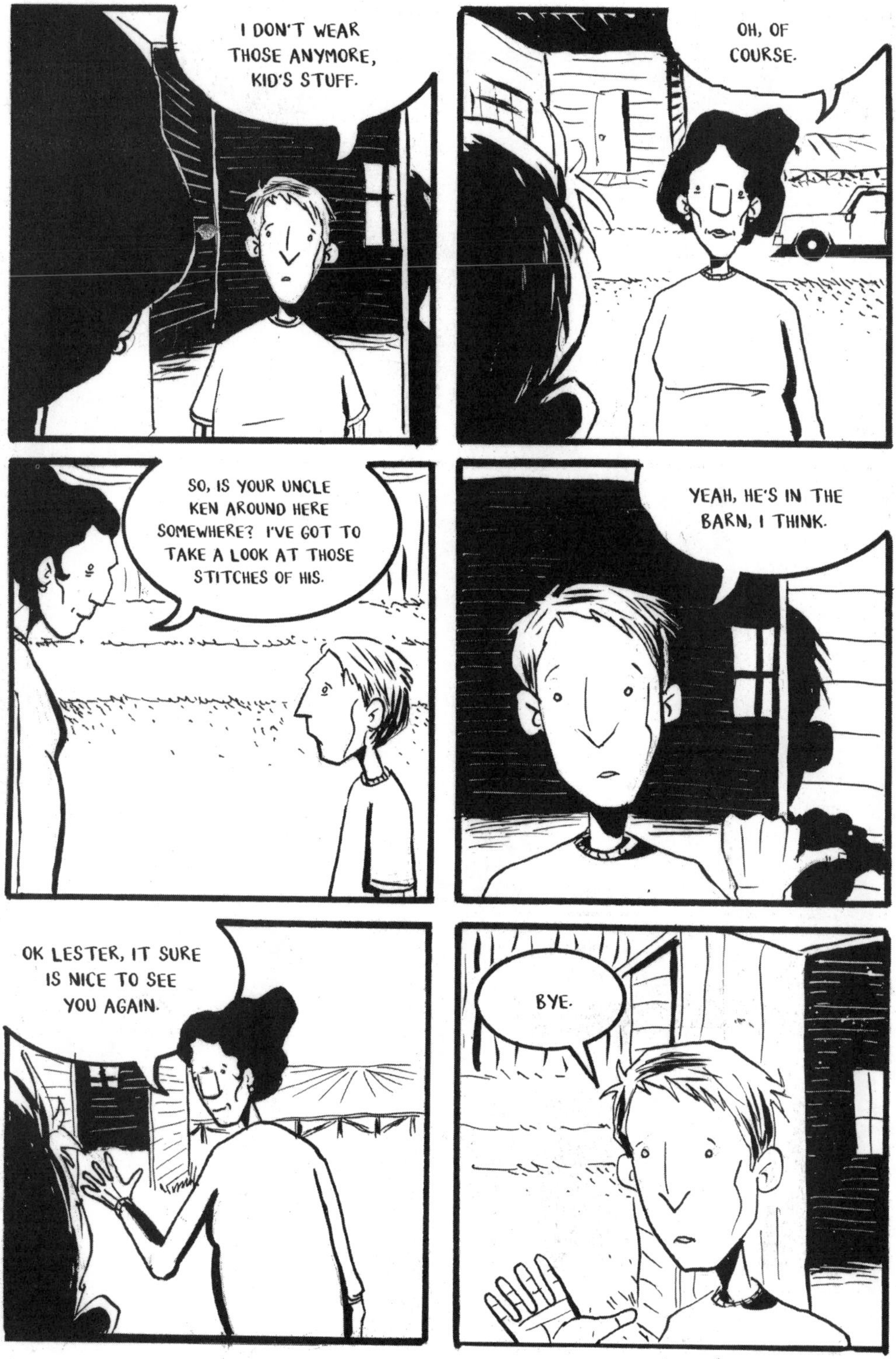
I DON'T WEAR THOSE ANYMORE, KID'S STUFF.
OH, OF COURSE.
SO, IS YOUR UNCLE KEN AROUND HERE SOMEWHERE? I'VE GOT TO TAKE A LOOK AT THOSE STITCHES OF HIS.
YEAH, HE'S IN THE BARN, I THINK.
OK LESTER, IT SURE IS NICE TO SEE YOU AGAIN.
BYE.

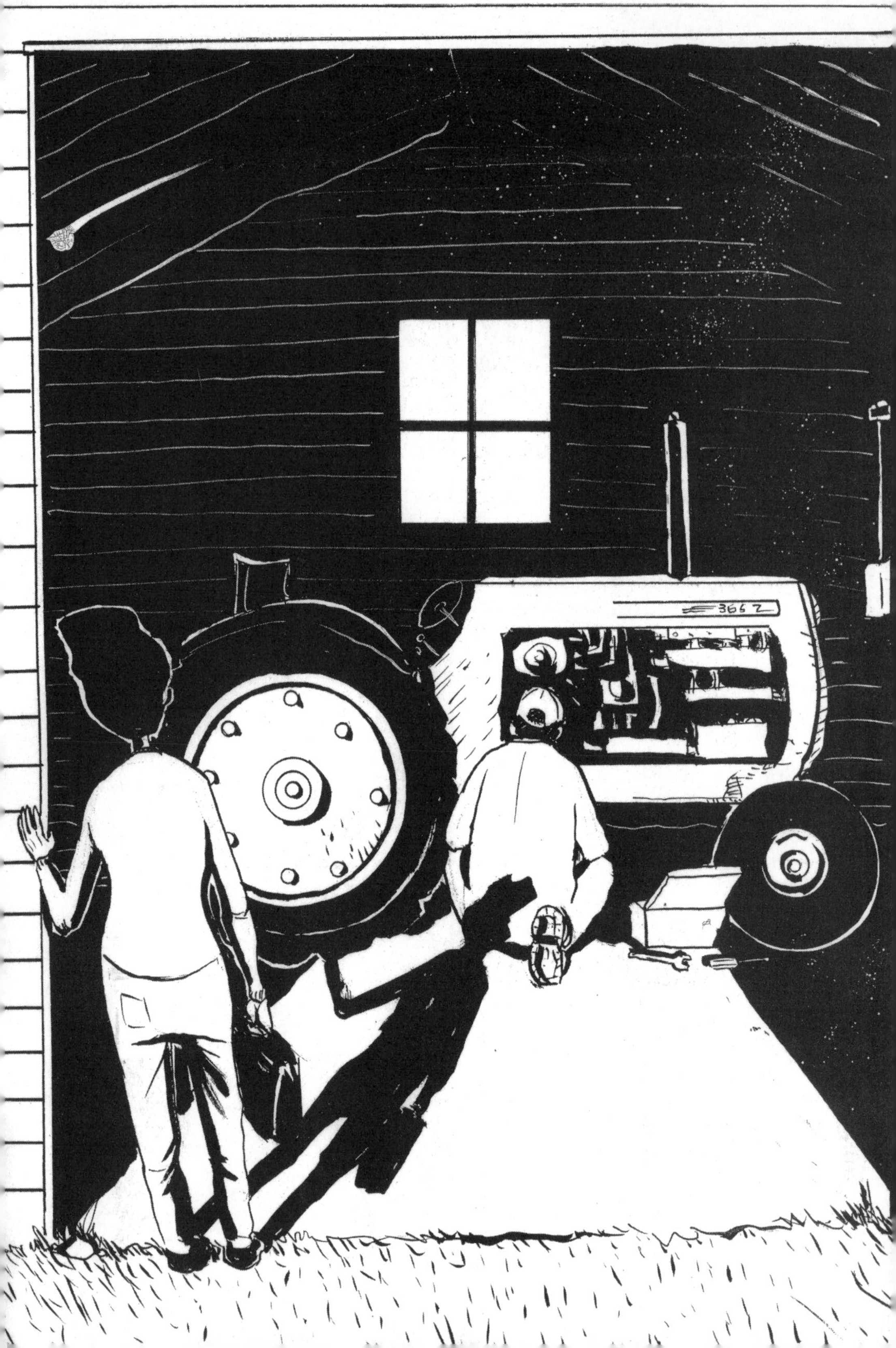

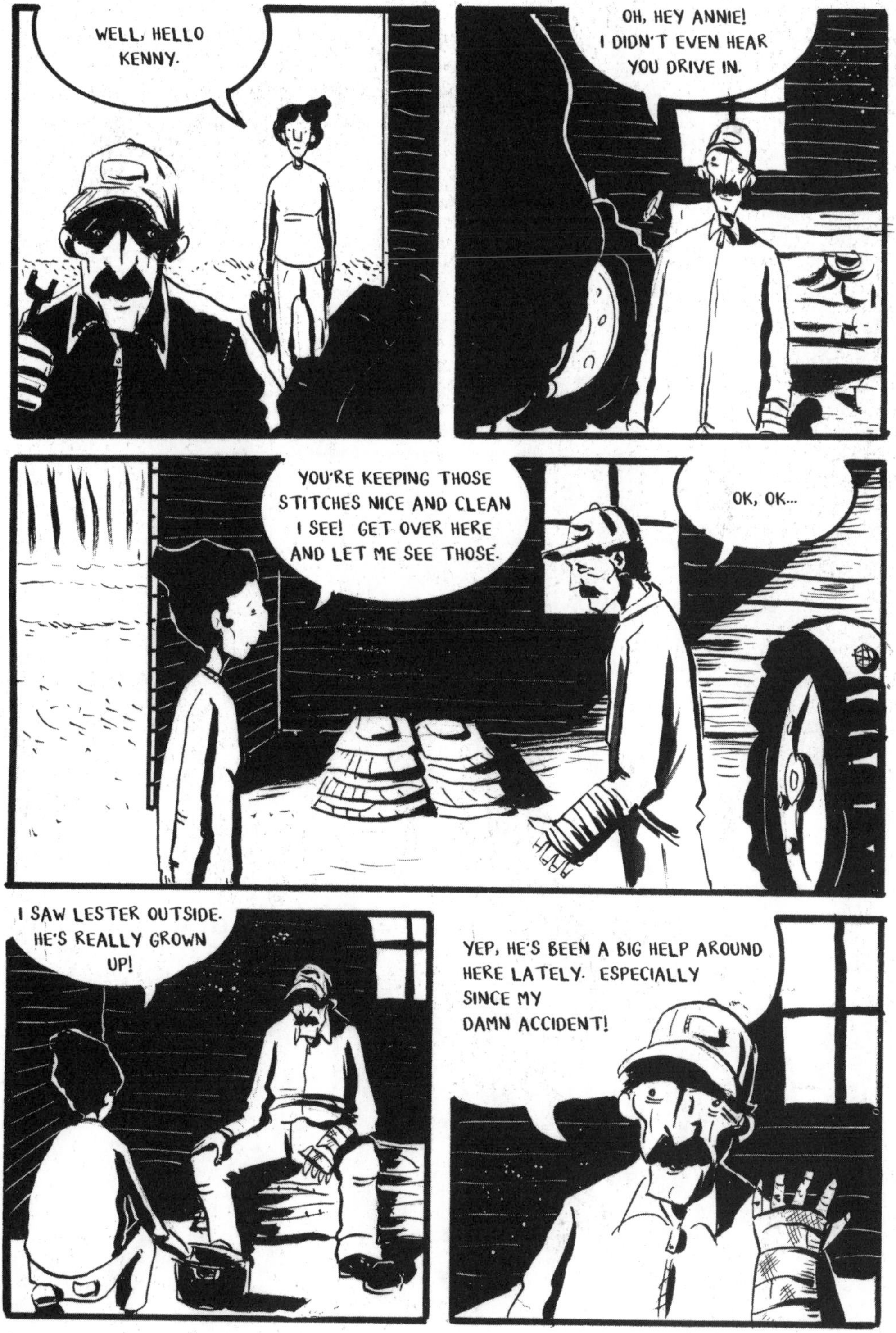
WELL, HELLO KENNY.
OH, HEY ANNIE! I DIDN'T EVEN HEAR YOU DRIVE IN.
YOU'RE KEEPING THOSE STITCHES NICE AND CLEAN I SEE! GET OVER HERE AND LET ME SEE THOSE.
OK, OK...
I SAW LESTER OUTSIDE. HE'S REALLY GROWN UP!
YEP, HE'S BEEN A BIG HELP AROUND HERE LATELY. ESPECIALLY SINCE MY DAMN ACCIDENT!

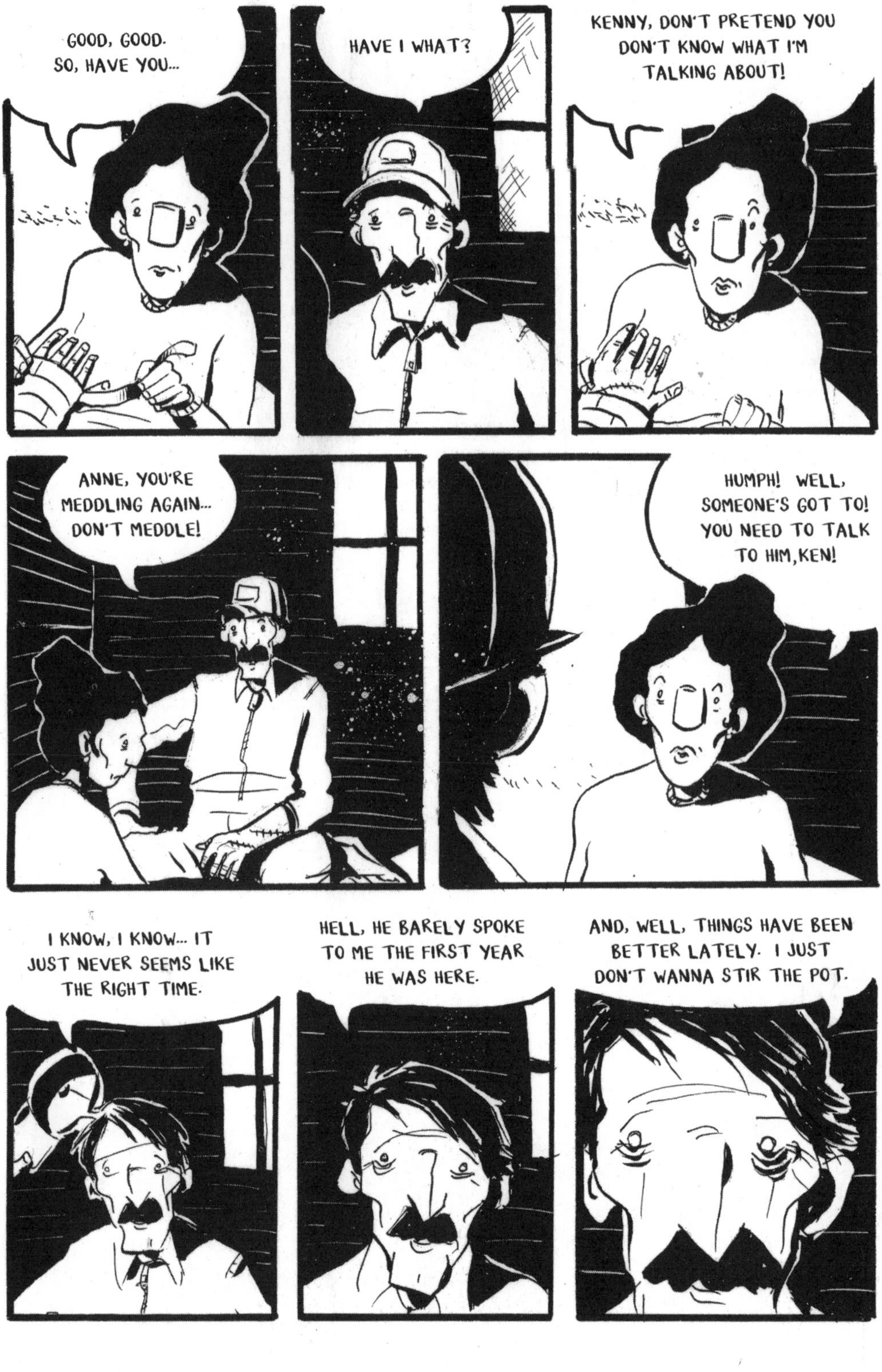
GOOD, GOOD.
SO, HAVE YOU...
HAVE I WHAT?
KENNY, DON'T PRETEND YOU DON'T KNOW WHAT I'M TALKING ABOUT!
ANNE, YOU'RE MEDDLING AGAIN... DON'T MEDDLE!
HUMPH! WELL, SOMEONE'S GOT TO! YOU NEED TO TALK TO HIM, KEN!
I KNOW, I KNOW... IT JUST NEVER SEEMS LIKE THE RIGHT TIME.
HELL, HE BARELY SPOKE TO ME THE FIRST YEAR HE WAS HERE.
AND, WELL, THINGS HAVE BEEN BETTER LATELY. I JUST DON'T WANNA STIR THE POT.

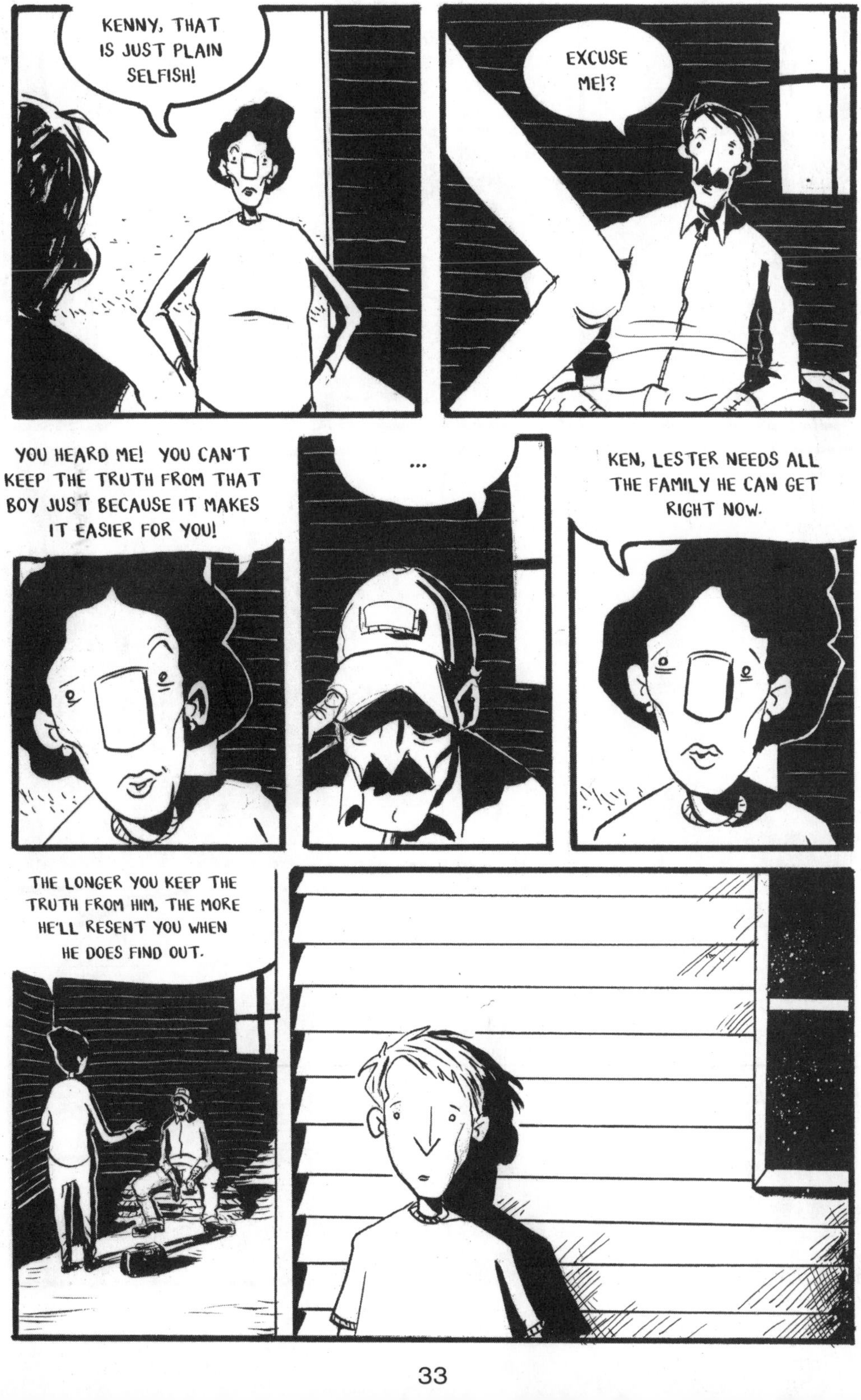
KENNY, THAT IS JUST PLAIN SELFISH!
EXCUSE ME!?
YOU HEARD ME! YOU CAN'T KEEP THE TRUTH FROM THAT BOY JUST BECAUSE IT MAKES IT EASIER FOR YOU!
...
KEN, LESTER NEEDS ALL THE FAMILY HE CAN GET RIGHT NOW.
THE LONGER YOU KEEP THE TRUTH FROM HIM, THE MORE HE'LL RESENT YOU WHEN HE DOES FIND OUT.

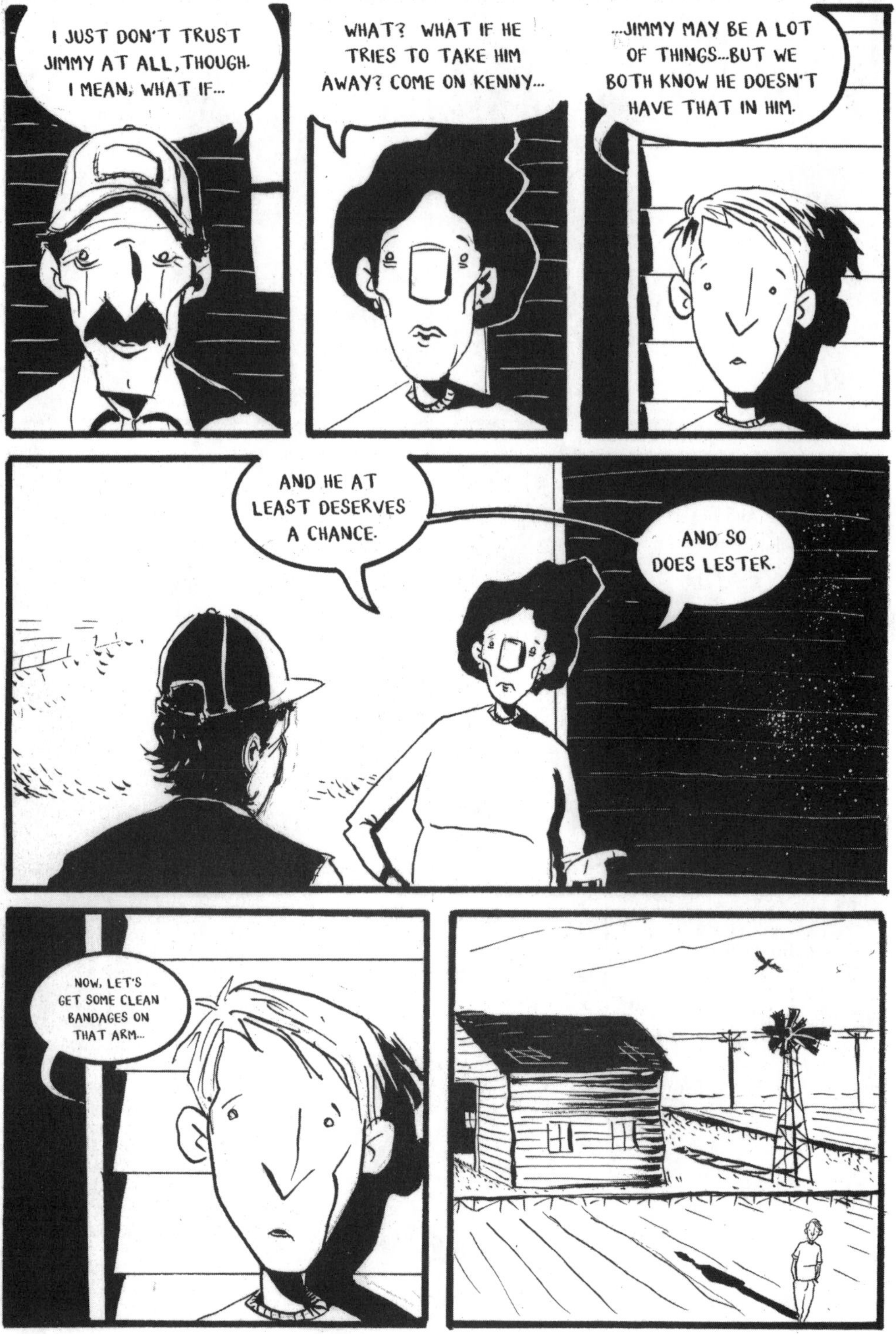
I JUST DON'T TRUST JIMMY AT ALL, THOUGH. I MEAN, WHAT IF...
WHAT? WHAT IF HE TRIES TO TAKE HIM AWAY? COME ON KENNY...
...JIMMY MAY BE A LOT OF THINGS...BUT WE BOTH KNOW HE DOESN'T HAVE THAT IN HIM.
AND HE AT LEAST DESERVES A CHANCE.
AND SO DOES LESTER.
NOW, LET'S GET SOME CLEAN BANDAGES ON THAT ARM...

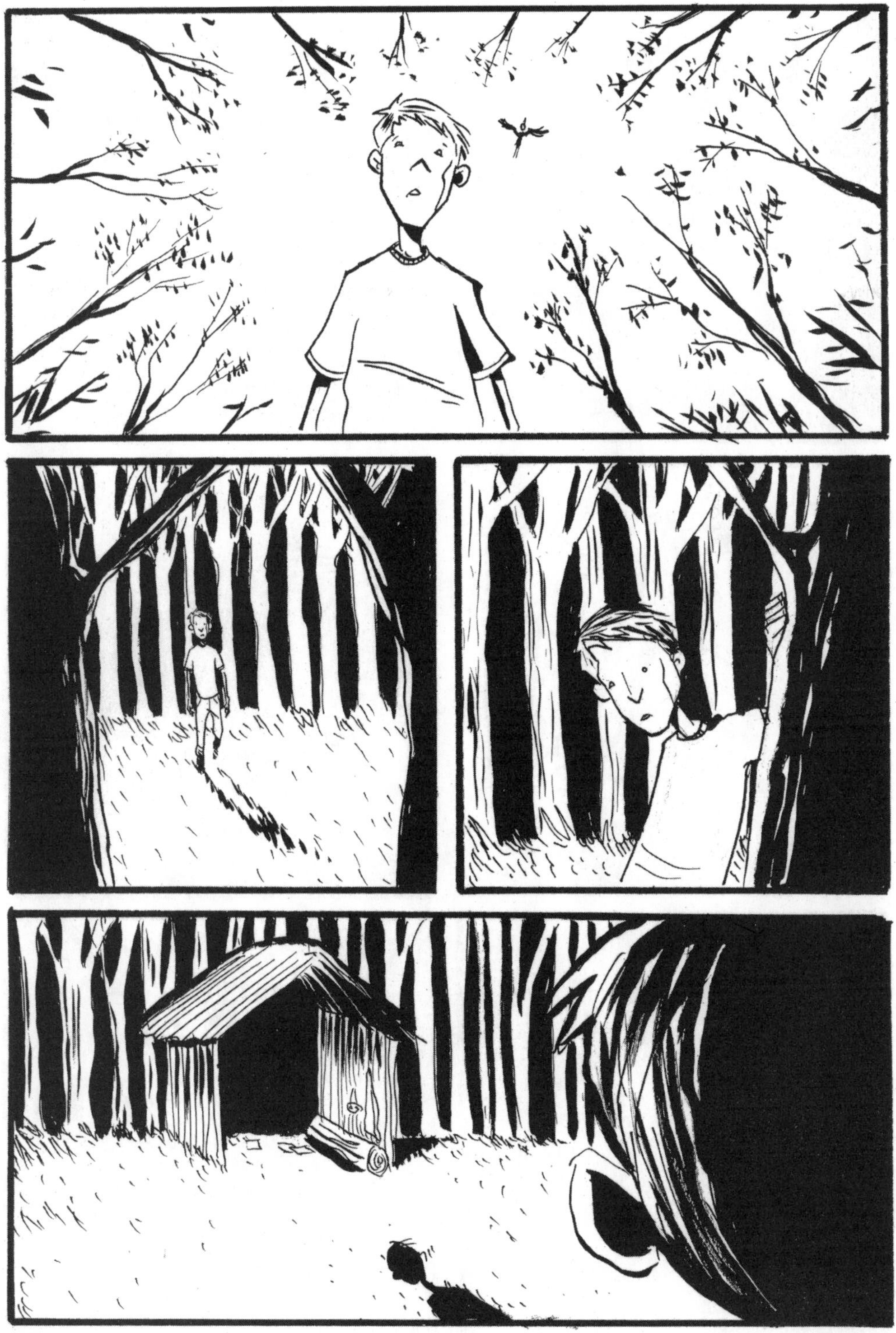

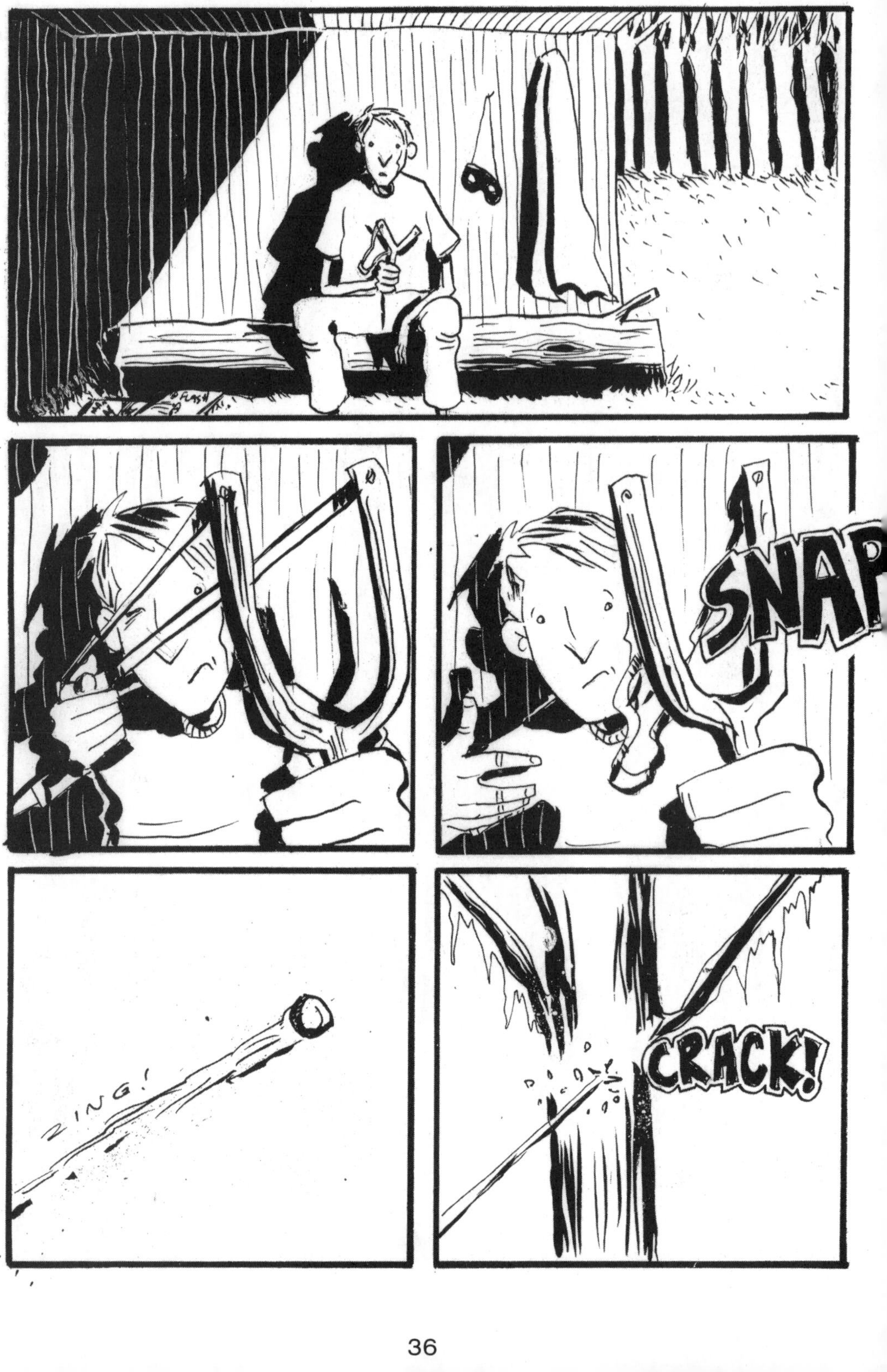
FLASH
SNAP
ZING!
CRACK!

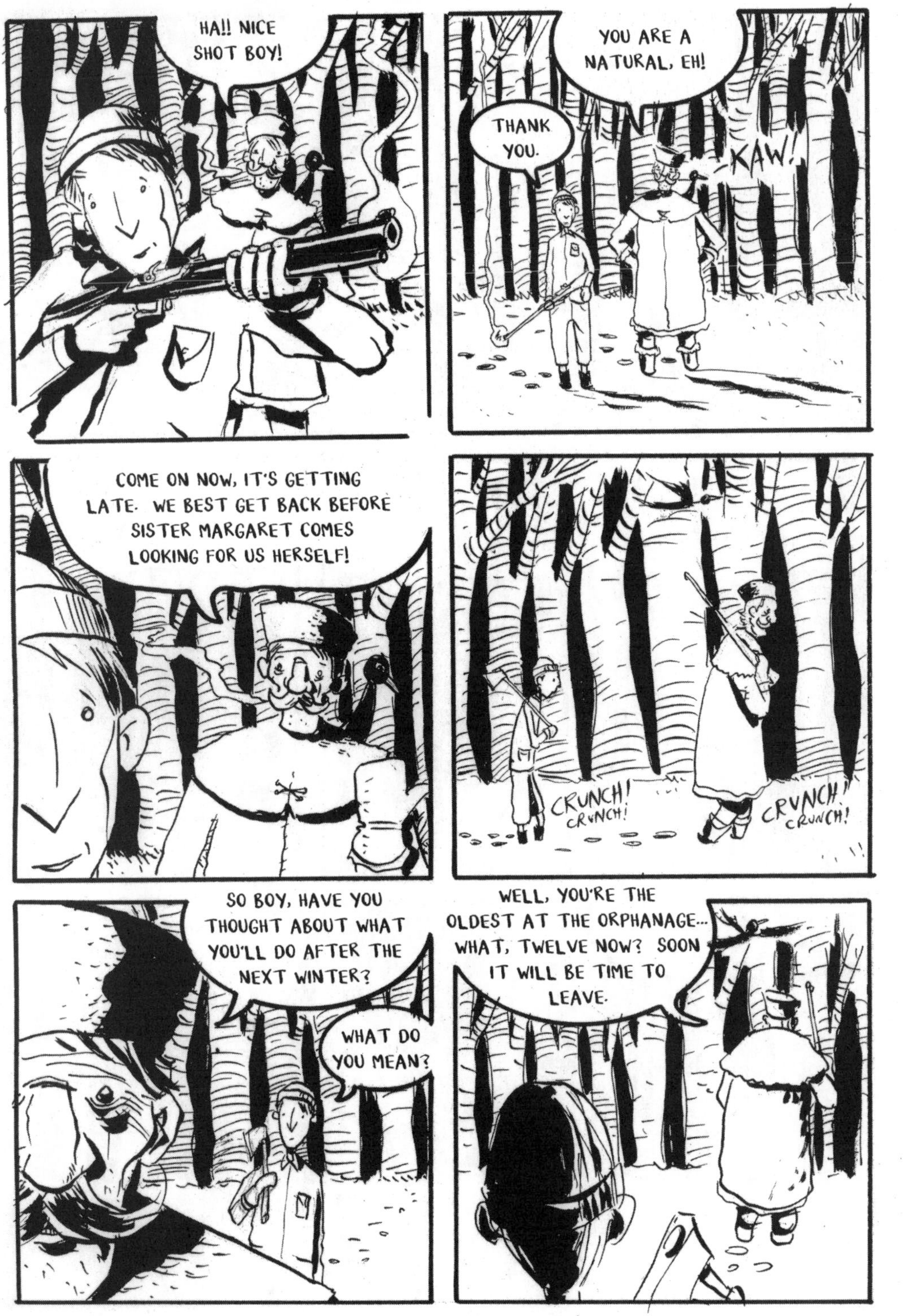
HA!! NICE SHOT BOY!
YOU ARE A NATURAL, EH!
THANK YOU.
KAW!
COME ON NOW, IT'S GETTING LATE. WE BEST GET BACK BEFORE SISTER MARGARET COMES LOOKING FOR US HERSELF!
CRUNCH! CRUNCH!
CRUNCH! CRUNCH!
SO BOY, HAVE YOU THOUGHT ABOUT WHAT YOU'LL DO AFTER THE NEXT WINTER?
WHAT DO YOU MEAN?
WELL, YOU'RE THE OLDEST AT THE ORPHANAGE... WHAT, TWELVE NOW? SOON IT WILL BE TIME TO LEAVE.

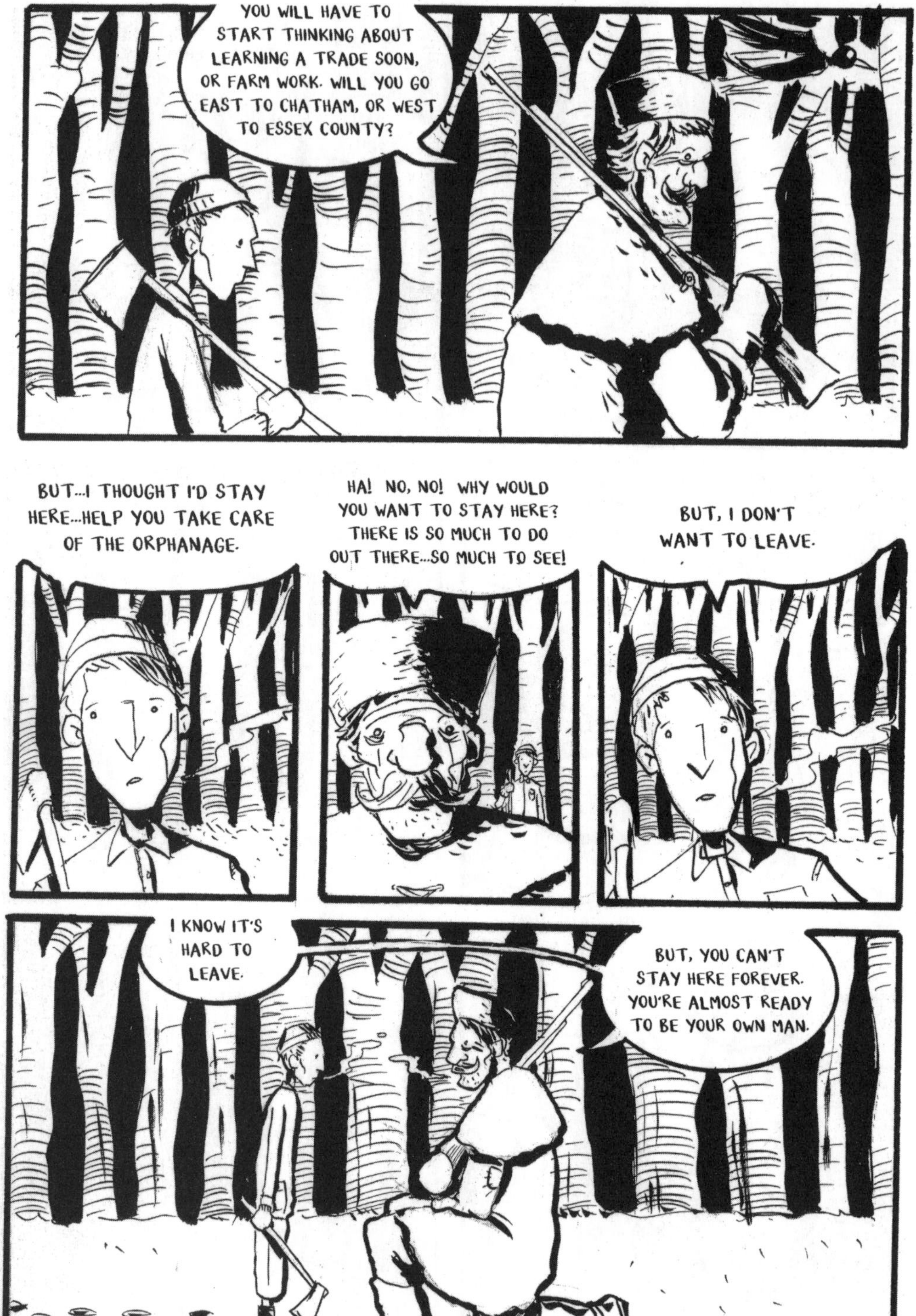
YOU WILL HAVE TO START THINKING ABOUT LEARNING A TRADE SOON, OR FARM WORK. WILL YOU GO EAST TO CHATHAM, OR WEST TO ESSEX COUNTY?
BUT...I THOUGHT I'D STAY HERE...HELP YOU TAKE CARE OF THE ORPHANAGE.
HA! NO, NO! WHY WOULD YOU WANT TO STAY HERE? THERE IS SO MUCH TO DO OUT THERE...SO MUCH TO SEE!
BUT, I DON'T WANT TO LEAVE.
I KNOW IT'S HARD TO LEAVE.
BUT, YOU CAN'T STAY HERE FOREVER. YOU'RE ALMOST READY TO BE YOUR OWN MAN.

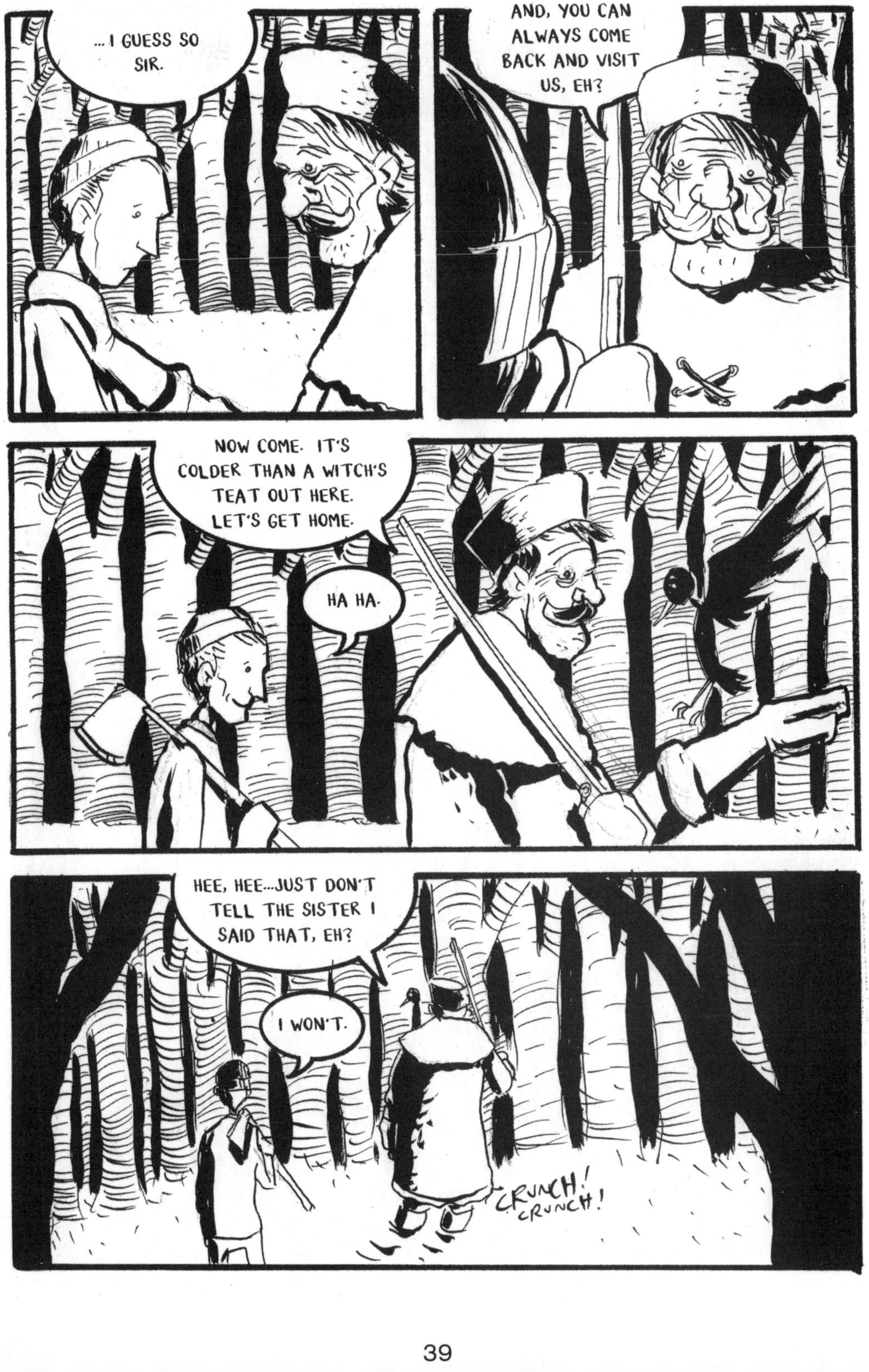
...I GUESS SO SIR.
AND, YOU CAN ALWAYS COME BACK AND VISIT US, EH?
NOW COME. IT'S COLDER THAN A WITCH'S TEAT OUT HERE. LET'S GET HOME.
HA HA.
HEE, HEE...JUST DON'T TELL THE SISTER I SAID THAT, EH?
I WON'T.
CRUNCH! CRUNCH!

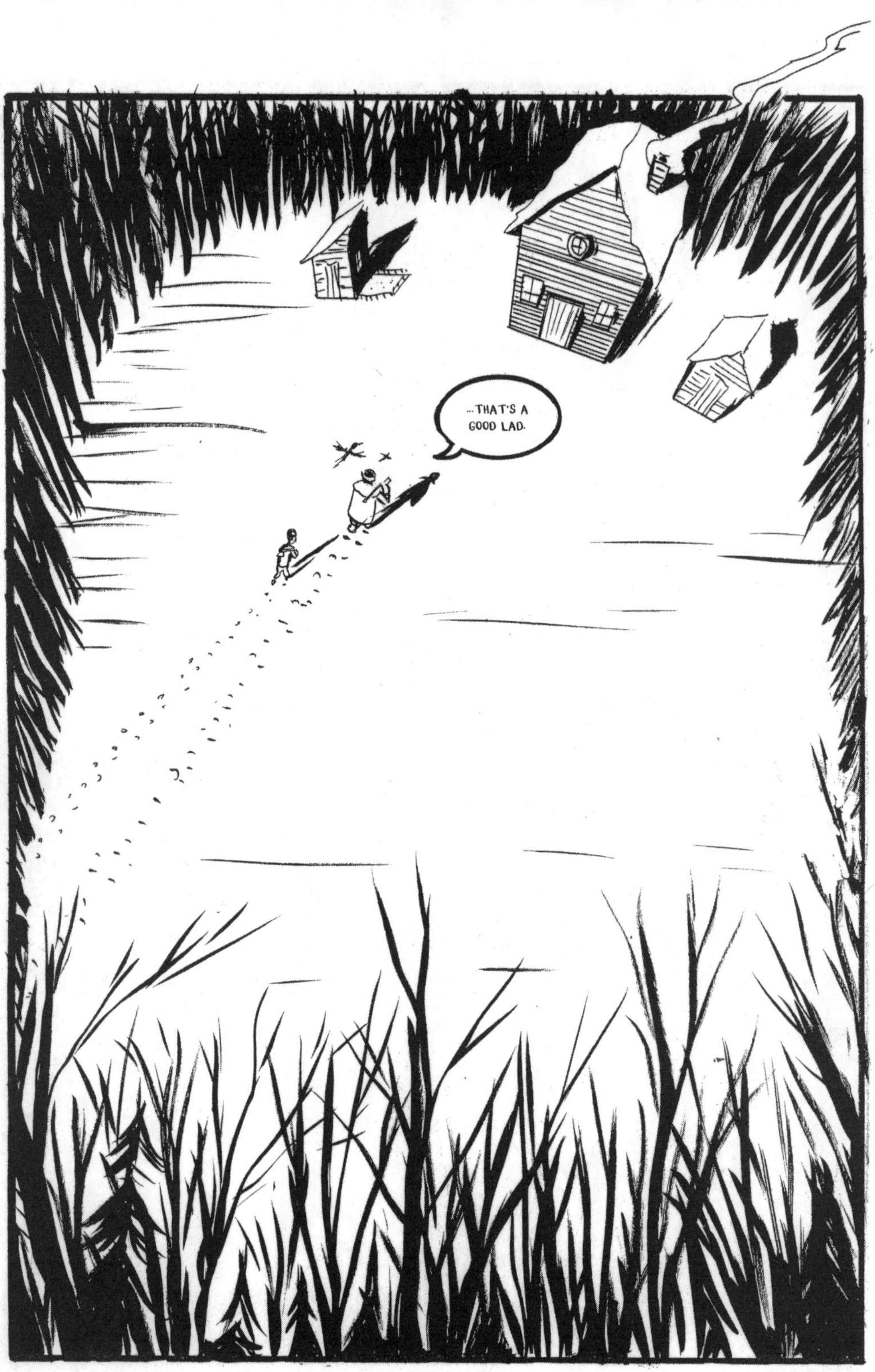
...THAT'S A GOOD LAD.

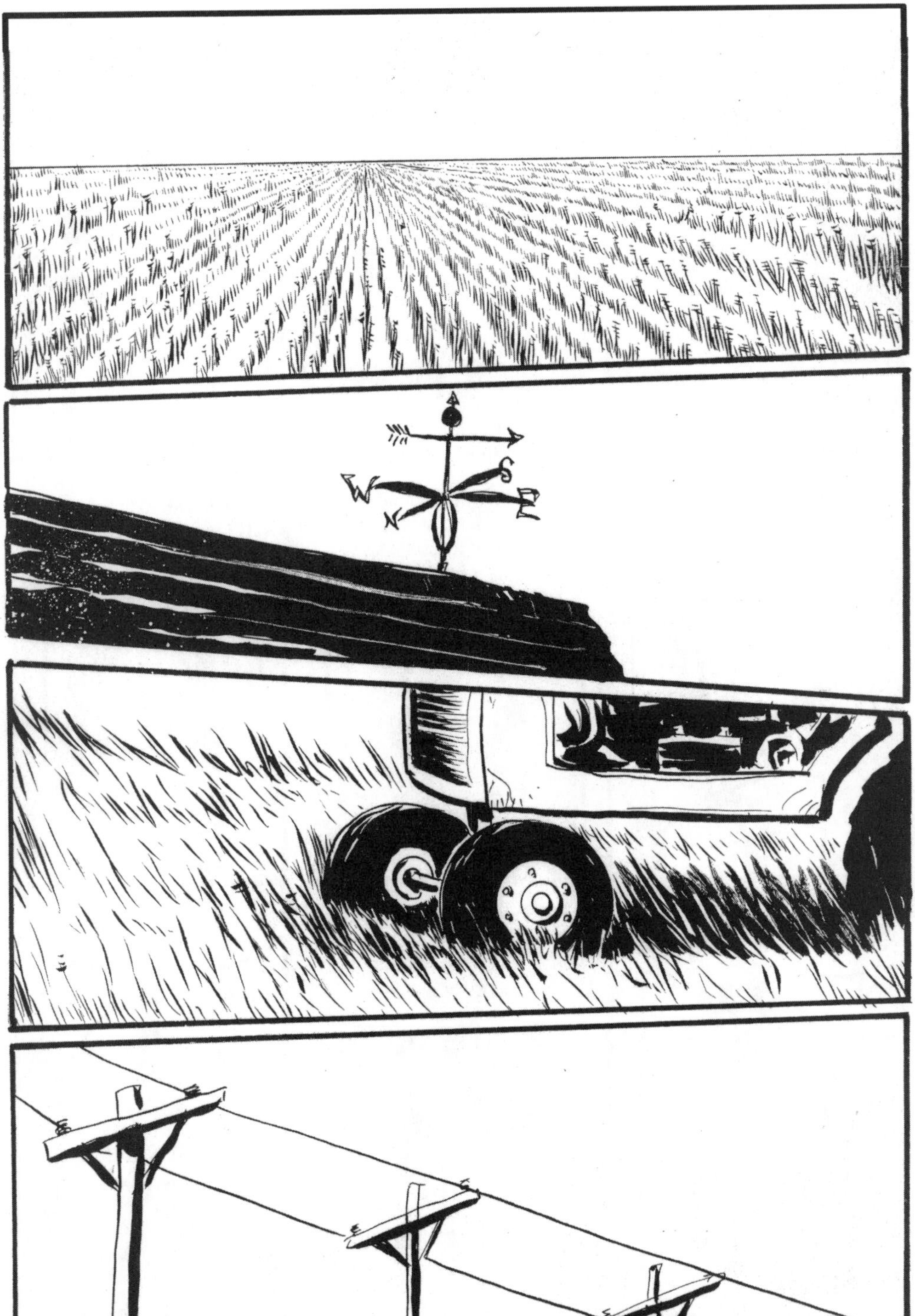
W
S
N
E

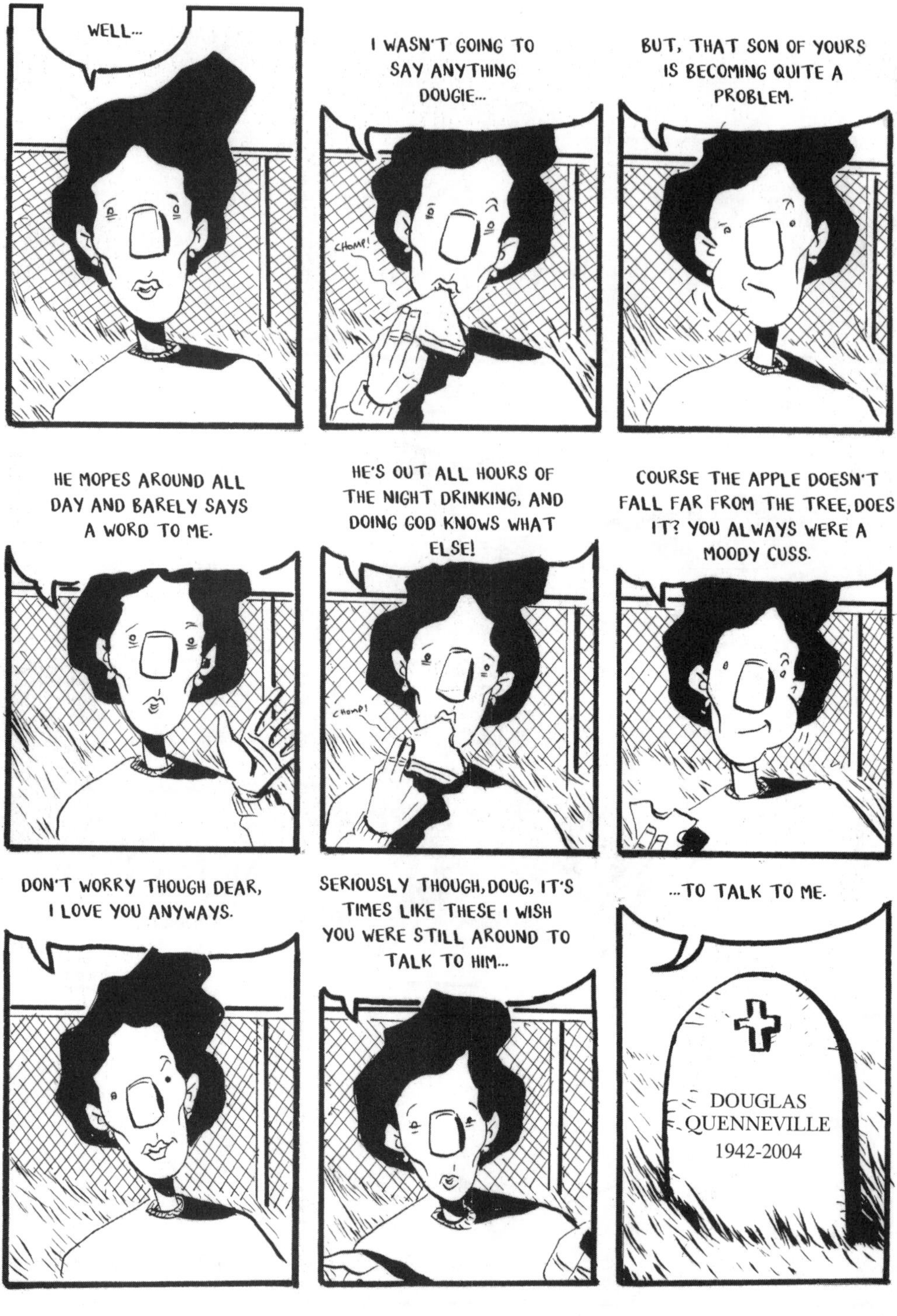
WELL...
I WASN'T GOING TO SAY ANYTHING DOUGIE...
CHOMP!
BUT, THAT SON OF YOURS IS BECOMING QUITE A PROBLEM.
HE MOPES AROUND ALL DAY AND BARELY SAYS A WORD TO ME.
HE'S OUT ALL HOURS OF THE NIGHT DRINKING, AND DOING GOD KNOWS WHAT ELSE!
CHOMP!
COURSE THE APPLE DOESN'T FALL FAR FROM THE TREE, DOES IT? YOU ALWAYS WERE A MOODY CUSS.
DON'T WORRY THOUGH DEAR, I LOVE YOU ANYWAYS.
SERIOUSLY THOUGH, DOUG, IT'S TIMES LIKE THESE I WISH YOU WERE STILL AROUND TO TALK TO HIM...
...TO TALK TO ME.
DOUGLAS QUENNEVILLE 1942-2004

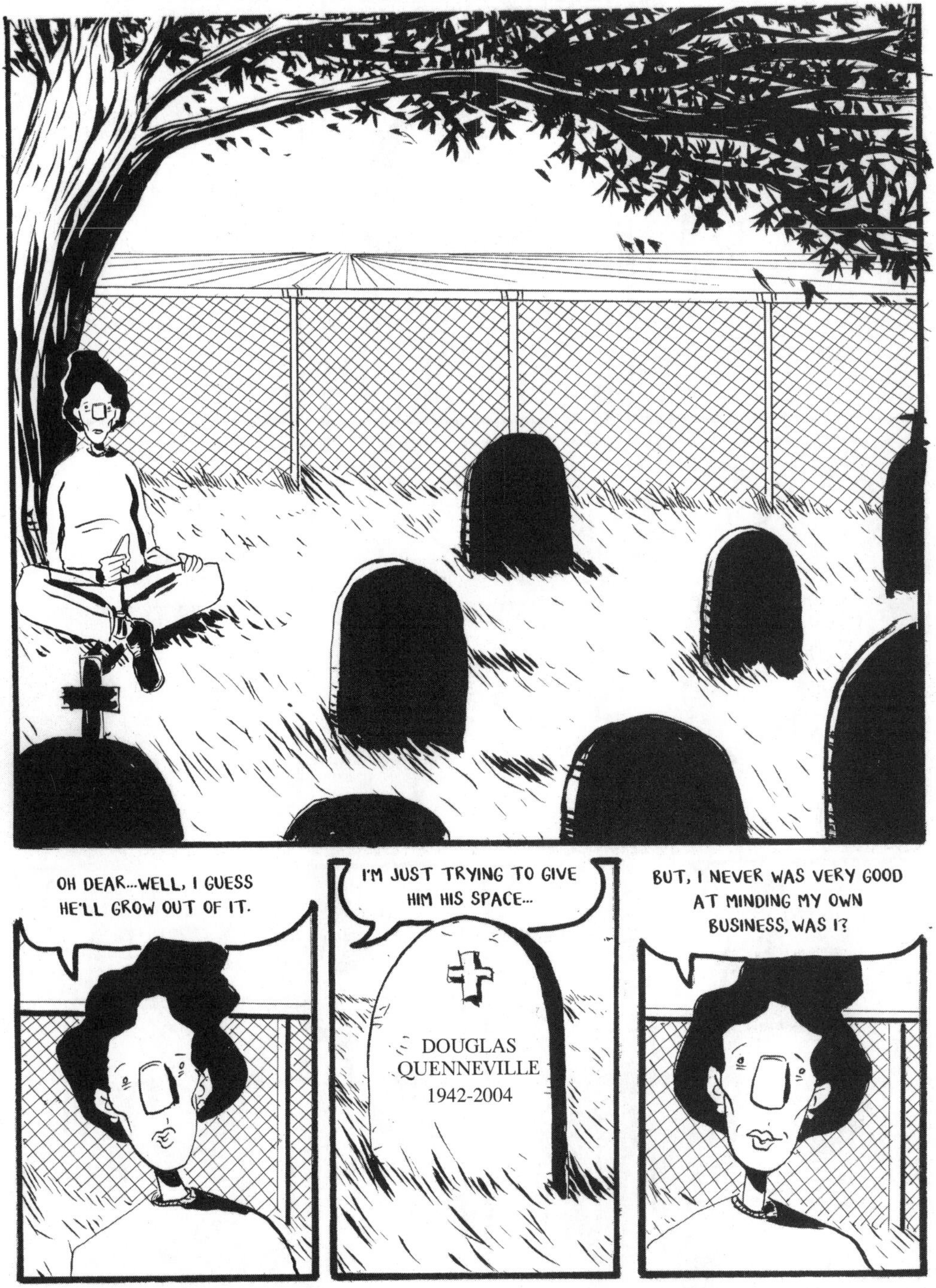
OH DEAR...WELL, I GUESS HE'LL GROW OUT OF IT.
I'M JUST TRYING TO GIVE HIM HIS SPACE...
DOUGLAS QUENNEVILLE 1942-2004
BUT, I NEVER WAS VERY GOOD AT MINDING MY OWN BUSINESS, WAS I?

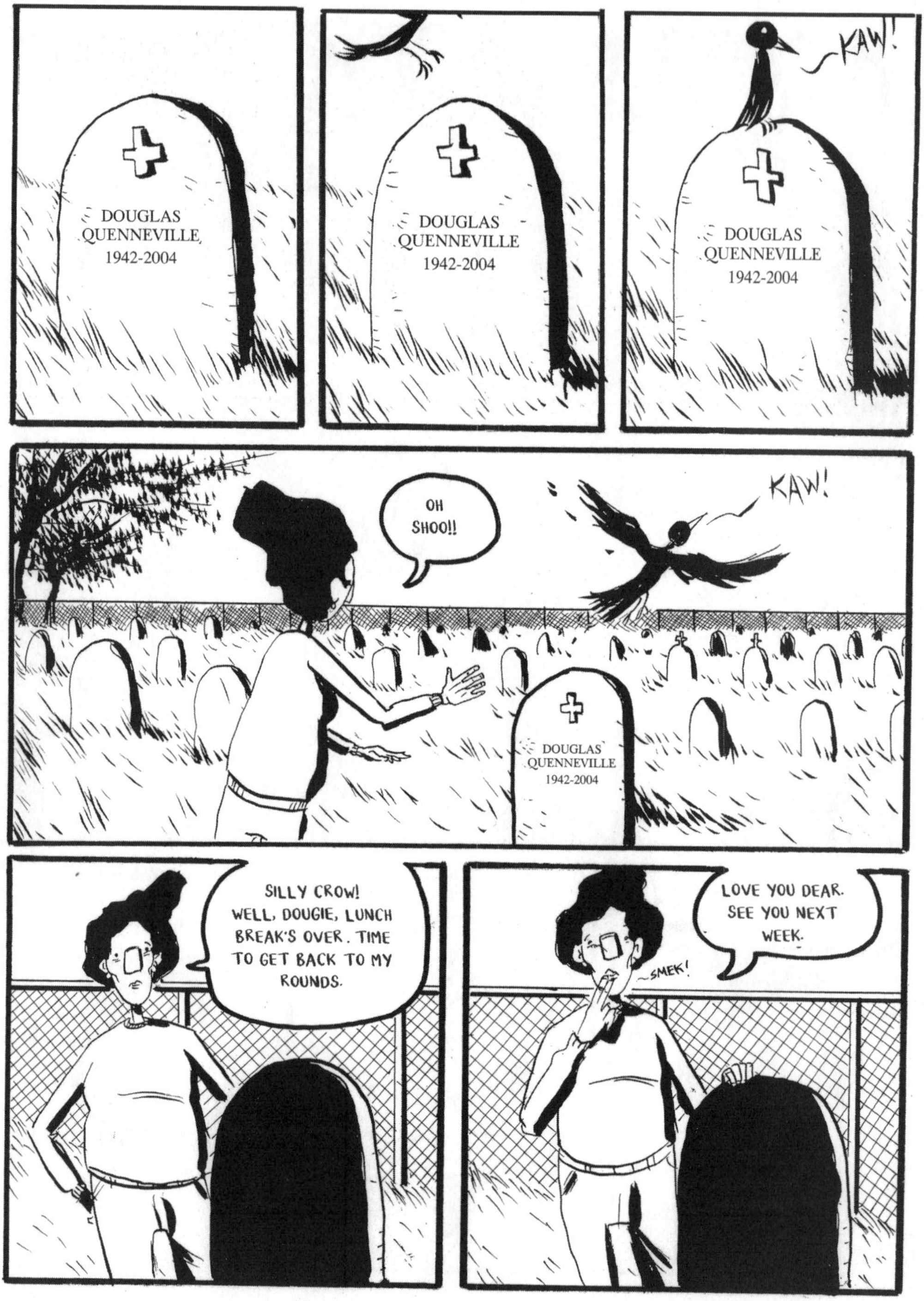
DOUGLAS QUENNEVILLE 1942-2004
DOUGLAS QUENNEVILLE 1942-2004
KAW!
DOUGLAS QUENNEVILLE 1942-2004
OH SHOO!!
KAW!
DOUGLAS QUENNEVILLE 1942-2004
SILLY CROW! WELL, DOUGIE, LUNCH BREAK'S OVER. TIME TO GET BACK TO MY ROUNDS.
LOVE YOU DEAR. SEE YOU NEXT WEEK.
SMEK!

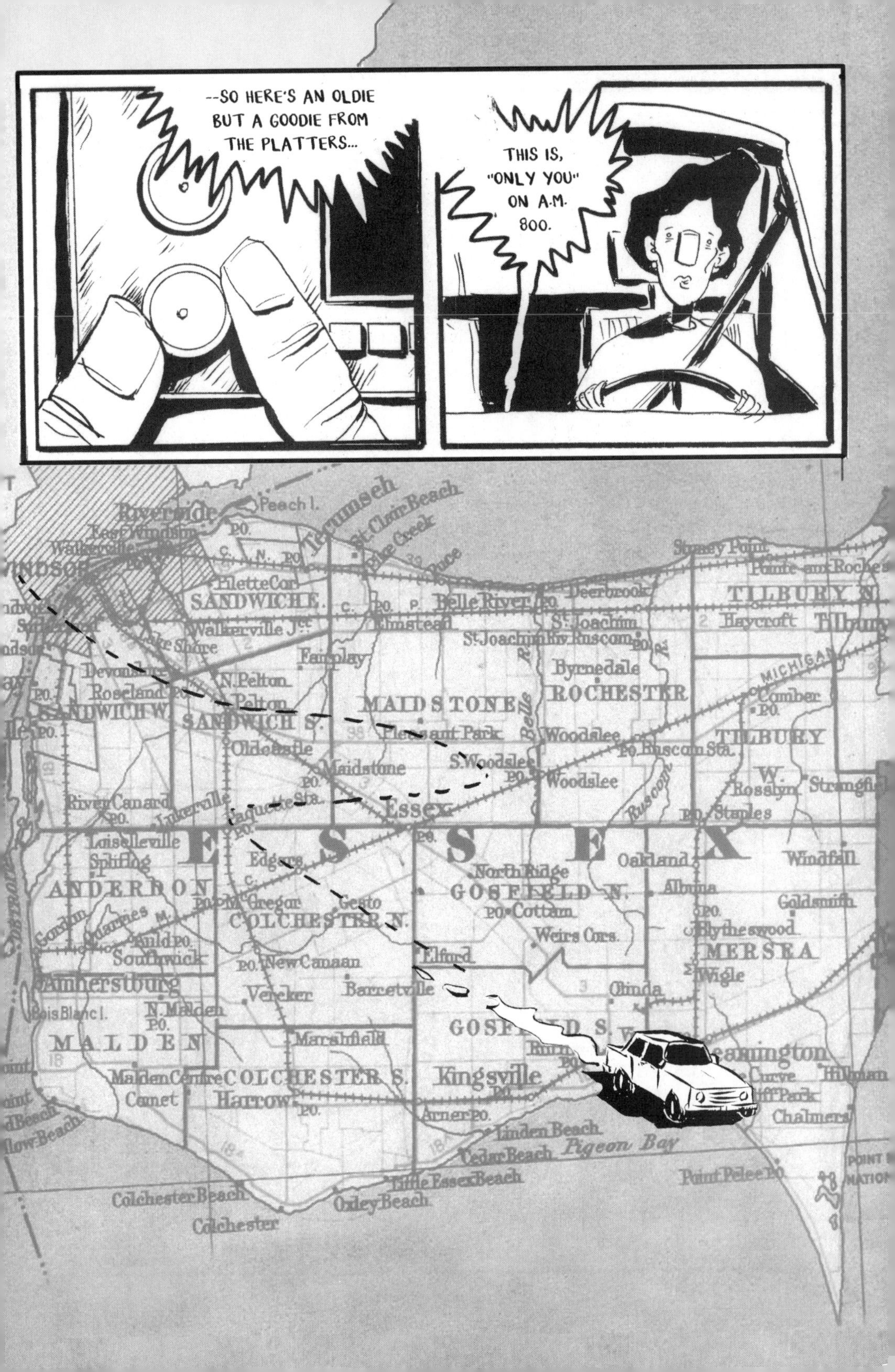
--SO HERE'S AN OLDIE BUT A GOODIE FROM THE PLATTERS...
THIS IS, "ONLY YOU" ON A.M. 800.
Tecumseh
St. Clair Beach
Peach I.
Riverside
SANDWICH E.
Belle River
Deerbrook
TILBURY N.
Pointe aux Roches
Haycroft
Tilbury
Walkerville Jct
Elmstead
St. Joachim
Fairplay
Byrnedale
ROCHESTER
Devonshire
Roseland
N. Pelton
Pelton
SANDWICH W.
SANDWICH S.
MAIDSTONE
Pleasant Park
Woodslee
Comber
TILBURY
Oldcastle
Maidstone
S. Woodslee
Ruscom Sta.
W.
Roslyn
Strangfield
River Canard
Essex
Staples
Loiselleville
E S S E X
Edgars
North Ridge
Oakland
Windfall
ANDERDON
GOSFIELD N.
Albuna
McGregor
Gesto
Goldsmith
COLCHESTER N.
Cottam
Blytheswood
Weirs Cors.
MERSEA
Auld
Southwick
New Canaan
Elford
Wigle
Amherstburg
Barretville
Olinda
Vereker
Bois Blanc I.
N. Malden
MALDEN
Marshfield
Leamington
Malden Centre
COLCHESTER S.
Kingsville
Hillman
Harrow
Chalmers
Linden Beach
Pigeon Bay
Cedar Beach
Point Pelee
Little Essex Beach
Colchester Beach
Oxley Beach
Colchester
MICHIGAN

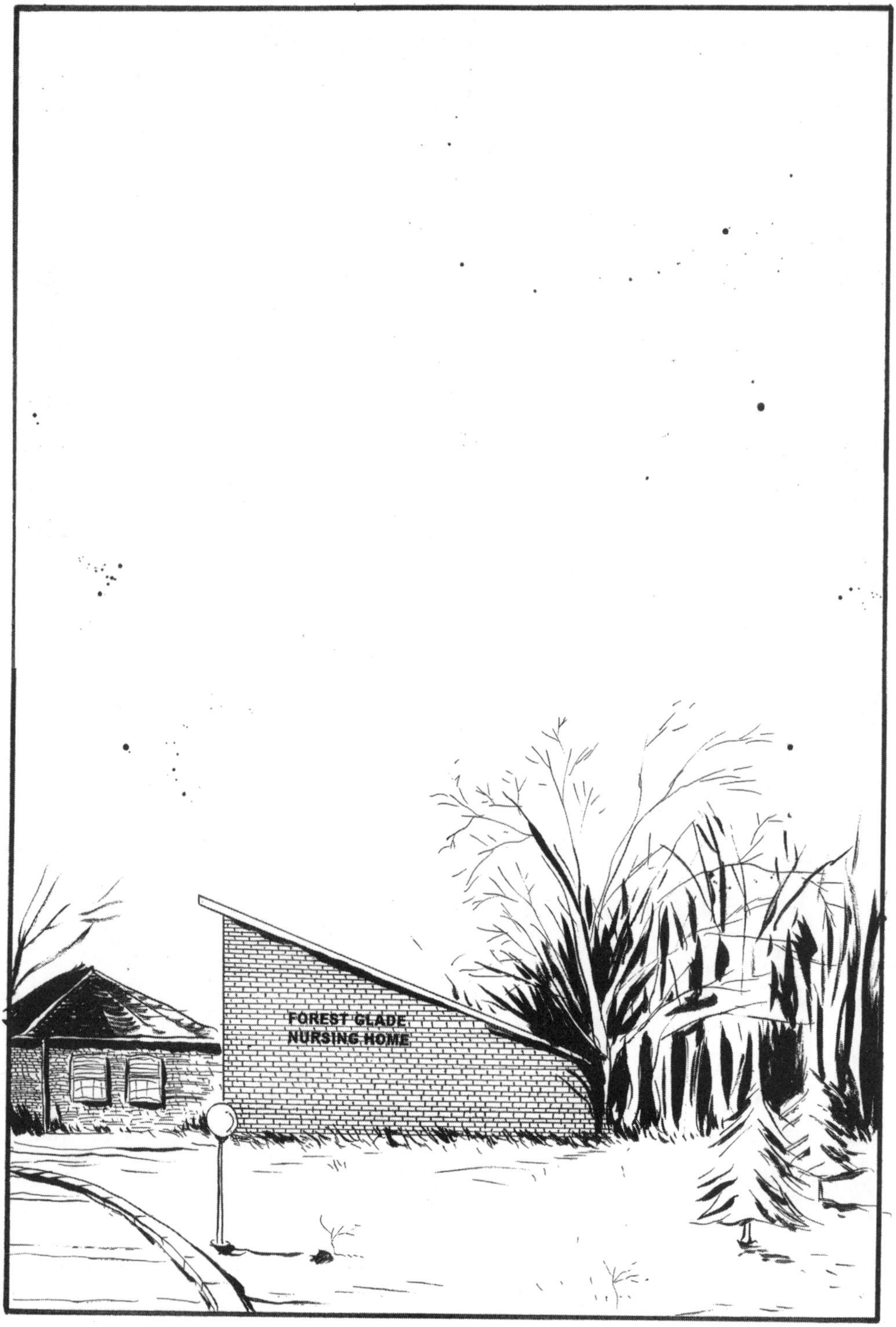
FOREST GLADE
NURSING HOME

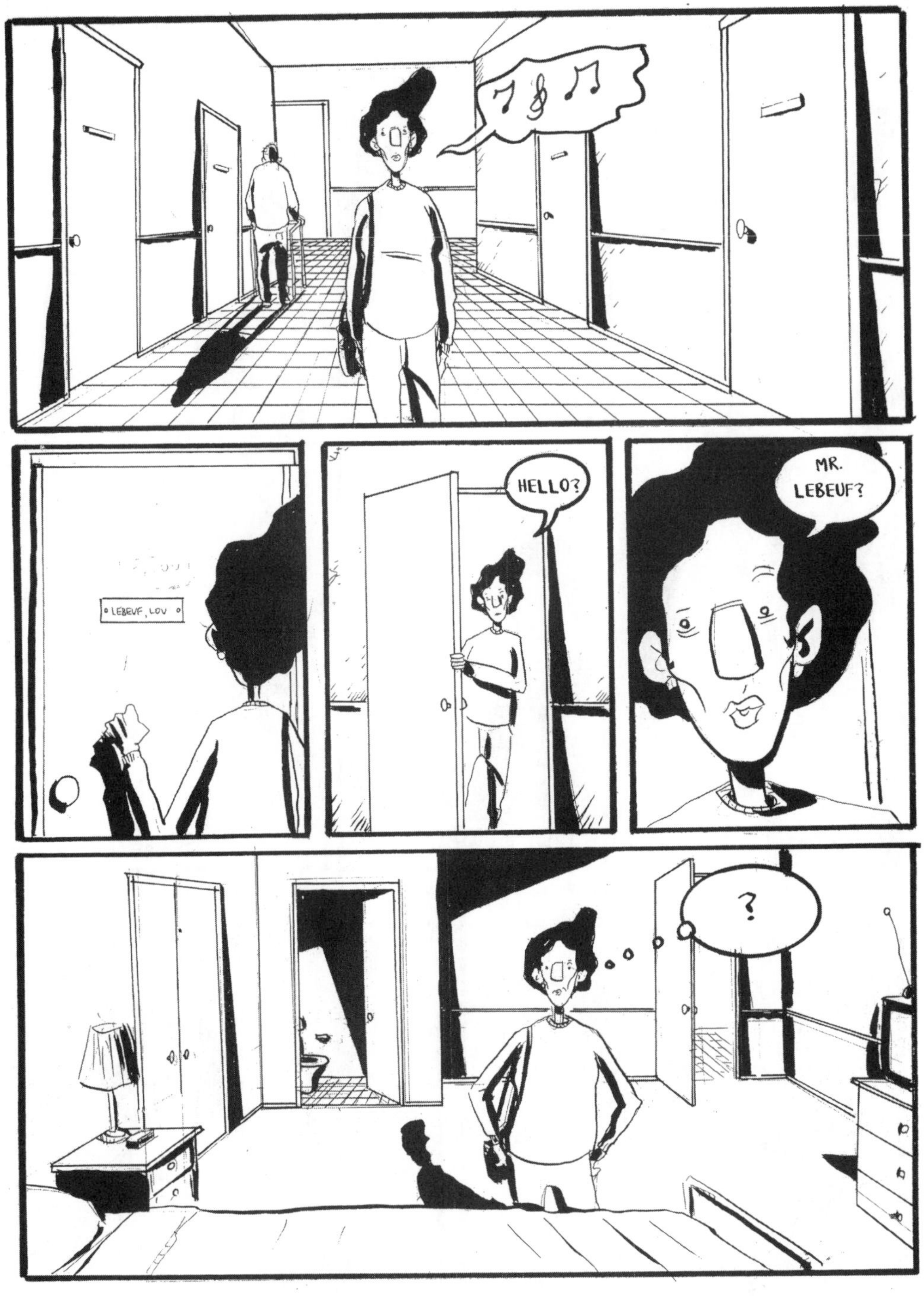
LEBEUF, LOU
HELLO?
MR. LEBEUF?
?

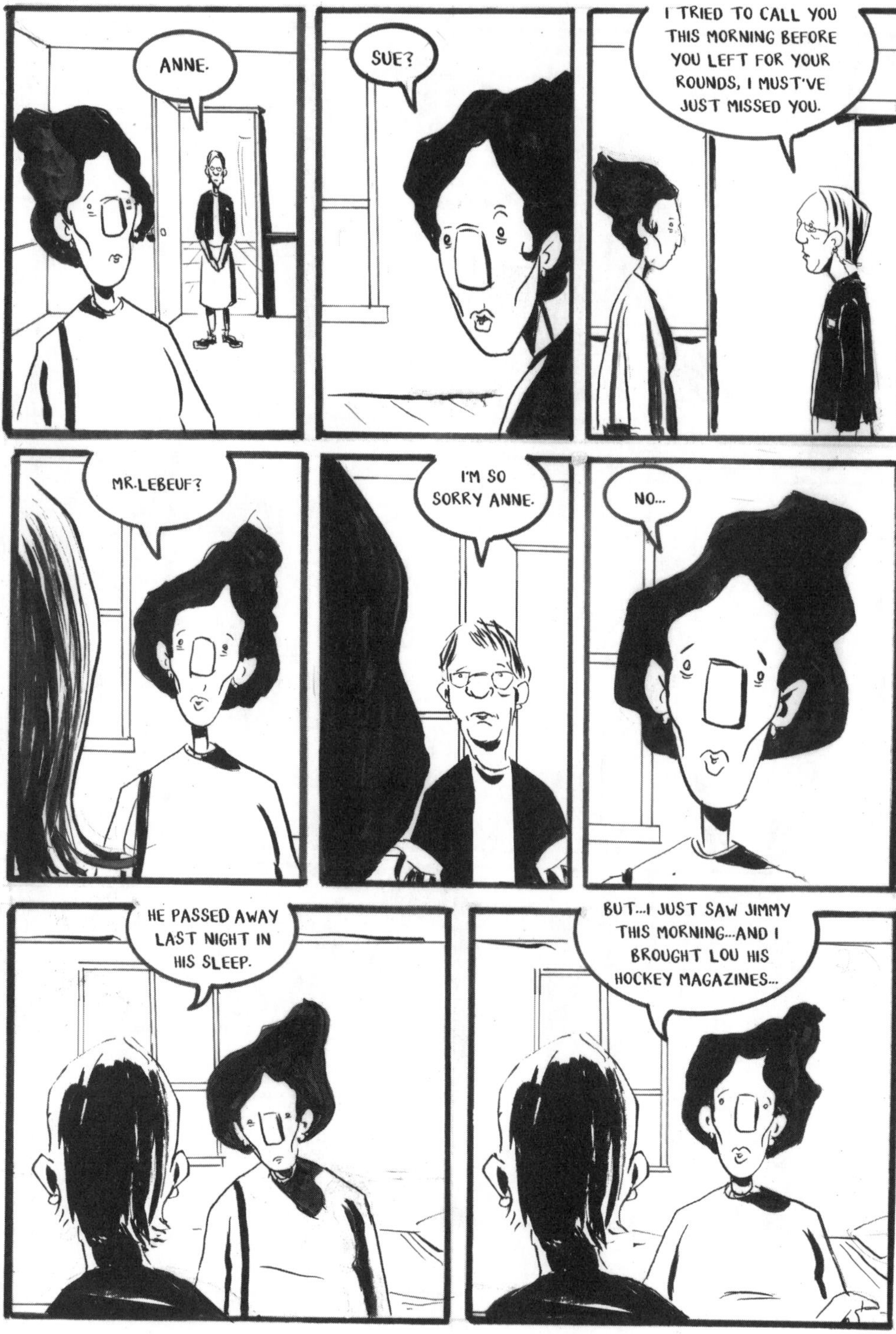
ANNE.
SUE?
I TRIED TO CALL YOU THIS MORNING BEFORE YOU LEFT FOR YOUR ROUNDS, I MUST'VE JUST MISSED YOU.
MR. LEBEUF?
I'M SO SORRY ANNE.
NO...
HE PASSED AWAY LAST NIGHT IN HIS SLEEP.
BUT...I JUST SAW JIMMY THIS MORNING...AND I BROUGHT LOU HIS HOCKEY MAGAZINES...

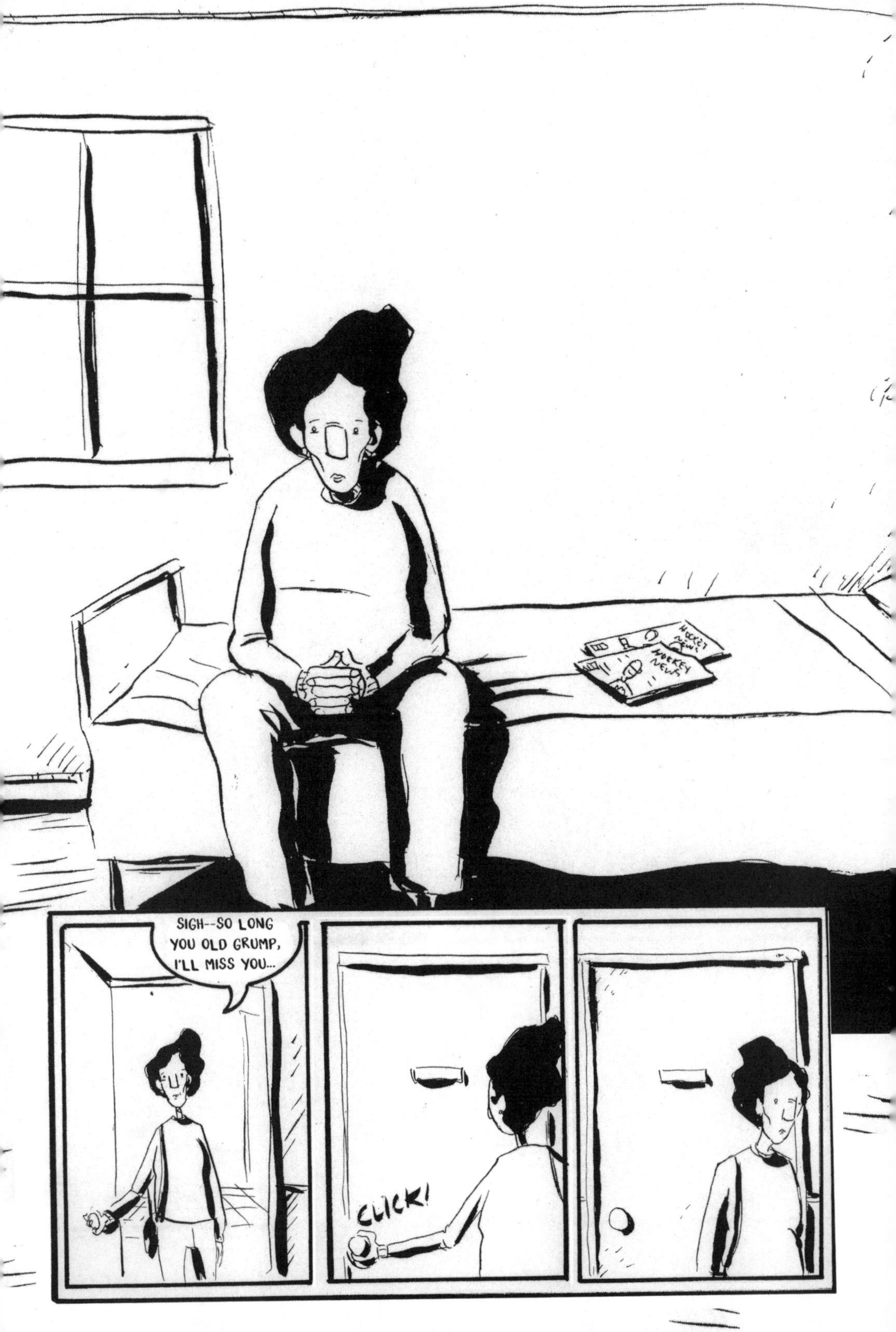
HOCKEY NEWS
HOCKEY NEWS
SIGH--SO LONG YOU OLD GRUMP, I'LL MISS YOU...
CLICK!

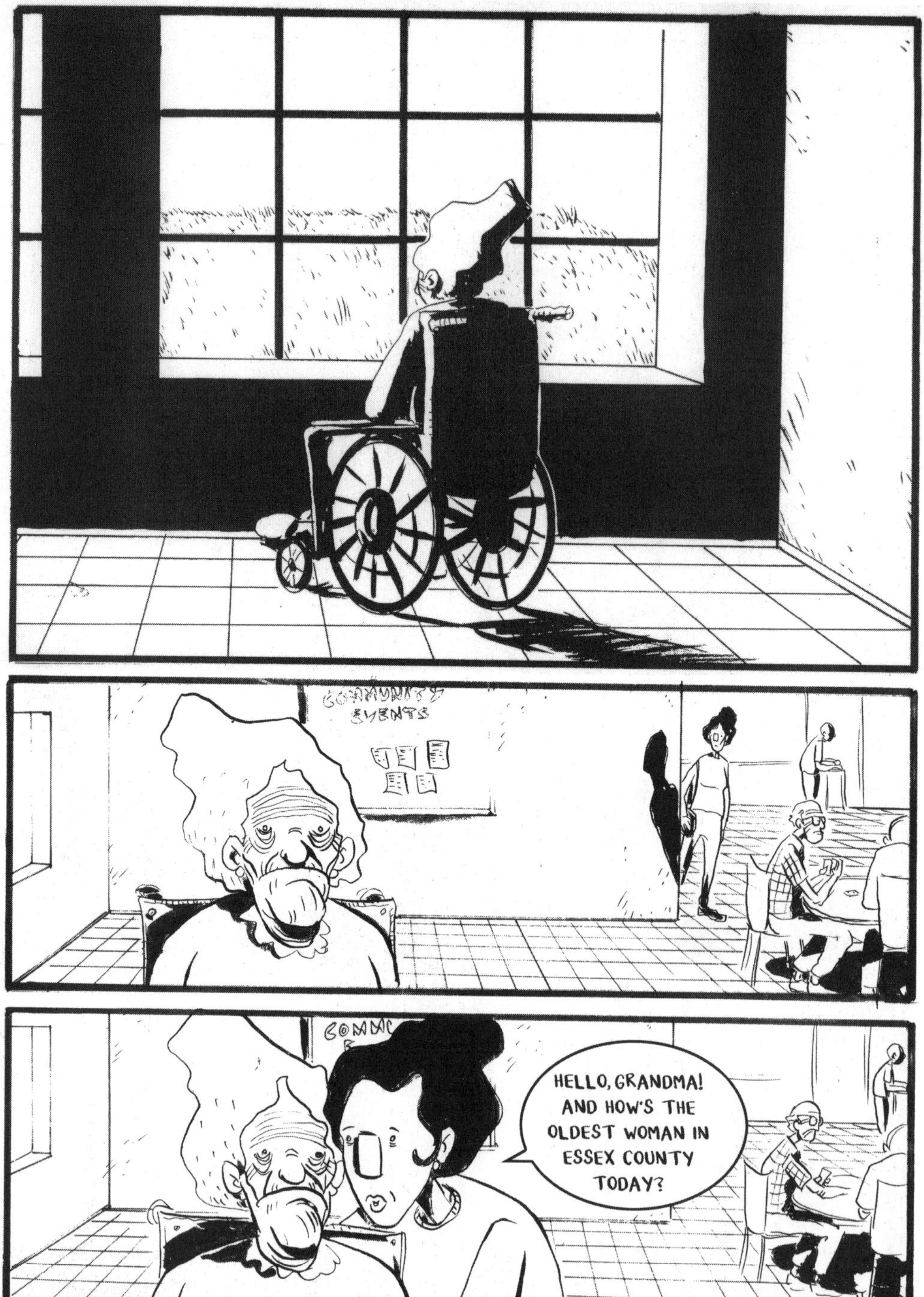
COMMUNITY EVENTS
HELLO, GRANDMA! AND HOW'S THE OLDEST WOMAN IN ESSEX COUNTY TODAY?

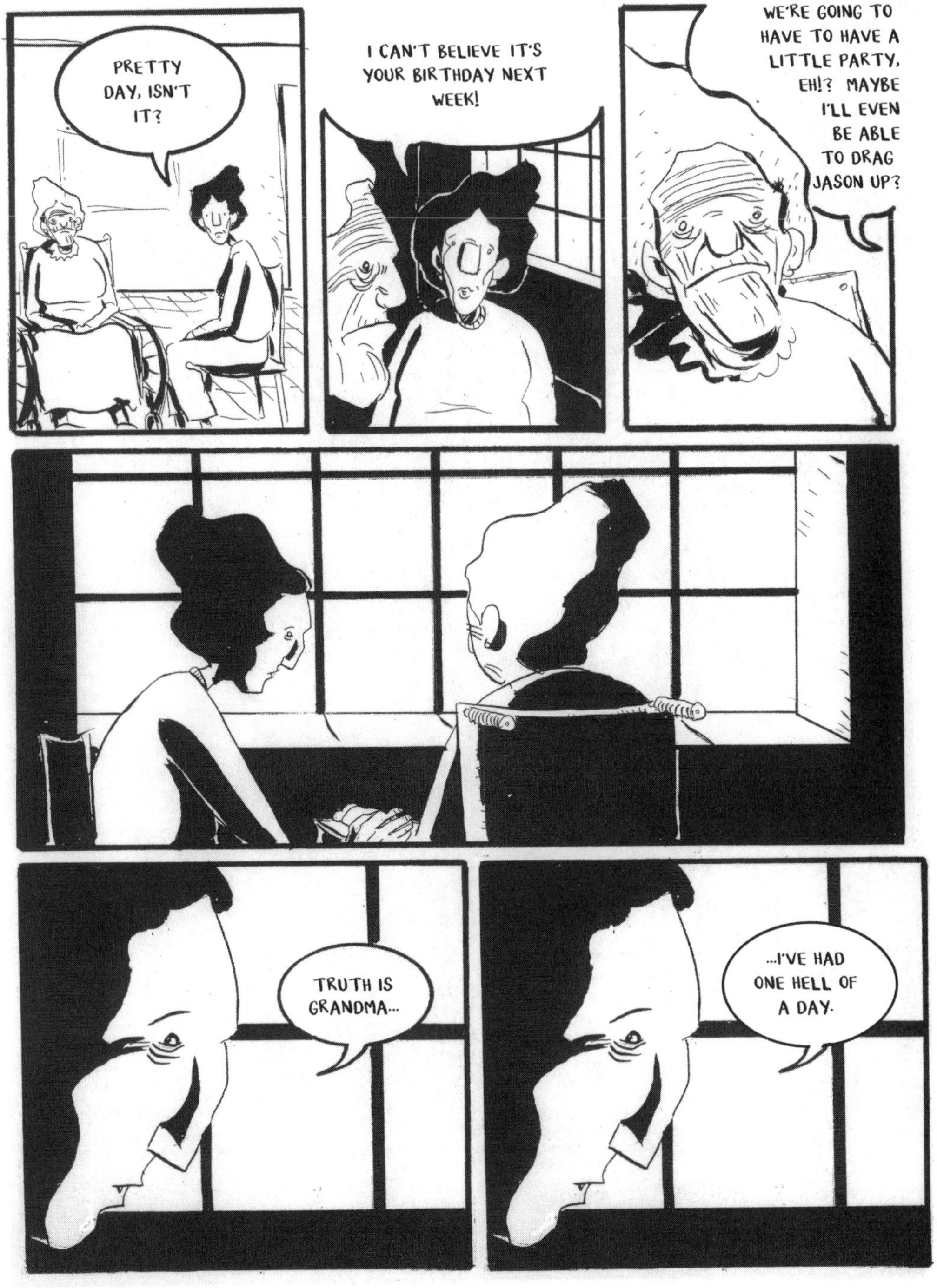
PRETTY DAY, ISN'T IT?
I CAN'T BELIEVE IT'S YOUR BIRTHDAY NEXT WEEK!
WE'RE GOING TO HAVE TO HAVE A LITTLE PARTY, EH!? MAYBE I'LL EVEN BE ABLE TO DRAG JASON UP?
TRUTH IS GRANDMA...
...I'VE HAD ONE HELL OF A DAY.

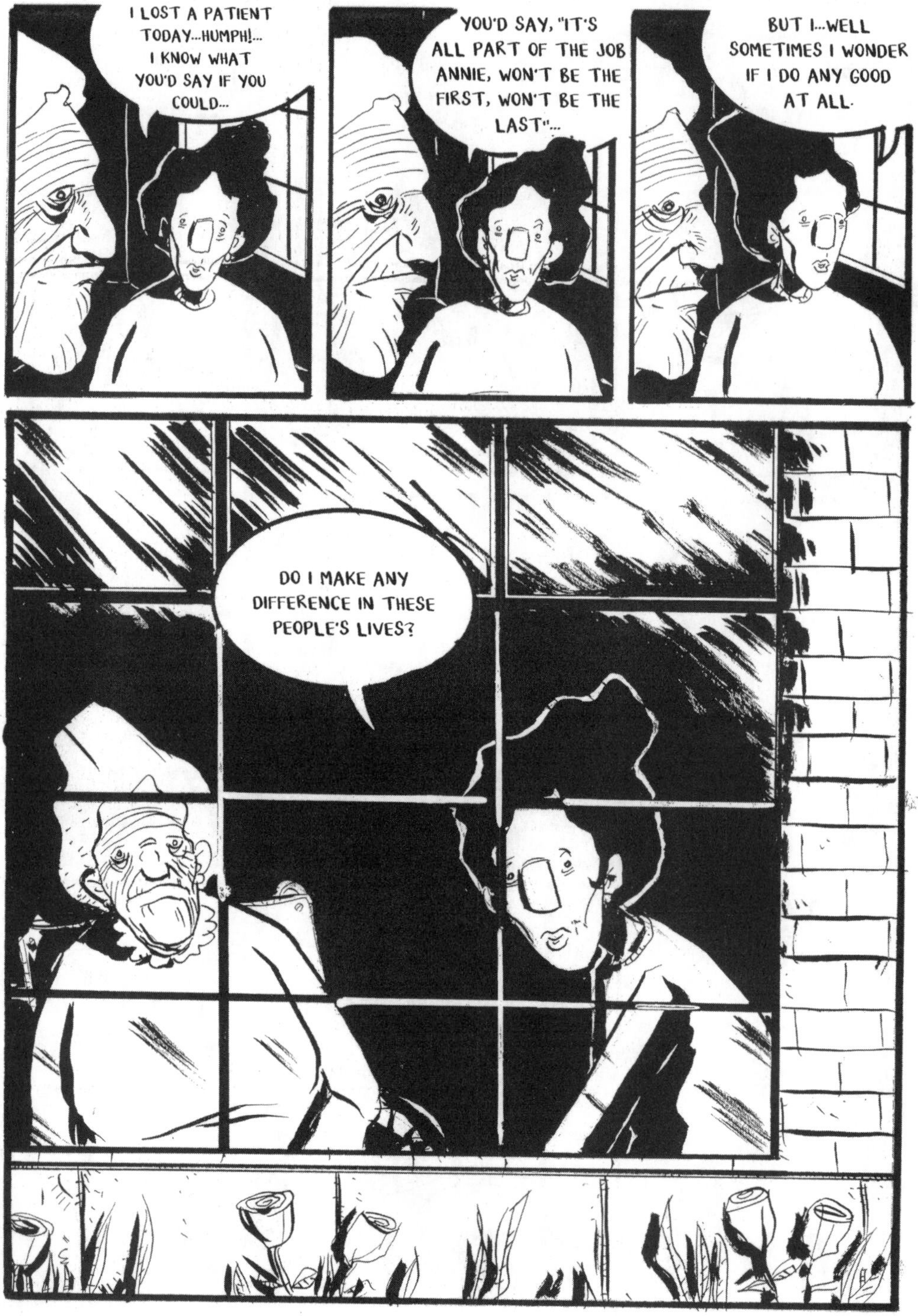
I LOST A PATIENT TODAY...HUMPH!... I KNOW WHAT YOU'D SAY IF YOU COULD...
YOU'D SAY, "IT'S ALL PART OF THE JOB ANNIE, WON'T BE THE FIRST, WON'T BE THE LAST"...
BUT I...WELL SOMETIMES I WONDER IF I DO ANY GOOD AT ALL.
DO I MAKE ANY DIFFERENCE IN THESE PEOPLE'S LIVES?

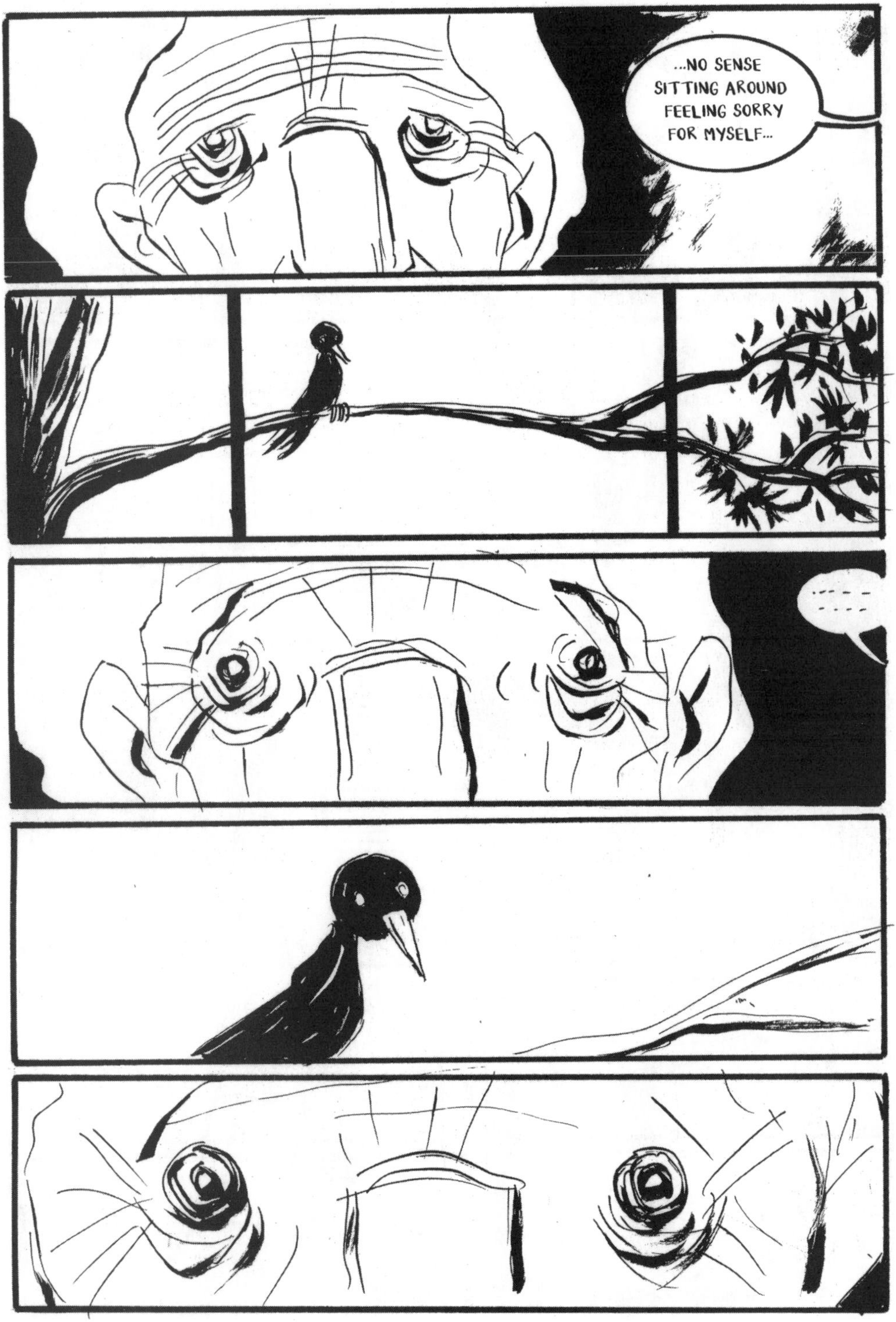
...NO SENSE
SITTING AROUND
FEELING SORRY
FOR MYSELF...

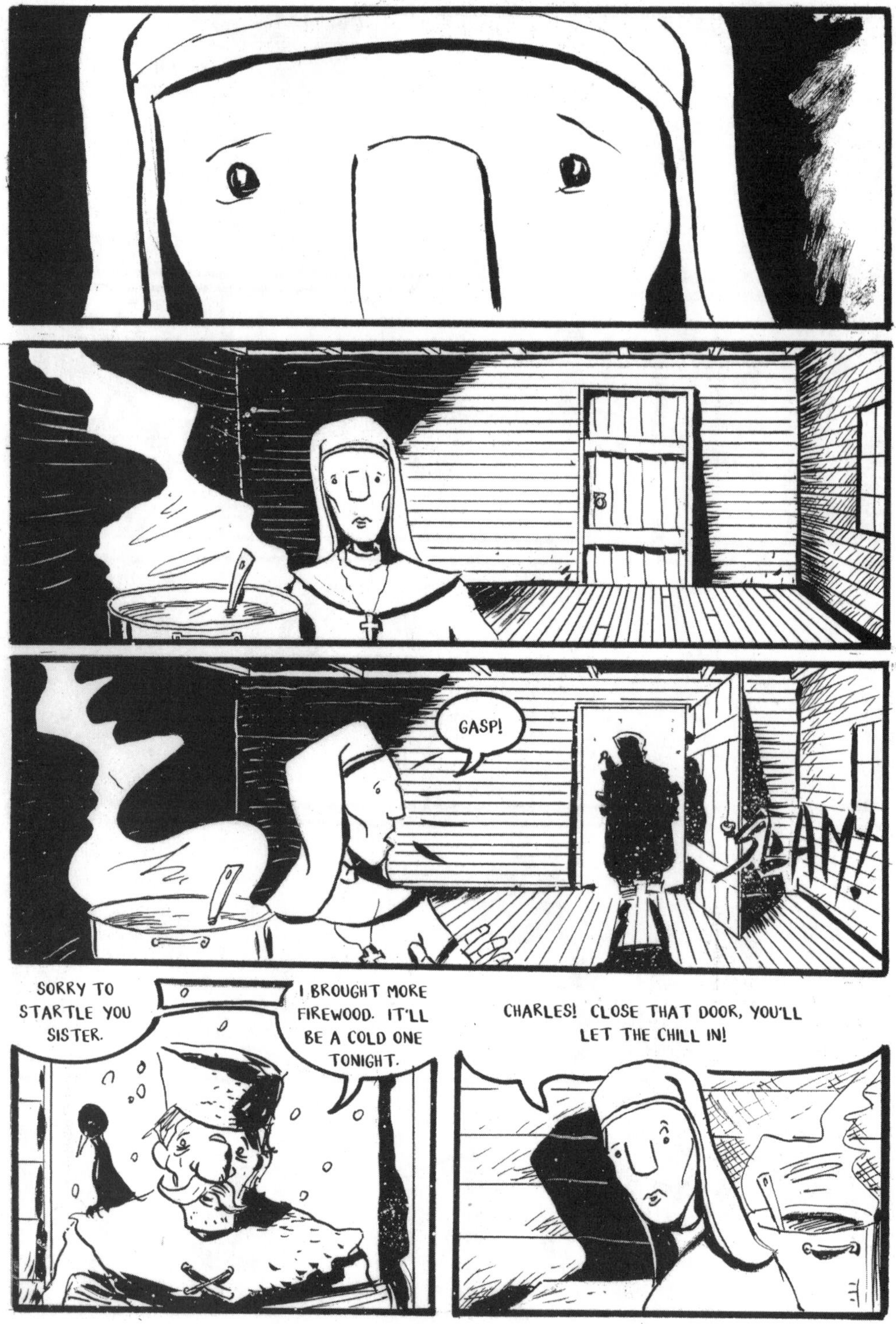
GASP!
SLAM!
SORRY TO STARTLE YOU SISTER.
I BROUGHT MORE FIREWOOD. IT'LL BE A COLD ONE TONIGHT.
CHARLES! CLOSE THAT DOOR, YOU'LL LET THE CHILL IN!

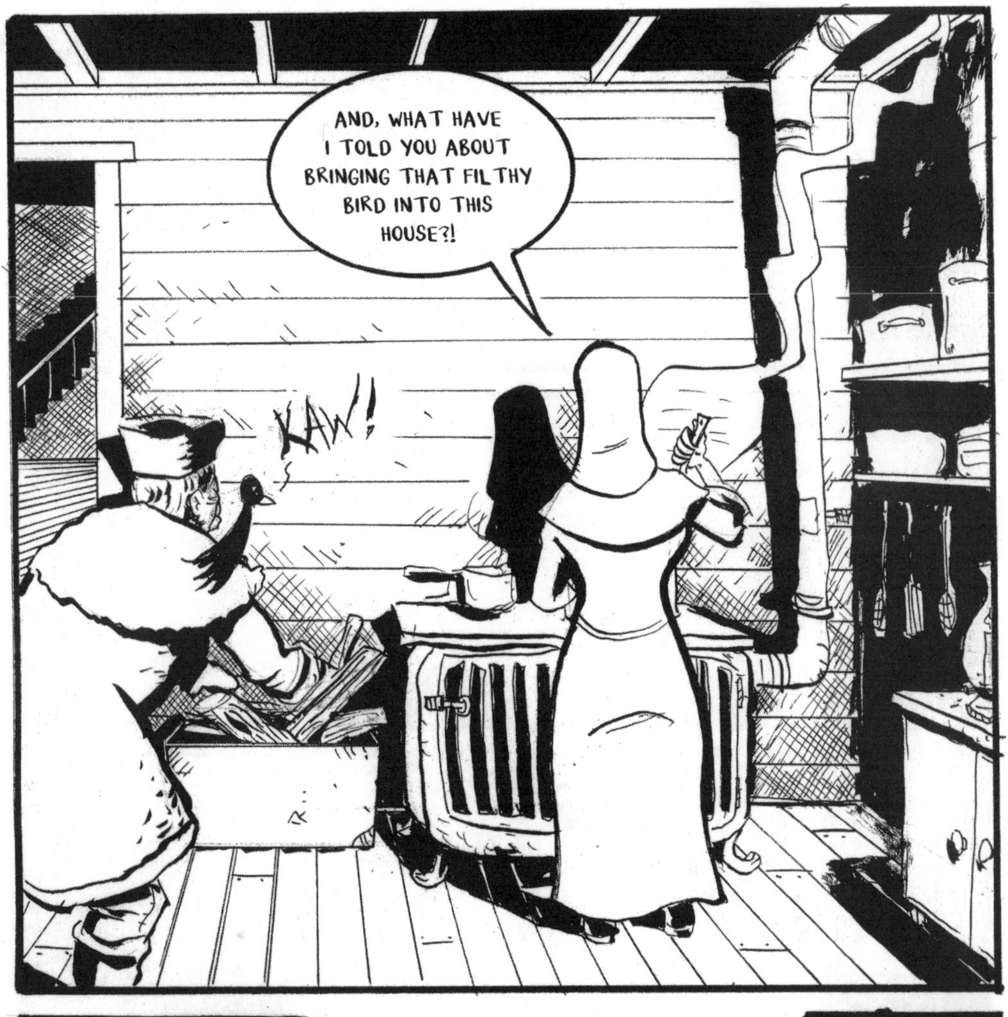
AND, WHAT HAVE I TOLD YOU ABOUT BRINGING THAT FILTHY BIRD INTO THIS HOUSE?!
KAW!

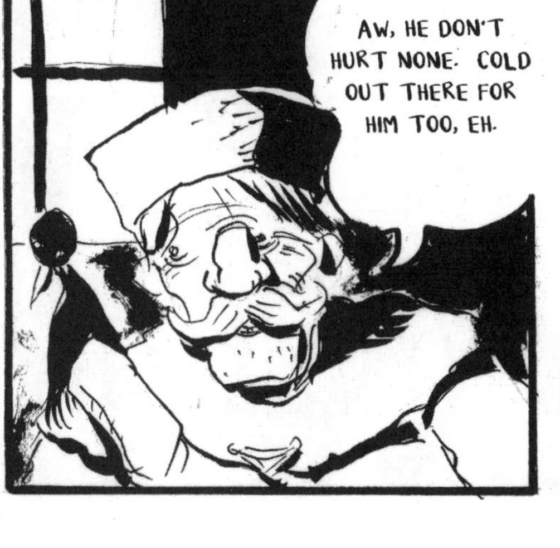
AW, HE DON'T HURT NONE. COLD OUT THERE FOR HIM TOO, EH.

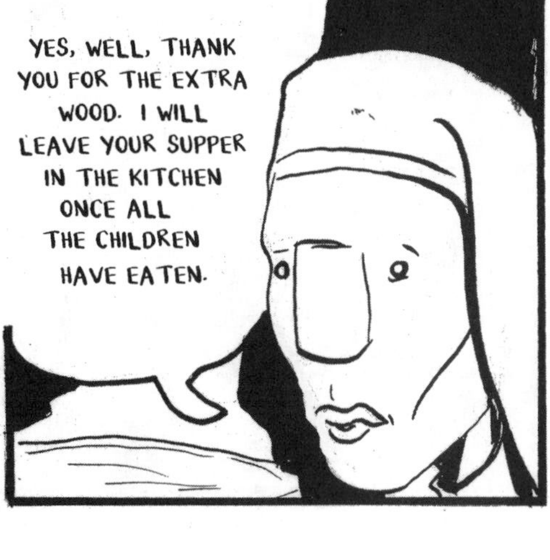
YES, WELL, THANK YOU FOR THE EXTRA WOOD. I WILL LEAVE YOUR SUPPER IN THE KITCHEN ONCE ALL THE CHILDREN HAVE EATEN.

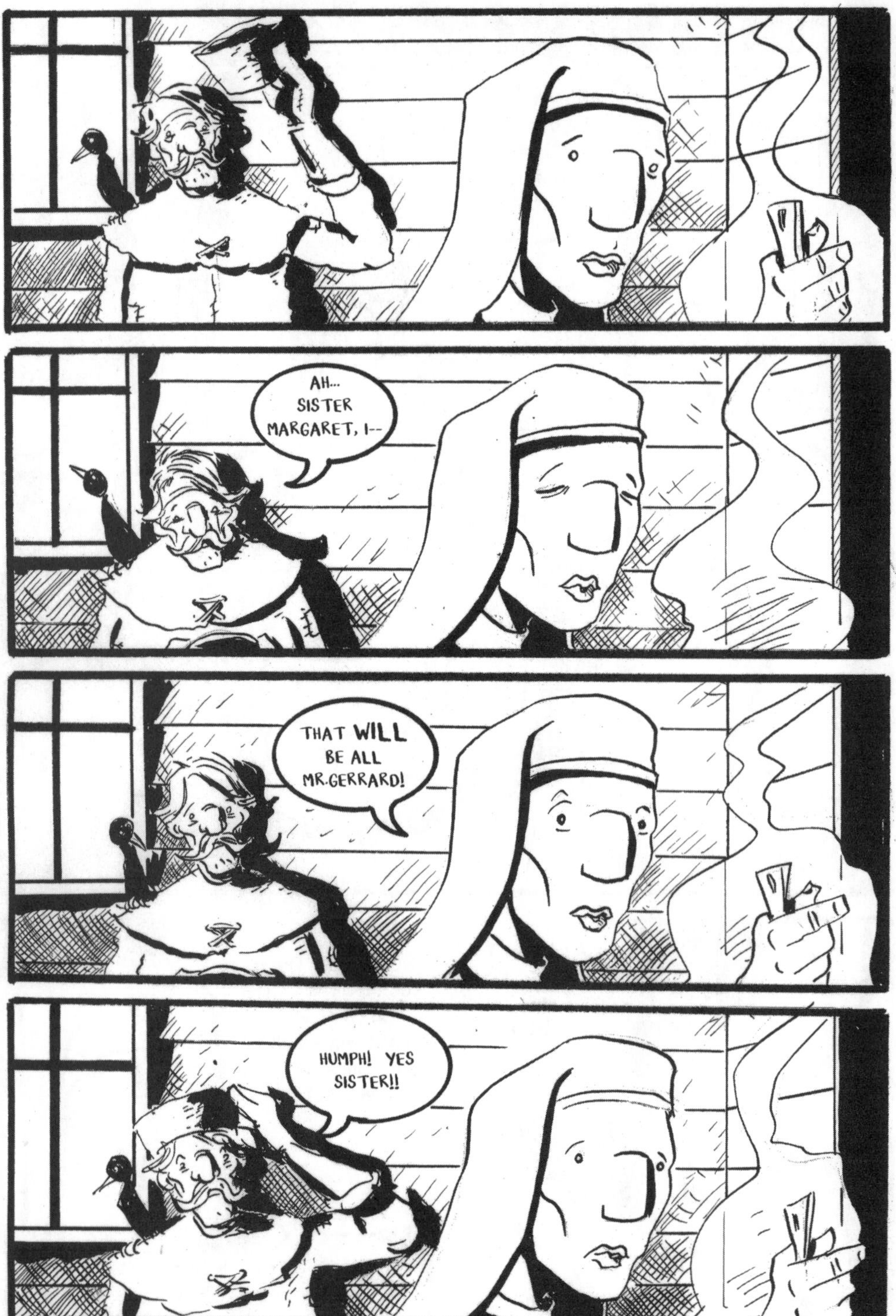
AH... SISTER MARGARET, I--
THAT WILL BE ALL MR.GERRARD!
HUMPH! YES SISTER!!

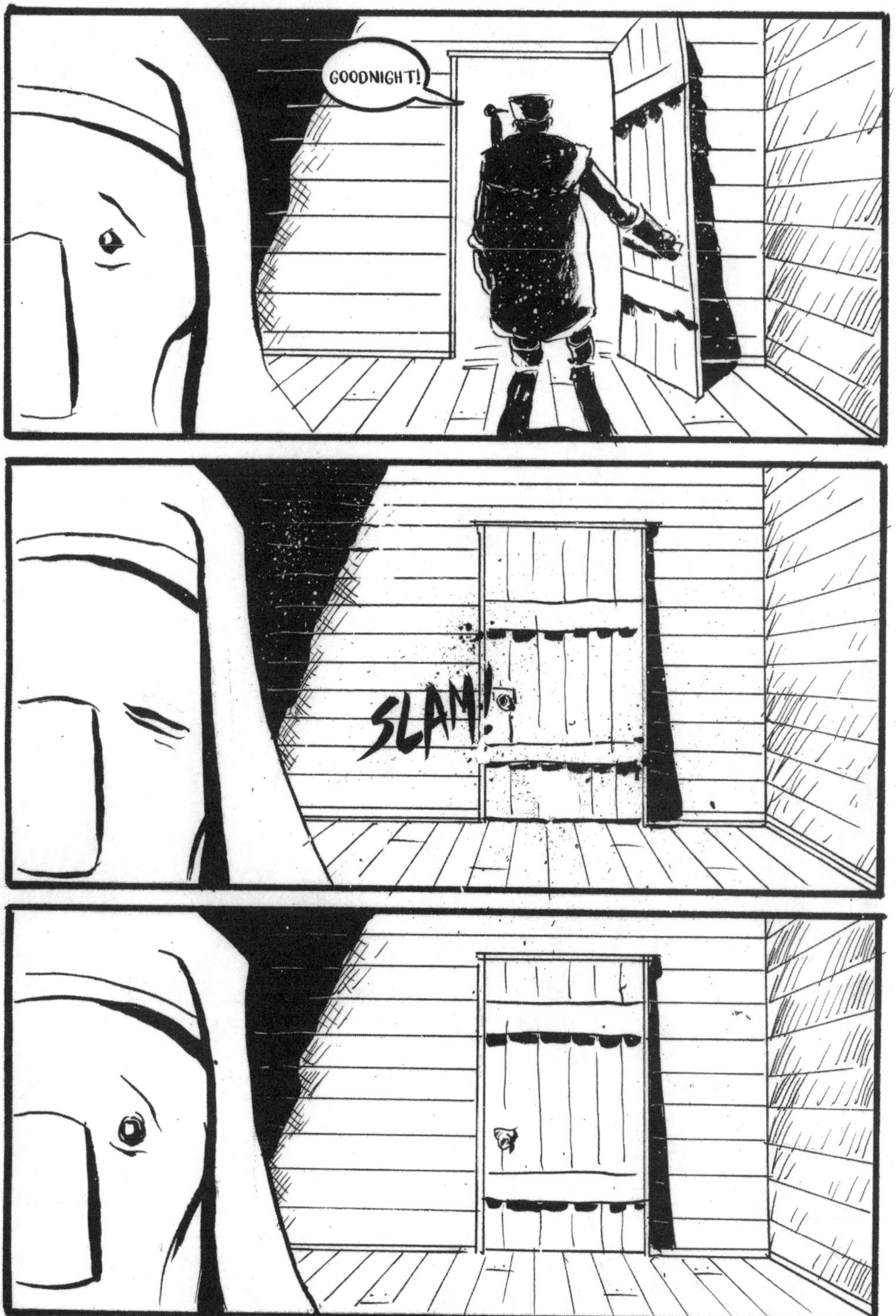
GOODNIGHT!
SLAM!

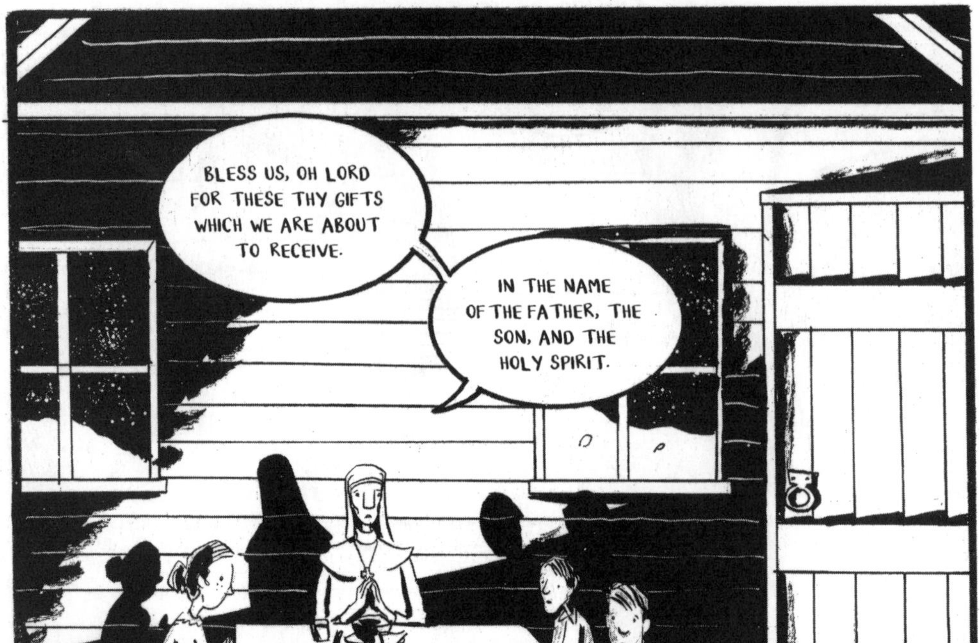
BLESS US, OH LORD FOR THESE THY GIFTS WHICH WE ARE ABOUT TO RECEIVE.
IN THE NAME OF THE FATHER, THE SON, AND THE HOLY SPIRIT.

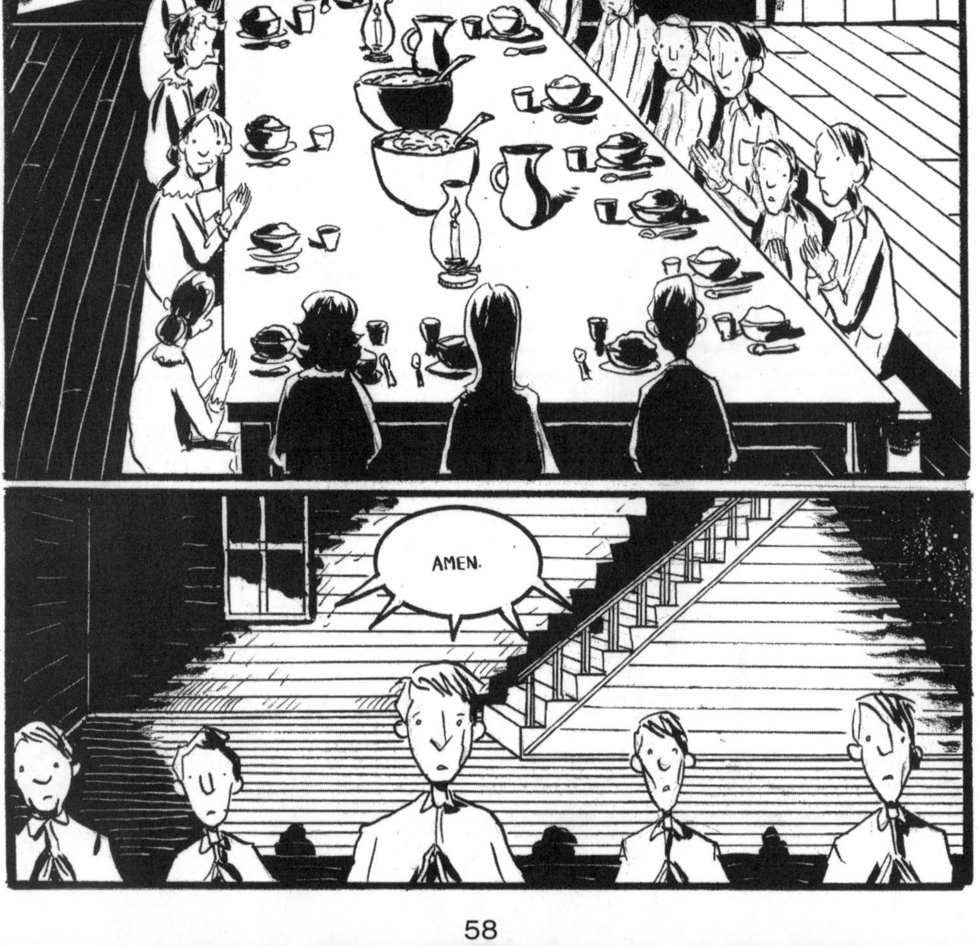
AMEN.

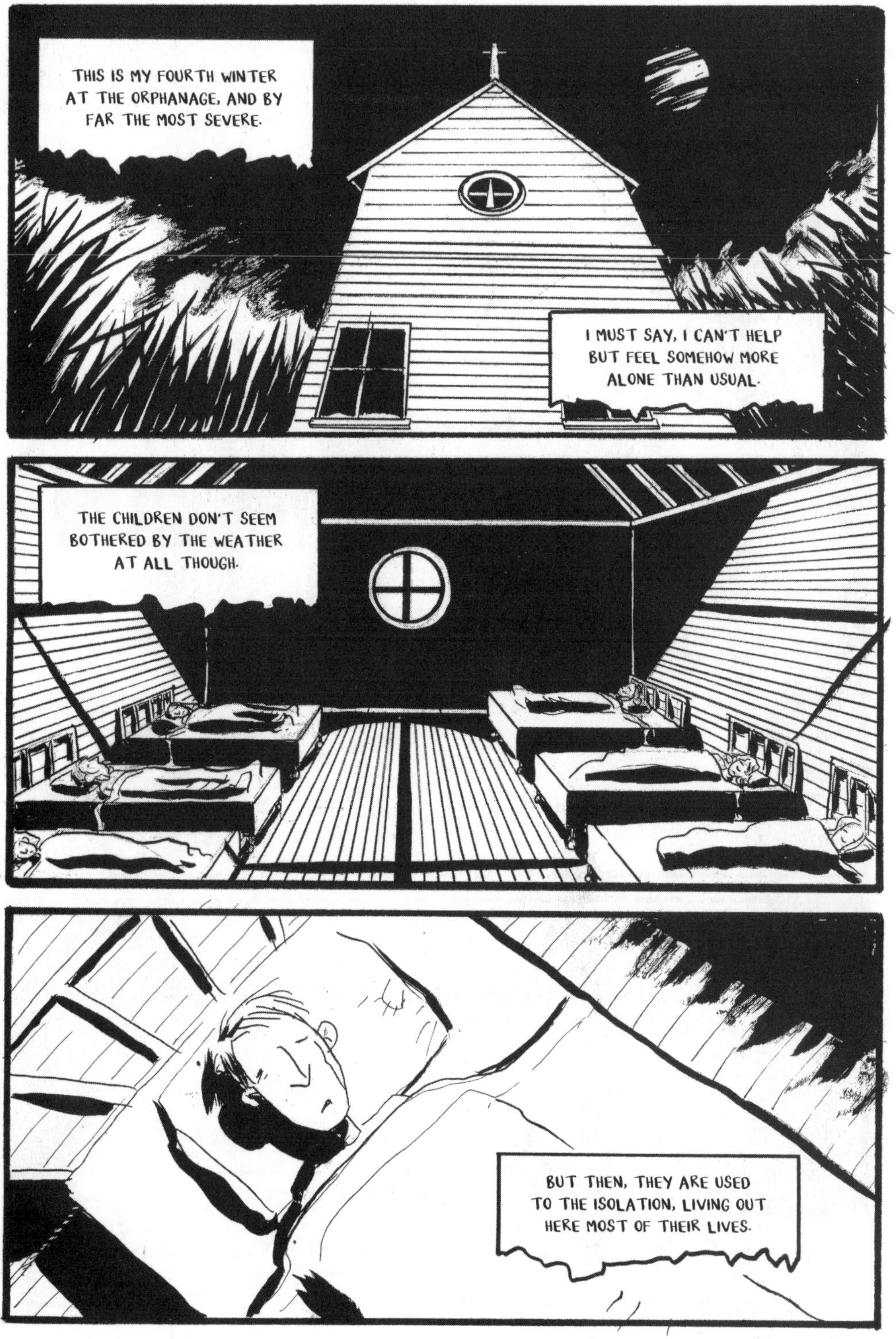
THIS IS MY FOURTH WINTER AT THE ORPHANAGE, AND BY FAR THE MOST SEVERE.
I MUST SAY, I CAN'T HELP BUT FEEL SOMEHOW MORE ALONE THAN USUAL.
THE CHILDREN DON'T SEEM BOTHERED BY THE WEATHER AT ALL THOUGH.
BUT THEN, THEY ARE USED TO THE ISOLATION, LIVING OUT HERE MOST OF THEIR LIVES.

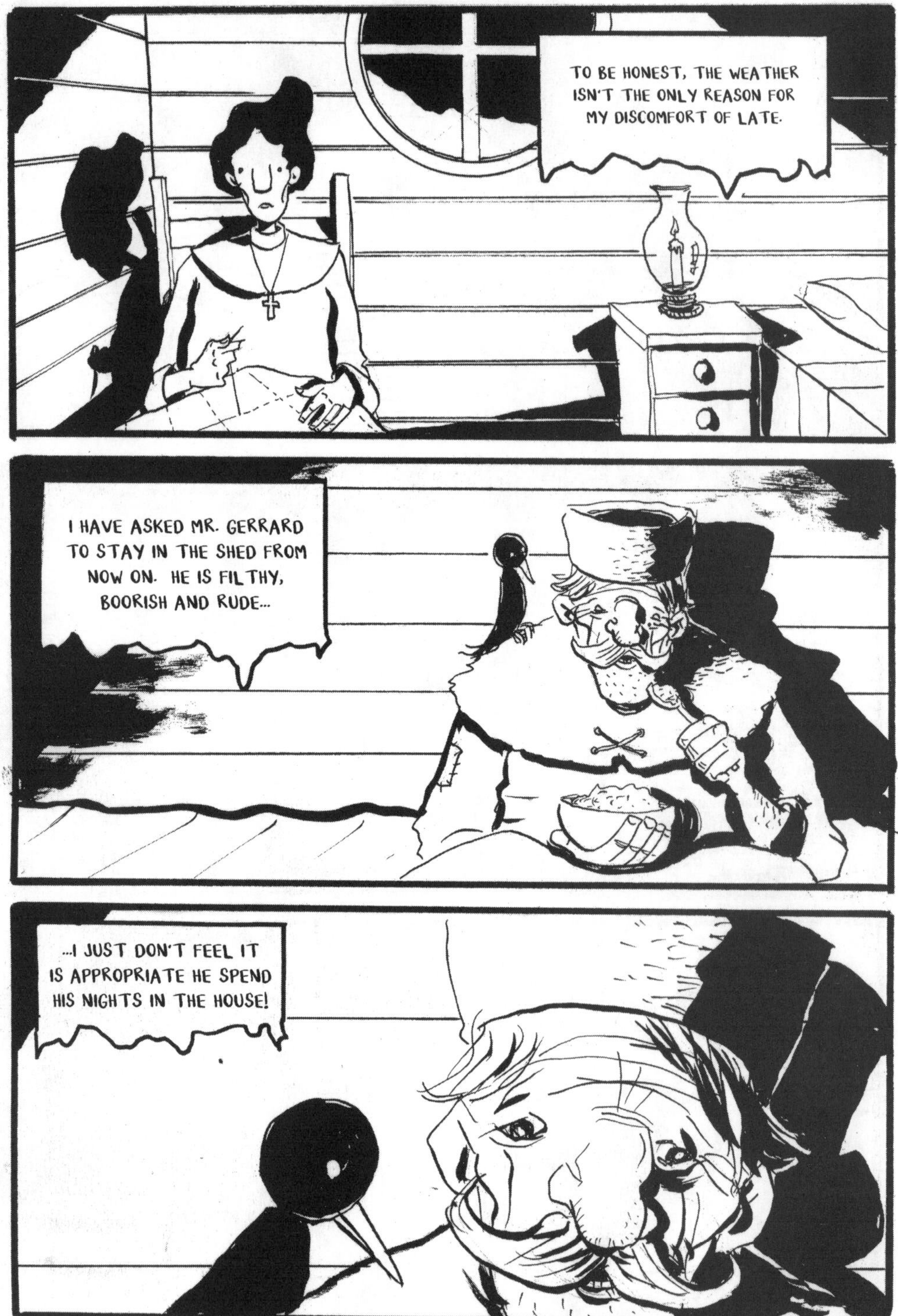
TO BE HONEST, THE WEATHER ISN'T THE ONLY REASON FOR MY DISCOMFORT OF LATE.
I HAVE ASKED MR. GERRARD TO STAY IN THE SHED FROM NOW ON. HE IS FILTHY, BOORISH AND RUDE...
...I JUST DON'T FEEL IT IS APPROPRIATE HE SPEND HIS NIGHTS IN THE HOUSE!

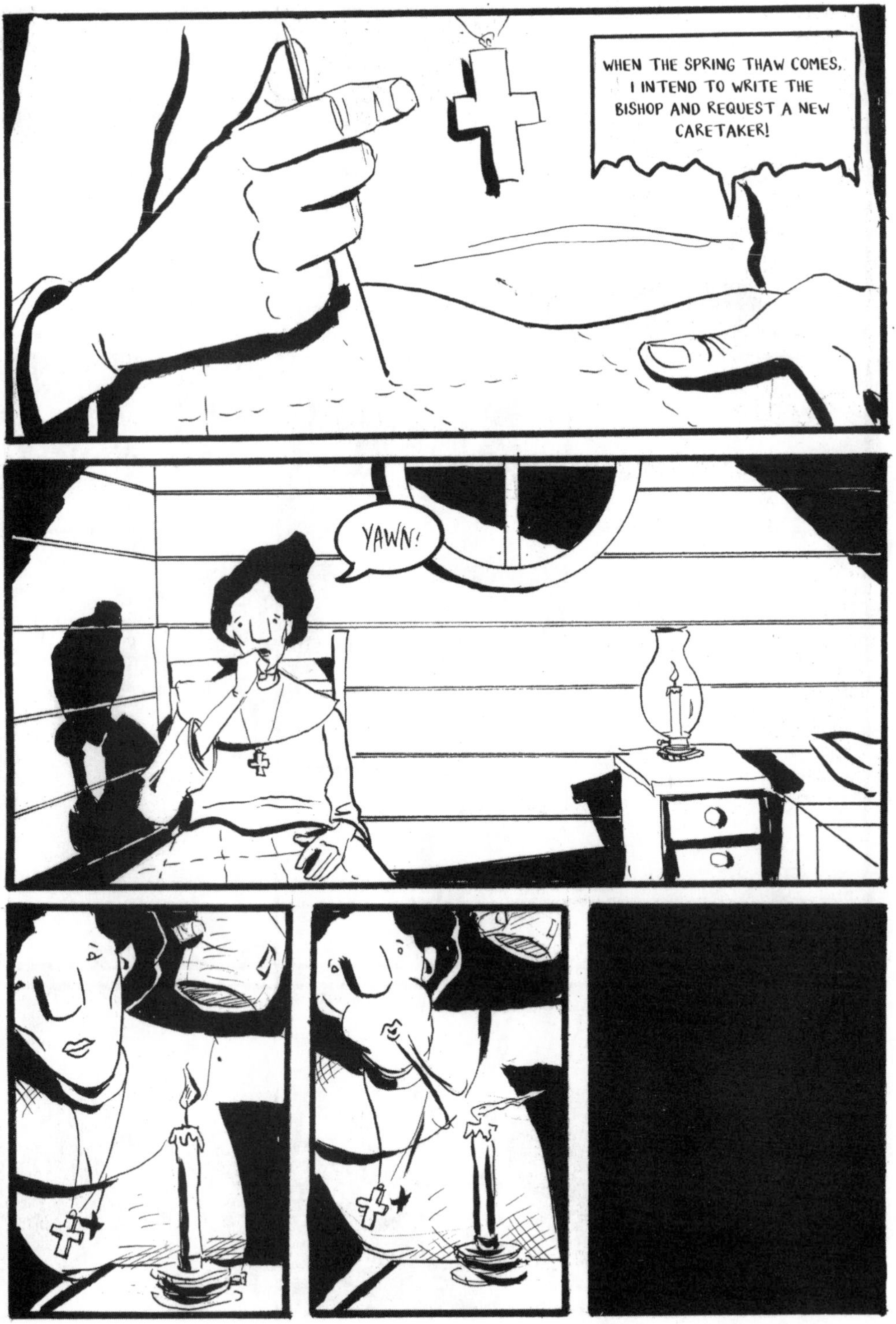
WHEN THE SPRING THAW COMES, I INTEND TO WRITE THE BISHOP AND REQUEST A NEW CARETAKER!
YAWN!

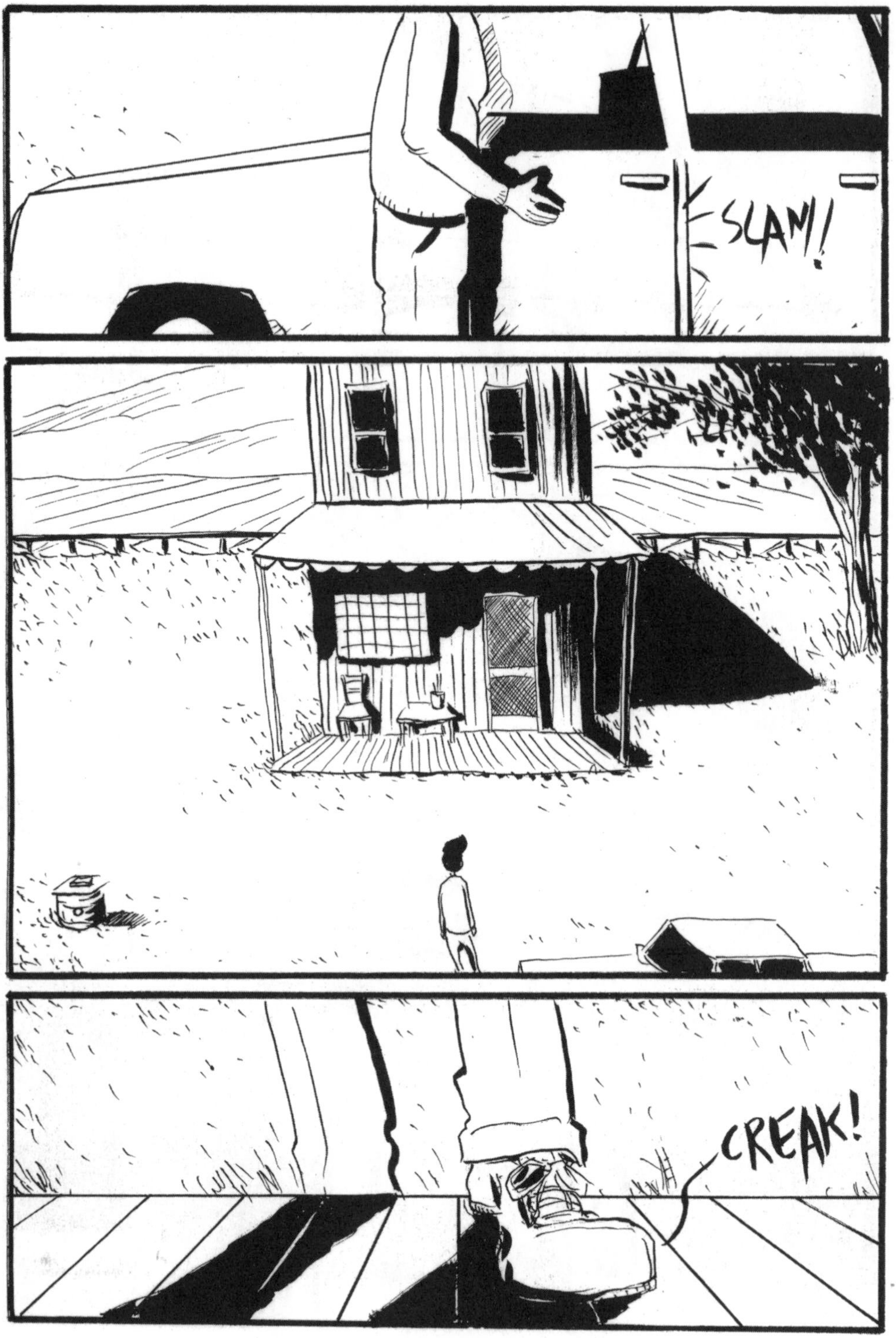
SLAM!
CREAK!

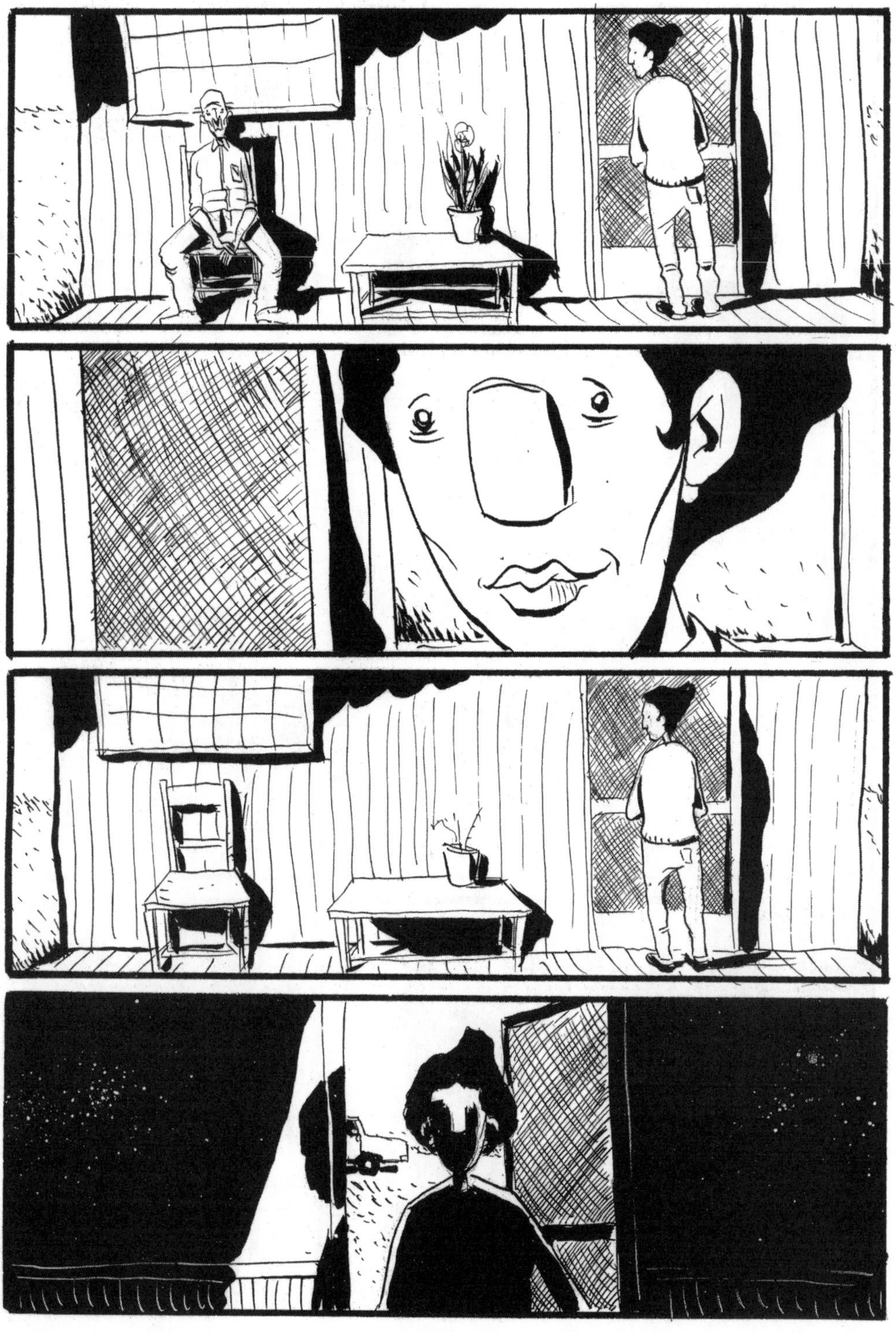

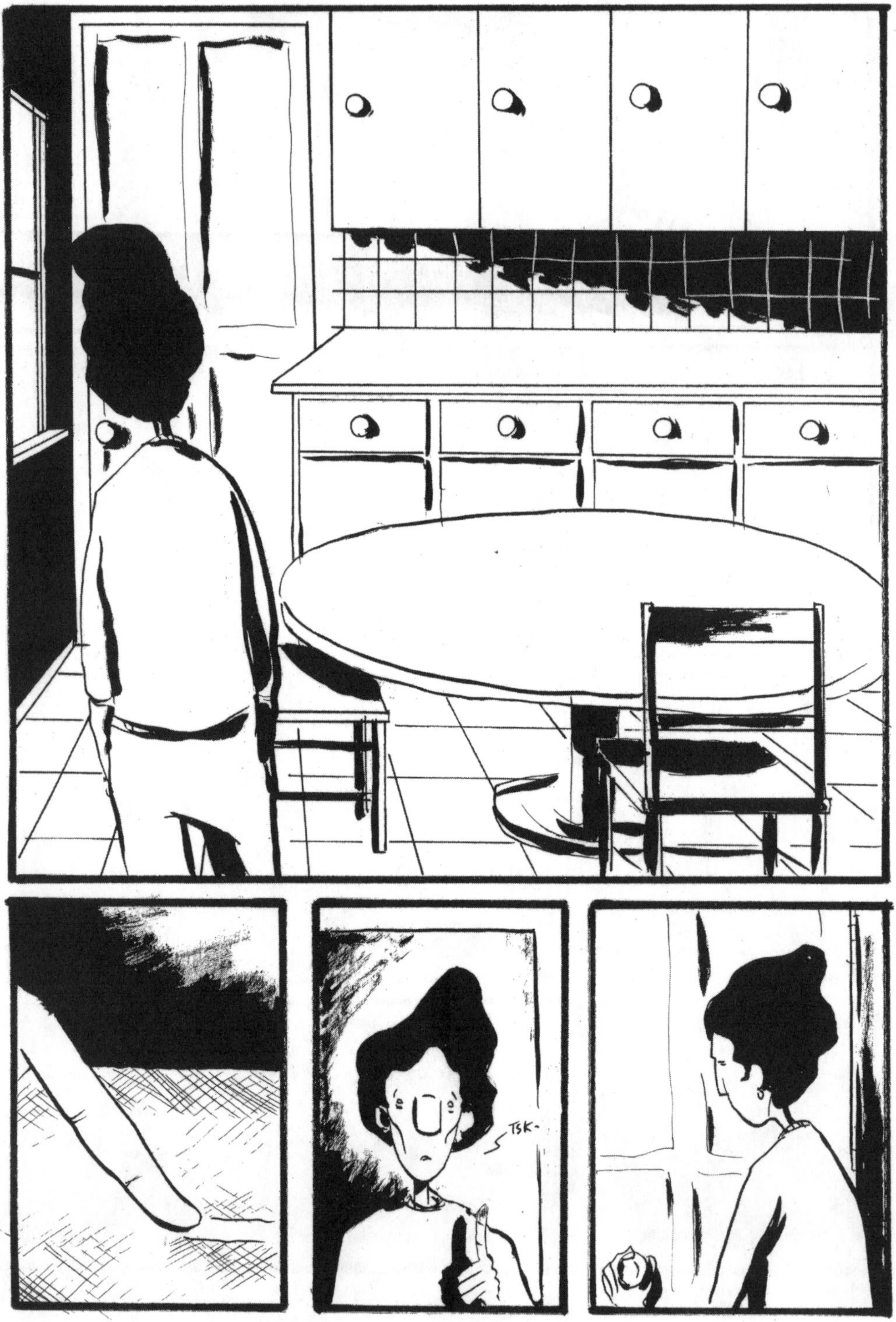
TSK-

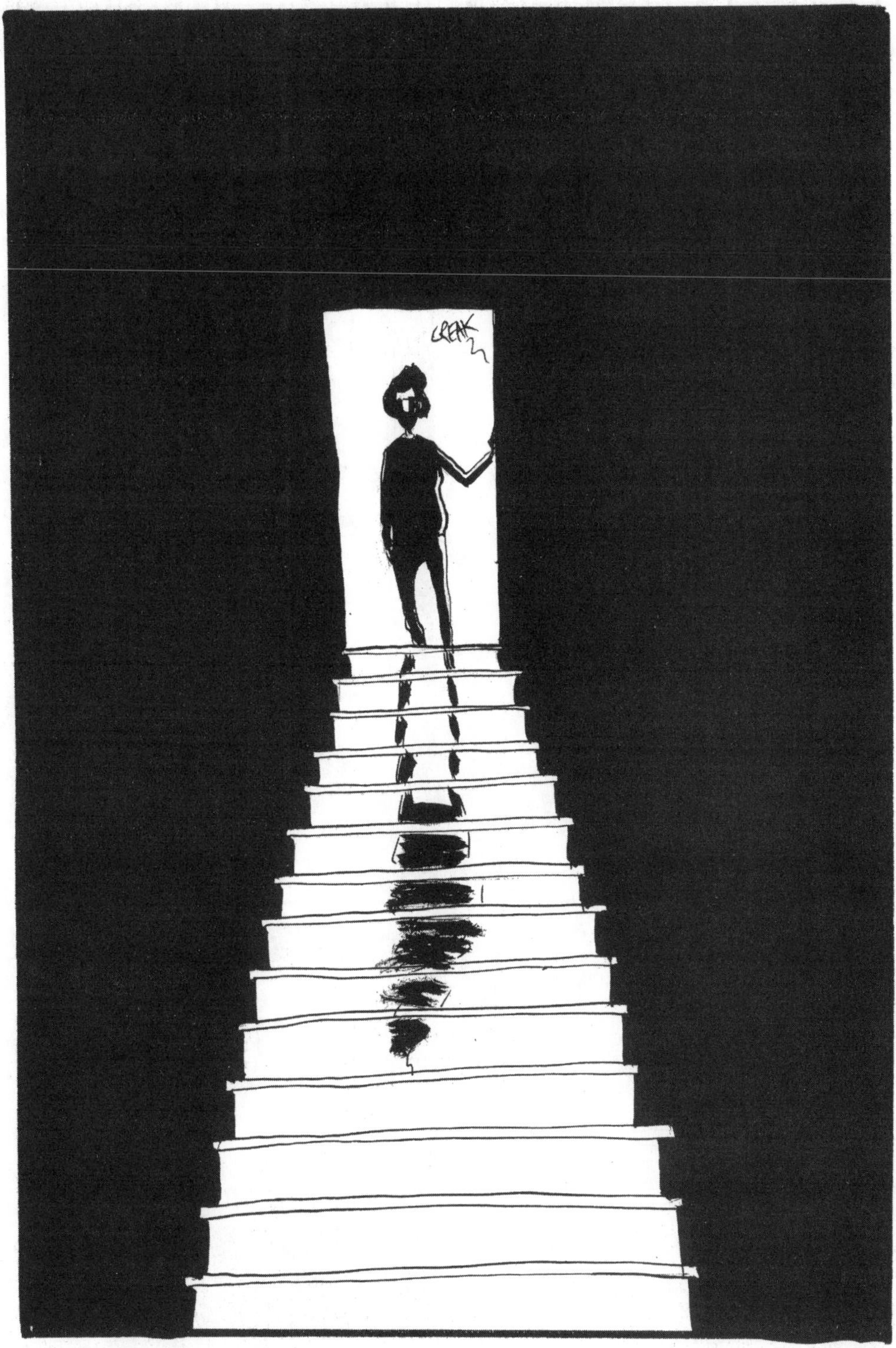
CREAK

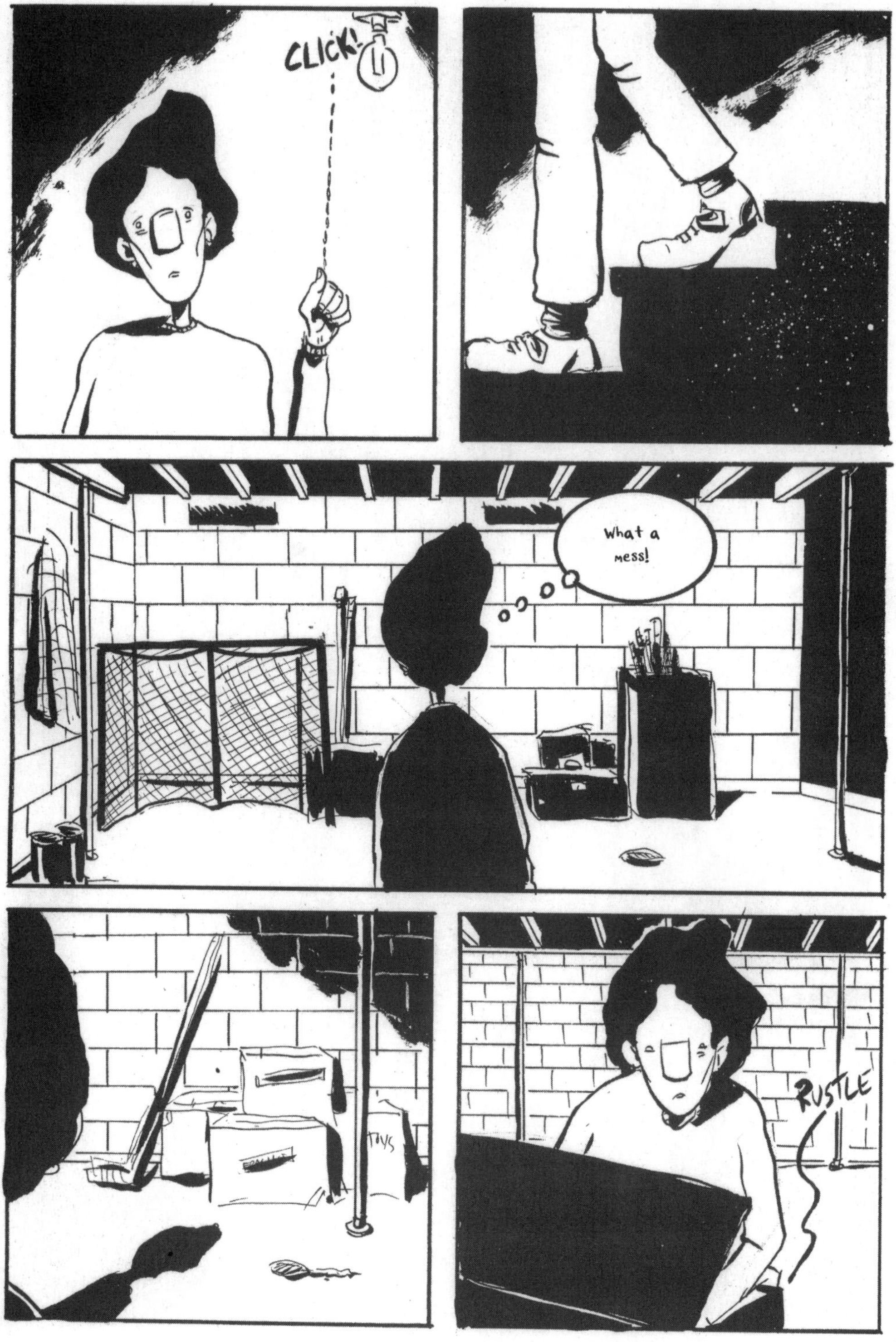
CLICK!
What a mess!
TOYS
RUSTLE

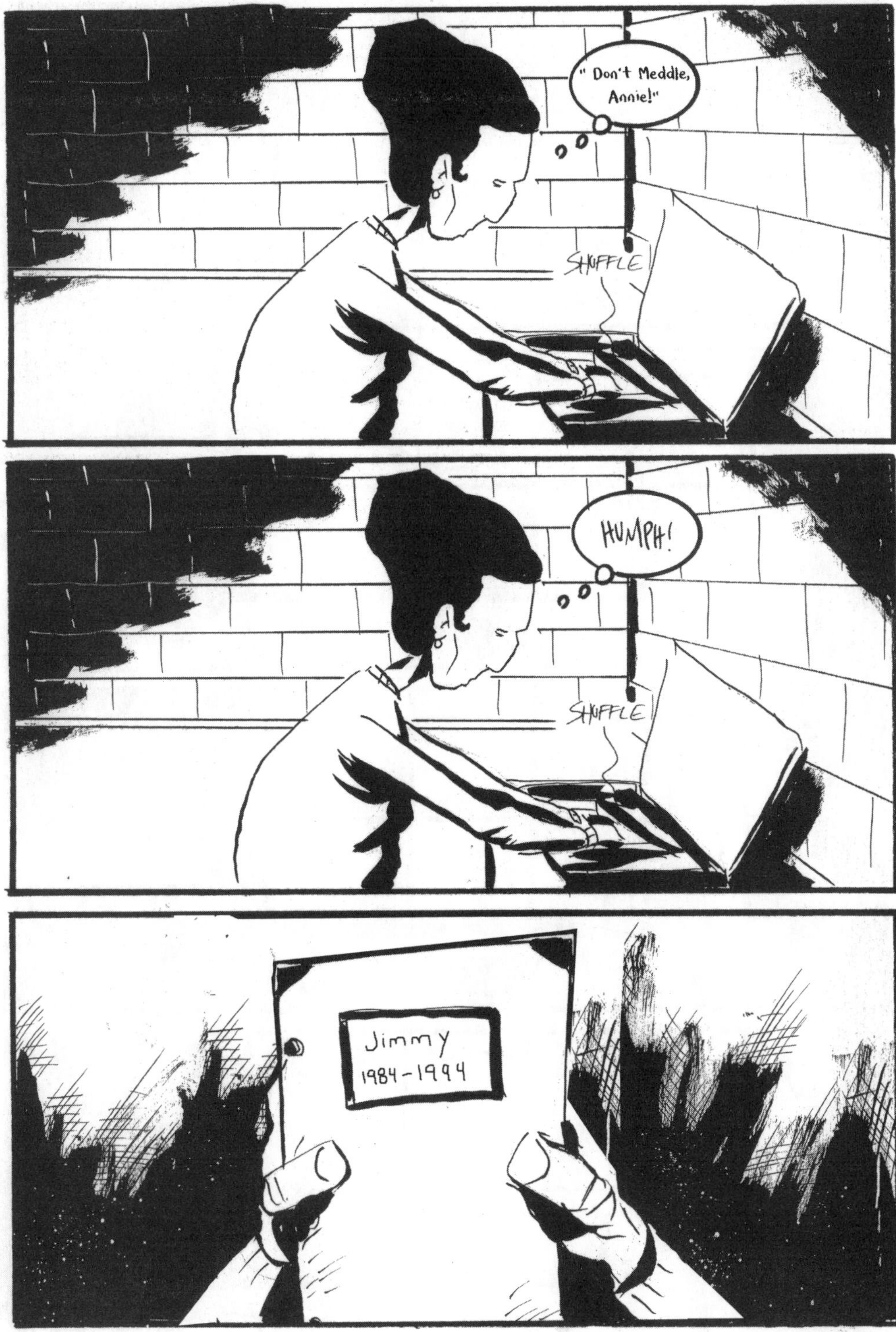
" Don't Meddle, Annie!"
SHUFFLE
HUMPH!
SHUFFLE
Jimmy
1984-1994

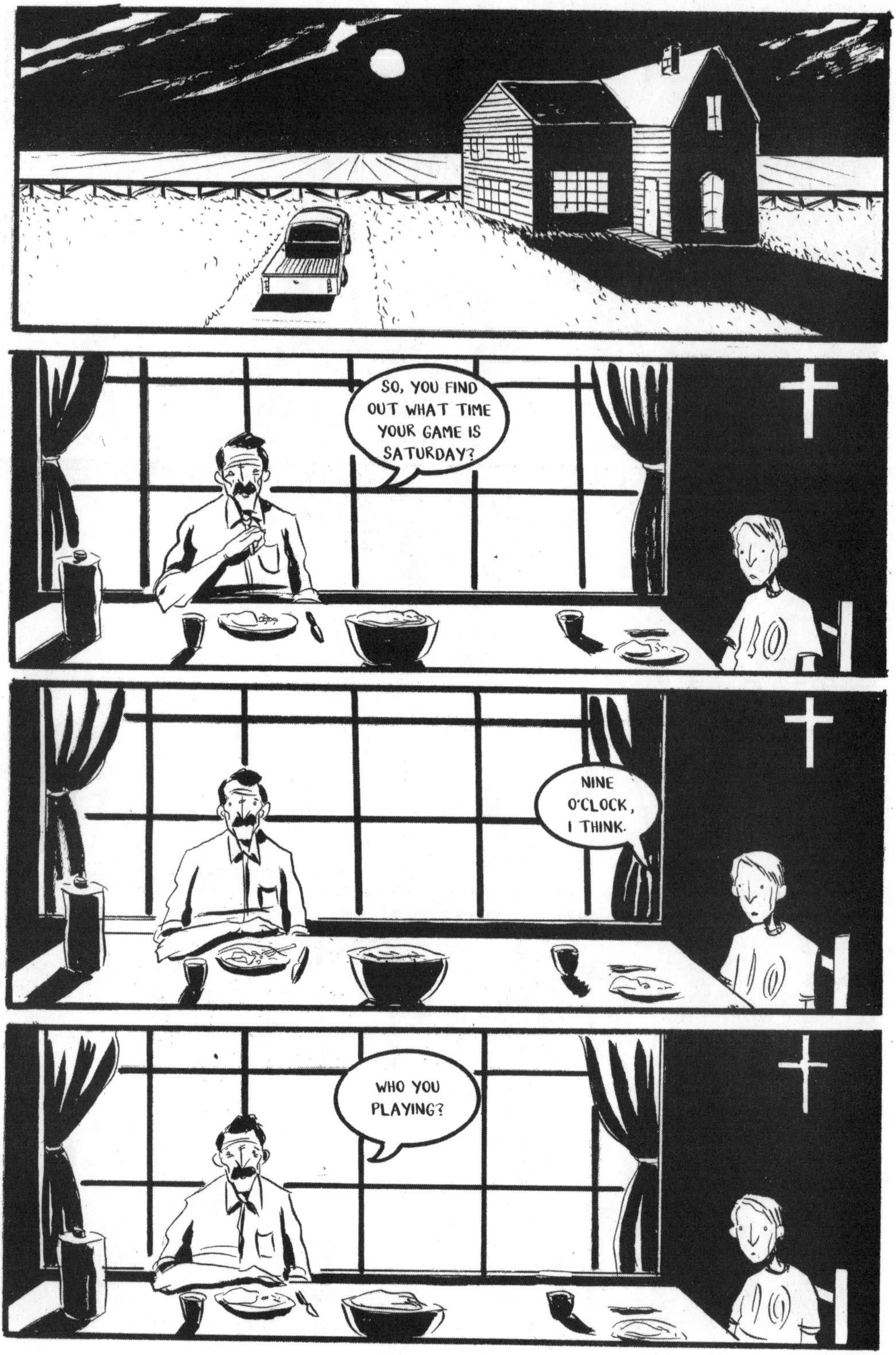
SO, YOU FIND OUT WHAT TIME YOUR GAME IS SATURDAY?
NINE O'CLOCK, I THINK.
WHO YOU PLAYING?

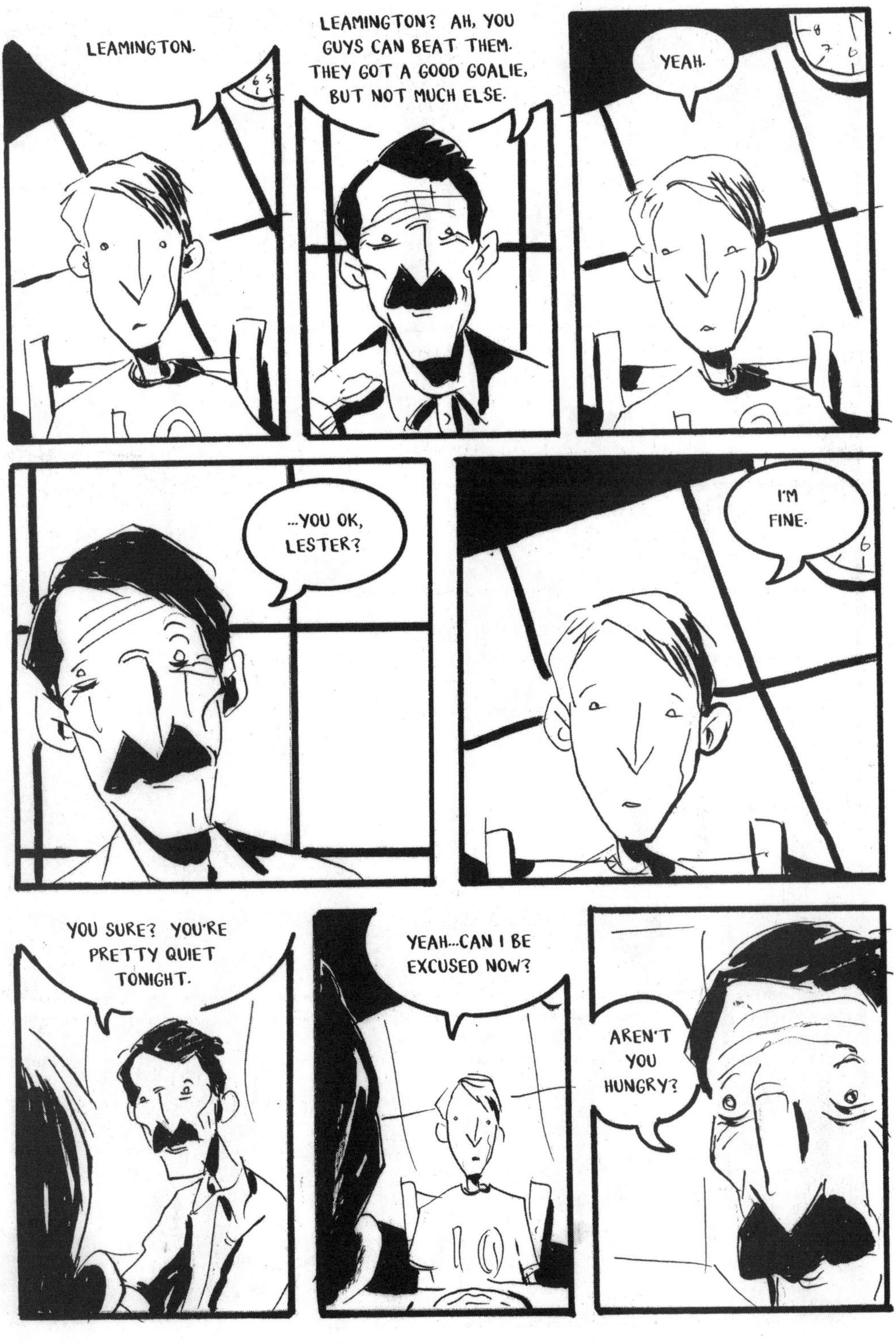
LEAMINGTON.
LEAMINGTON? AH, YOU GUYS CAN BEAT THEM. THEY GOT A GOOD GOALIE, BUT NOT MUCH ELSE.
YEAH.
...YOU OK, LESTER?
I'M FINE.
YOU SURE? YOU'RE PRETTY QUIET TONIGHT.
YEAH...CAN I BE EXCUSED NOW?
AREN'T YOU HUNGRY?

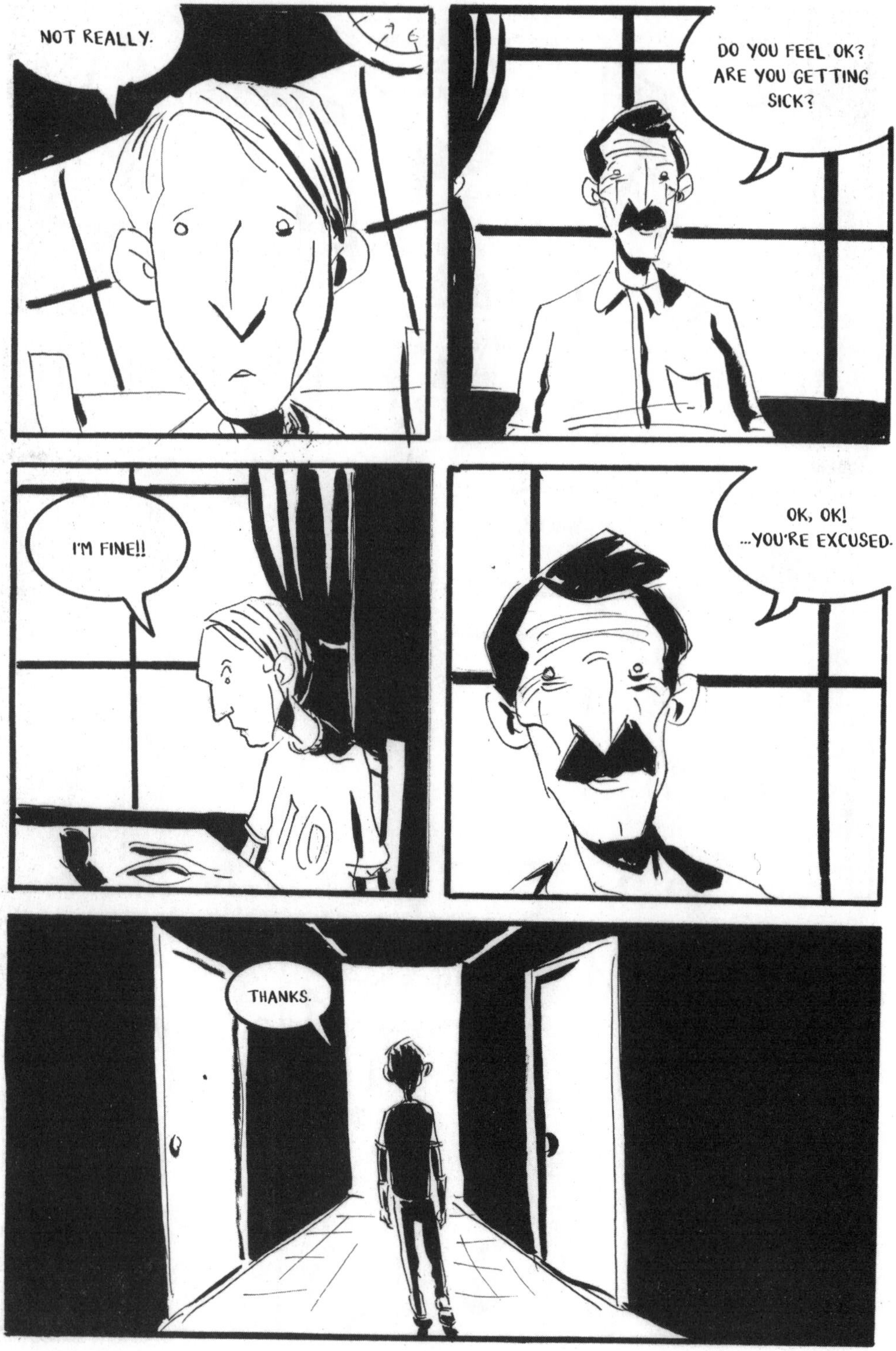
NOT REALLY.
DO YOU FEEL OK? ARE YOU GETTING SICK?
I'M FINE!!
OK, OK! ...YOU'RE EXCUSED.
THANKS.

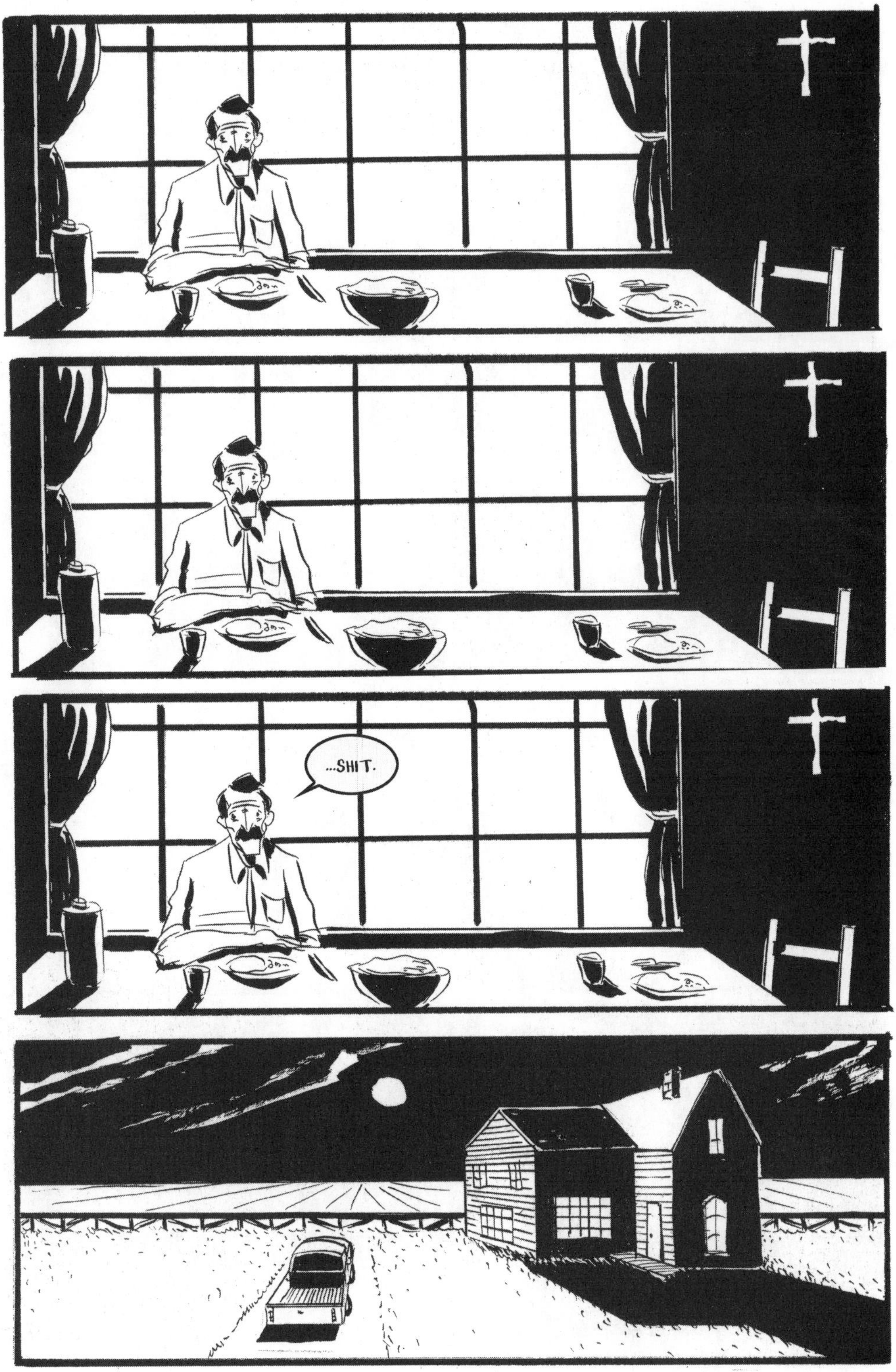
...SHIT.

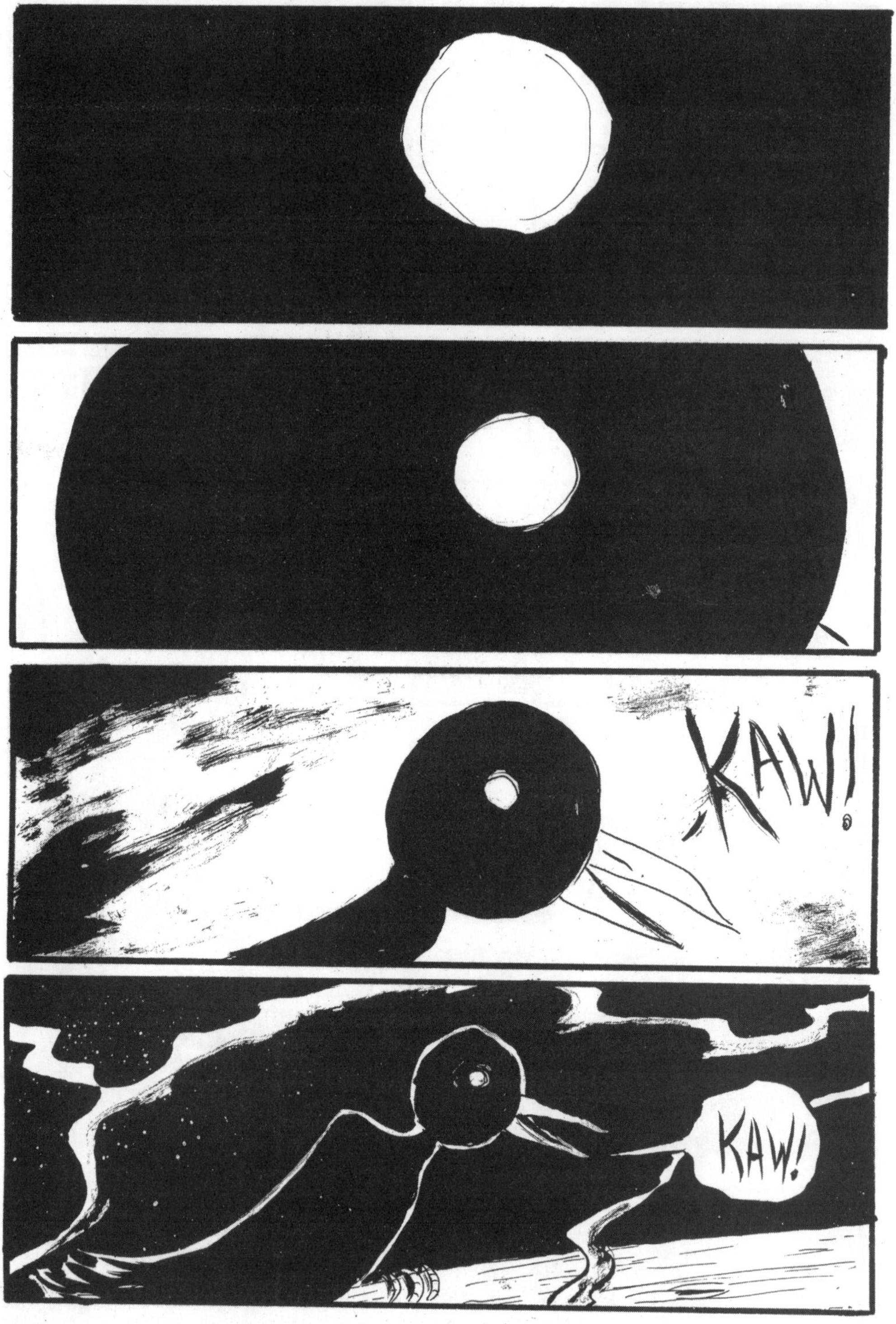
KAW!
KAW!

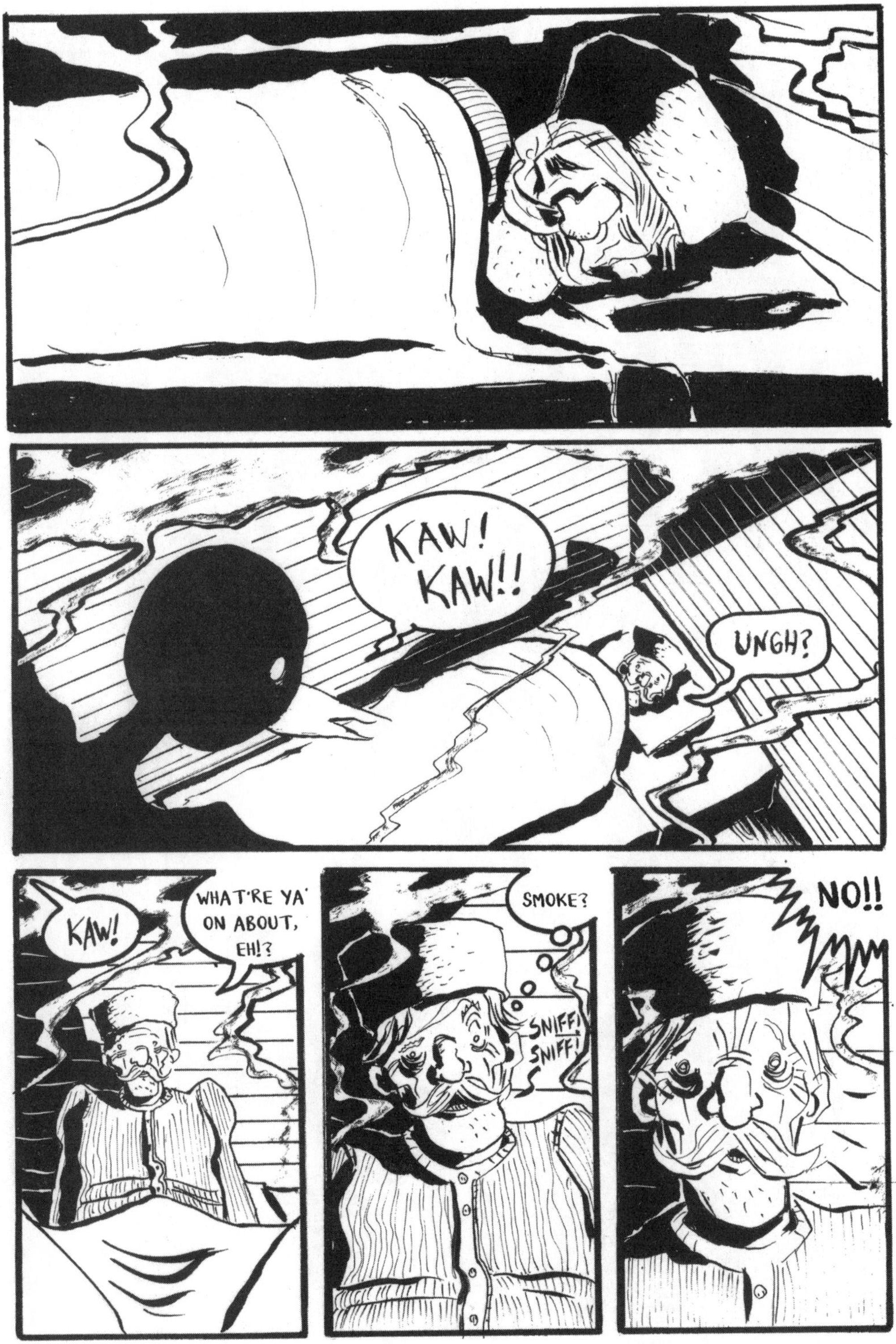
KAW! KAW!!
UNGH?
KAW!
WHAT'RE YA' ON ABOUT, EH!?
SMOKE?
SNIFF! SNIFF!
NO!!

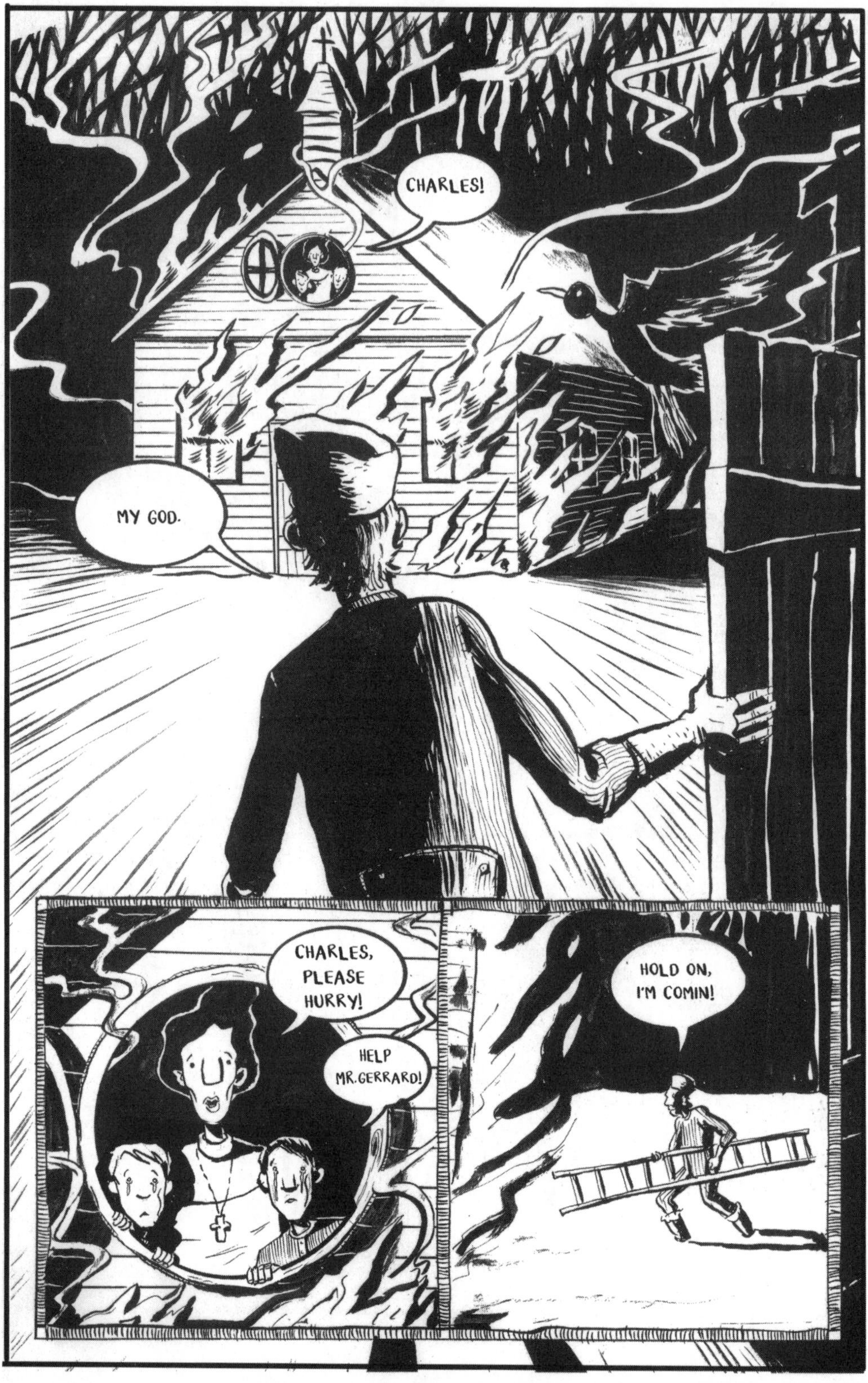
CHARLES!
MY GOD.
CHARLES, PLEASE HURRY!
HELP MR.GERRARD!
HOLD ON, I'M COMIN!

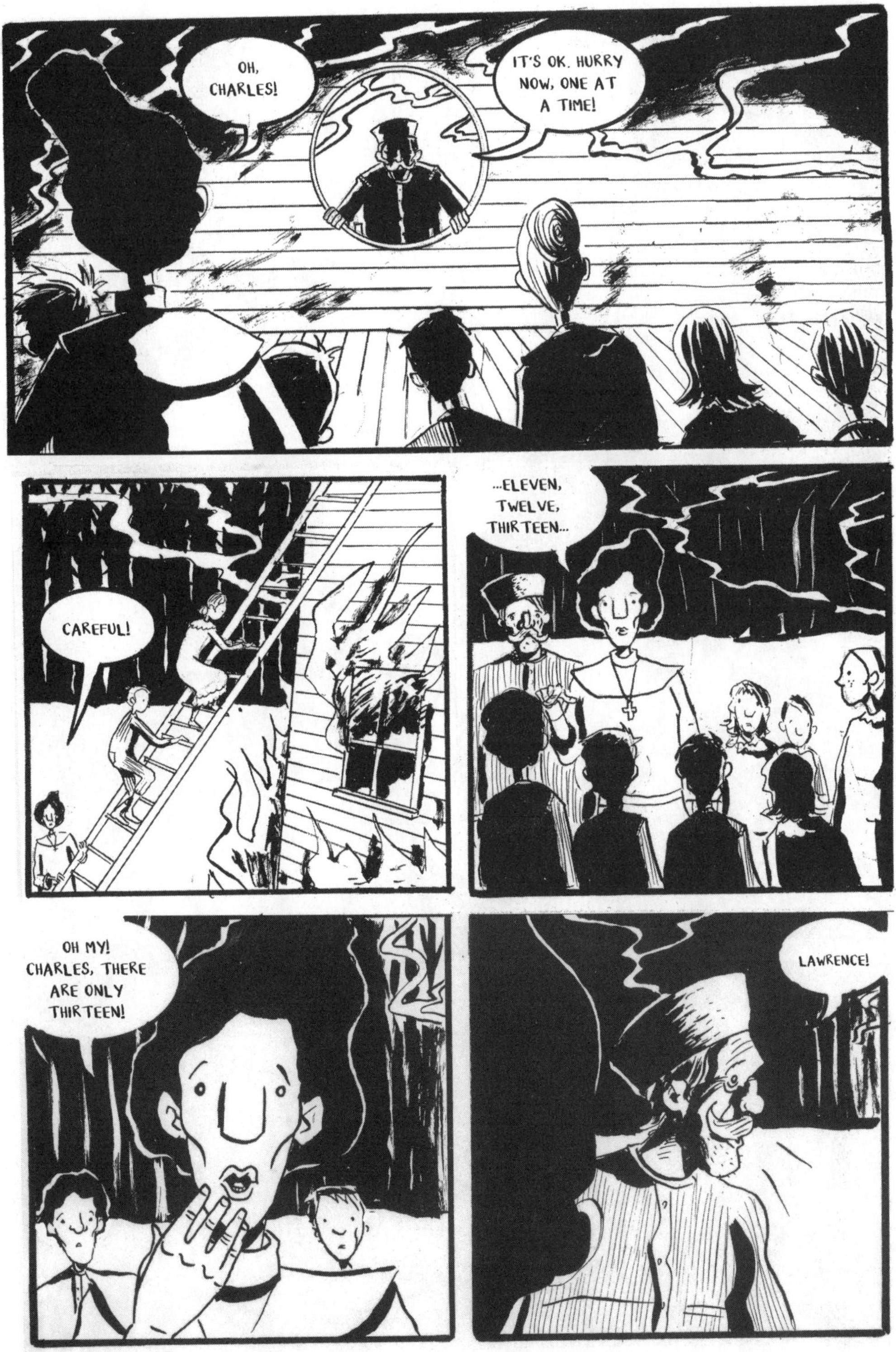
OH, CHARLES!
IT'S OK. HURRY NOW, ONE AT A TIME!
CAREFUL!
...ELEVEN, TWELVE, THIRTEEN...
OH MY! CHARLES, THERE ARE ONLY THIRTEEN!
LAWRENCE!

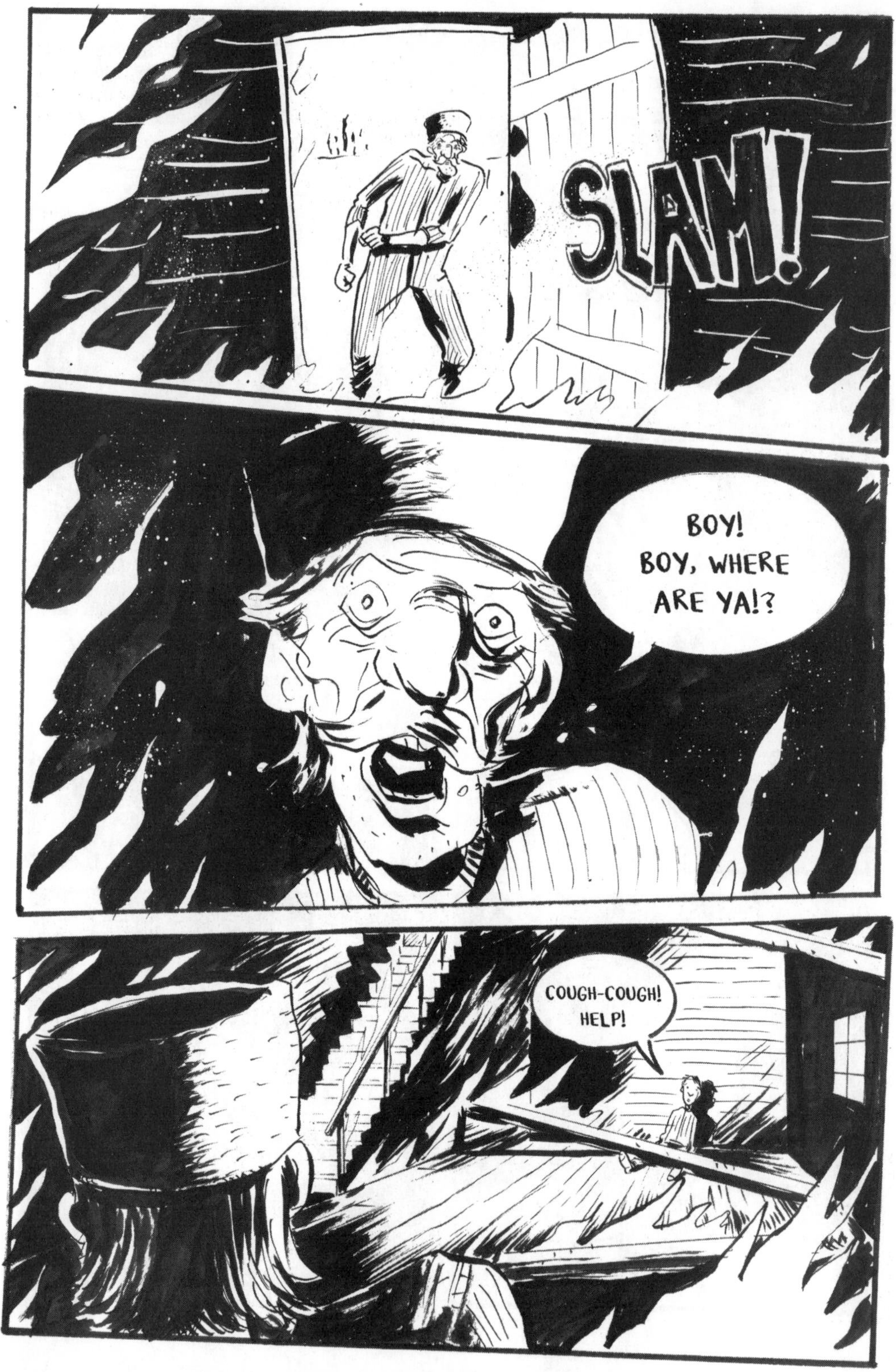
SLAM!
BOY!
BOY, WHERE
ARE YA!?
COUGH-COUGH!
HELP!

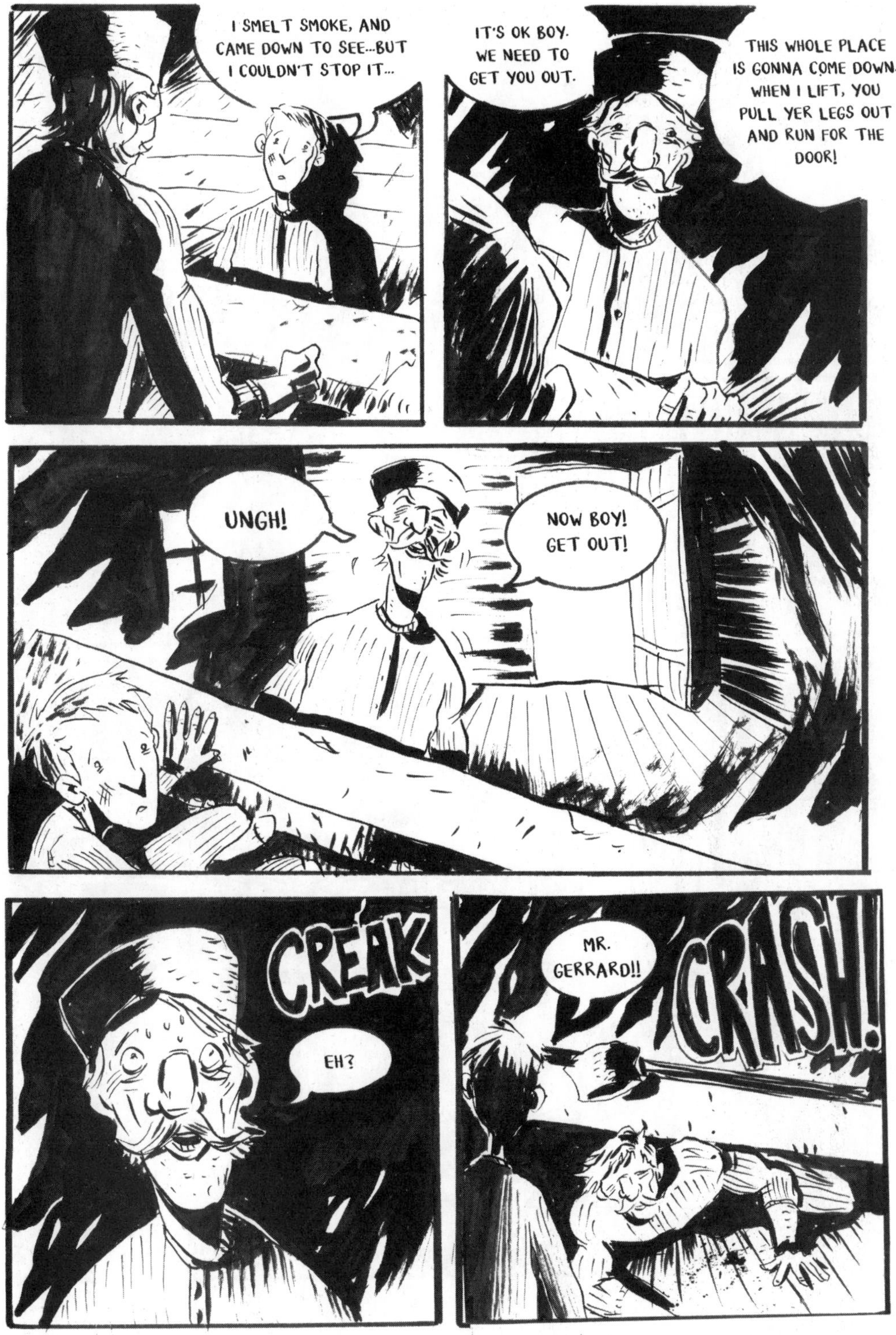
I SMELT SMOKE, AND CAME DOWN TO SEE...BUT I COULDN'T STOP IT...
IT'S OK BOY. WE NEED TO GET YOU OUT.
THIS WHOLE PLACE IS GONNA COME DOWN. WHEN I LIFT, YOU PULL YER LEGS OUT AND RUN FOR THE DOOR!
UNGH!
NOW BOY! GET OUT!
CREAK
EH?
MR. GERRARD!!
CRASH!

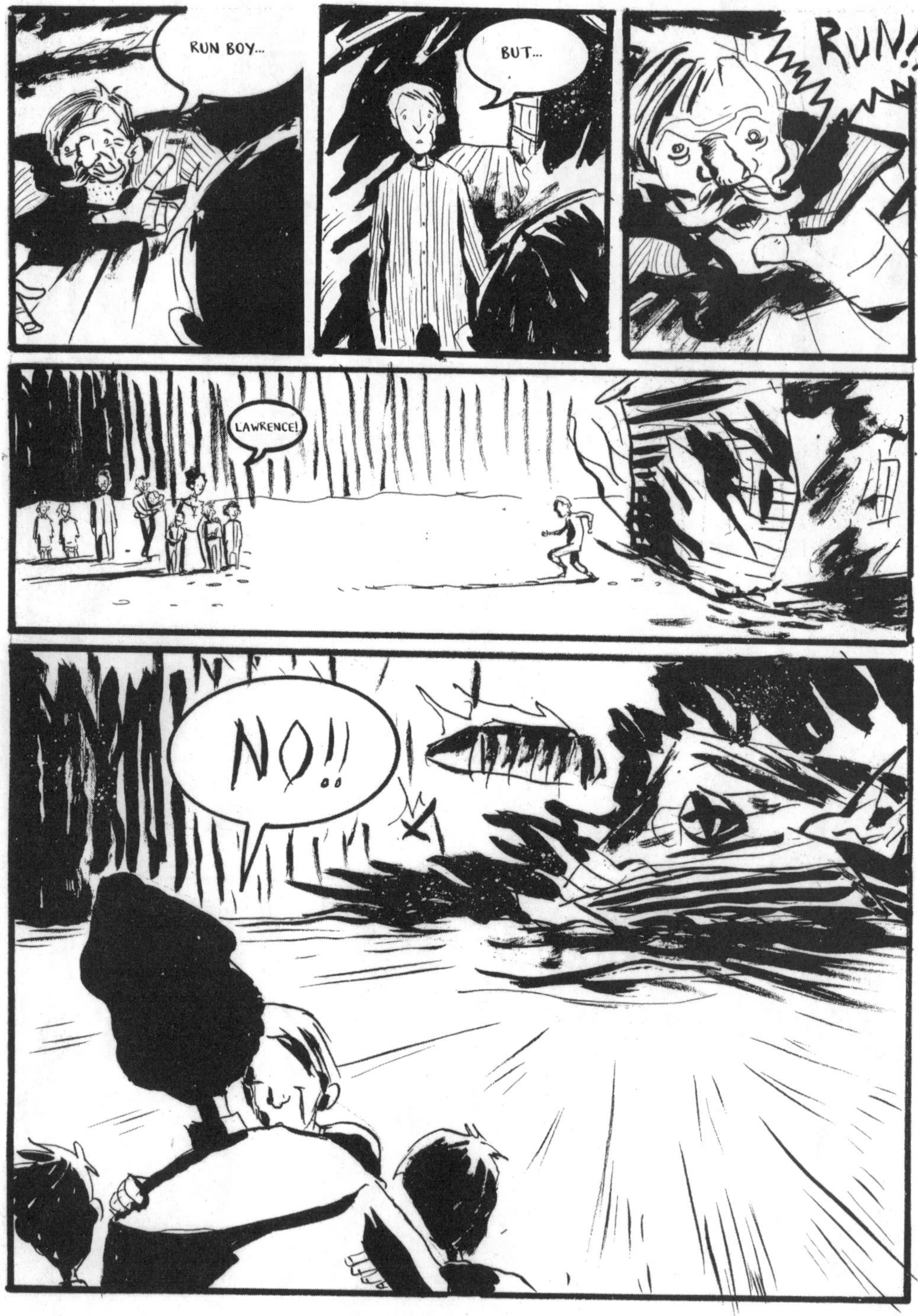
RUN BOY...
BUT...
RUN!!
LAWRENCE!
NO!!

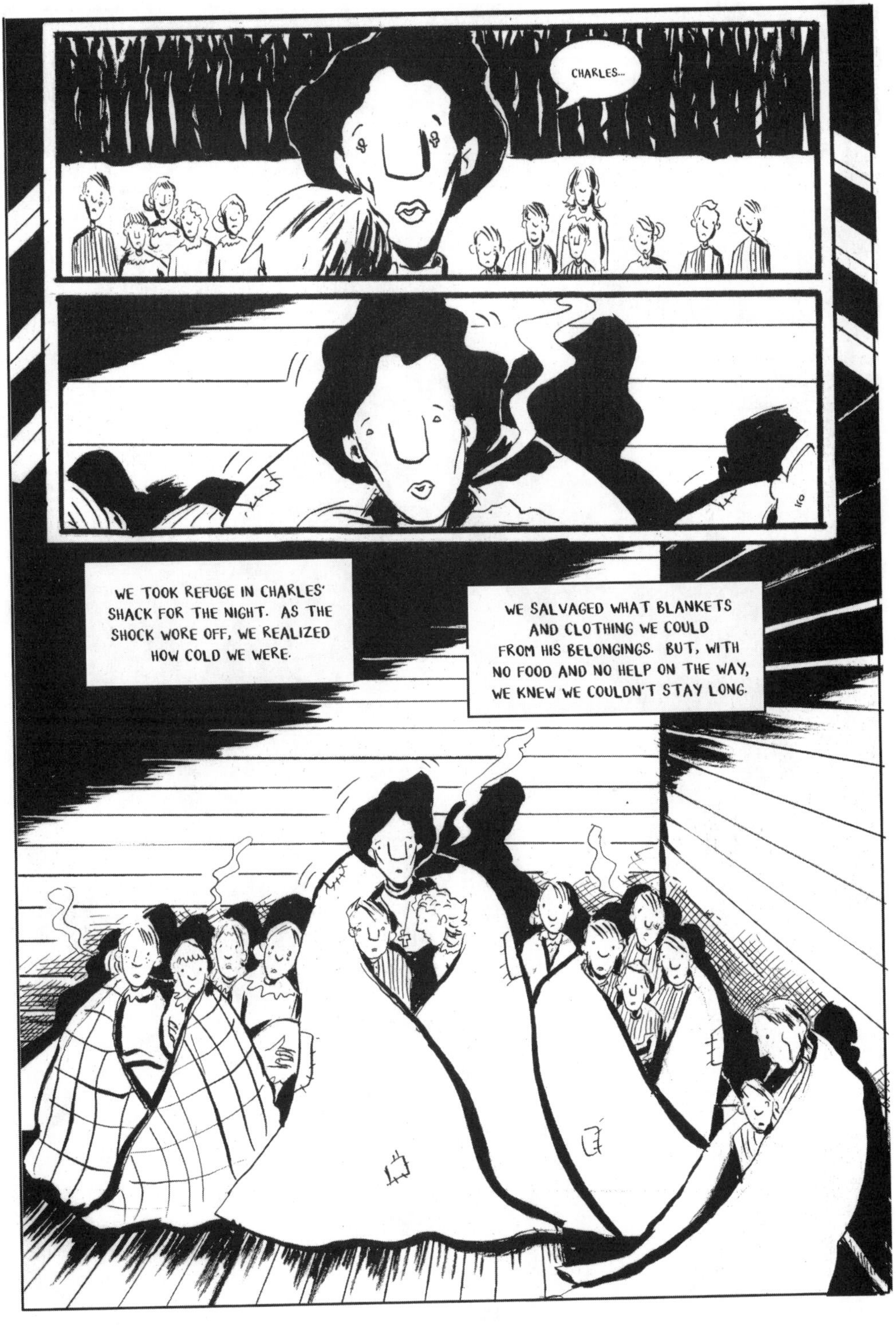
CHARLES...
WE TOOK REFUGE IN CHARLES' SHACK FOR THE NIGHT. AS THE SHOCK WORE OFF, WE REALIZED HOW COLD WE WERE.
WE SALVAGED WHAT BLANKETS AND CLOTHING WE COULD FROM HIS BELONGINGS. BUT, WITH NO FOOD AND NO HELP ON THE WAY, WE KNEW WE COULDN'T STAY LONG.

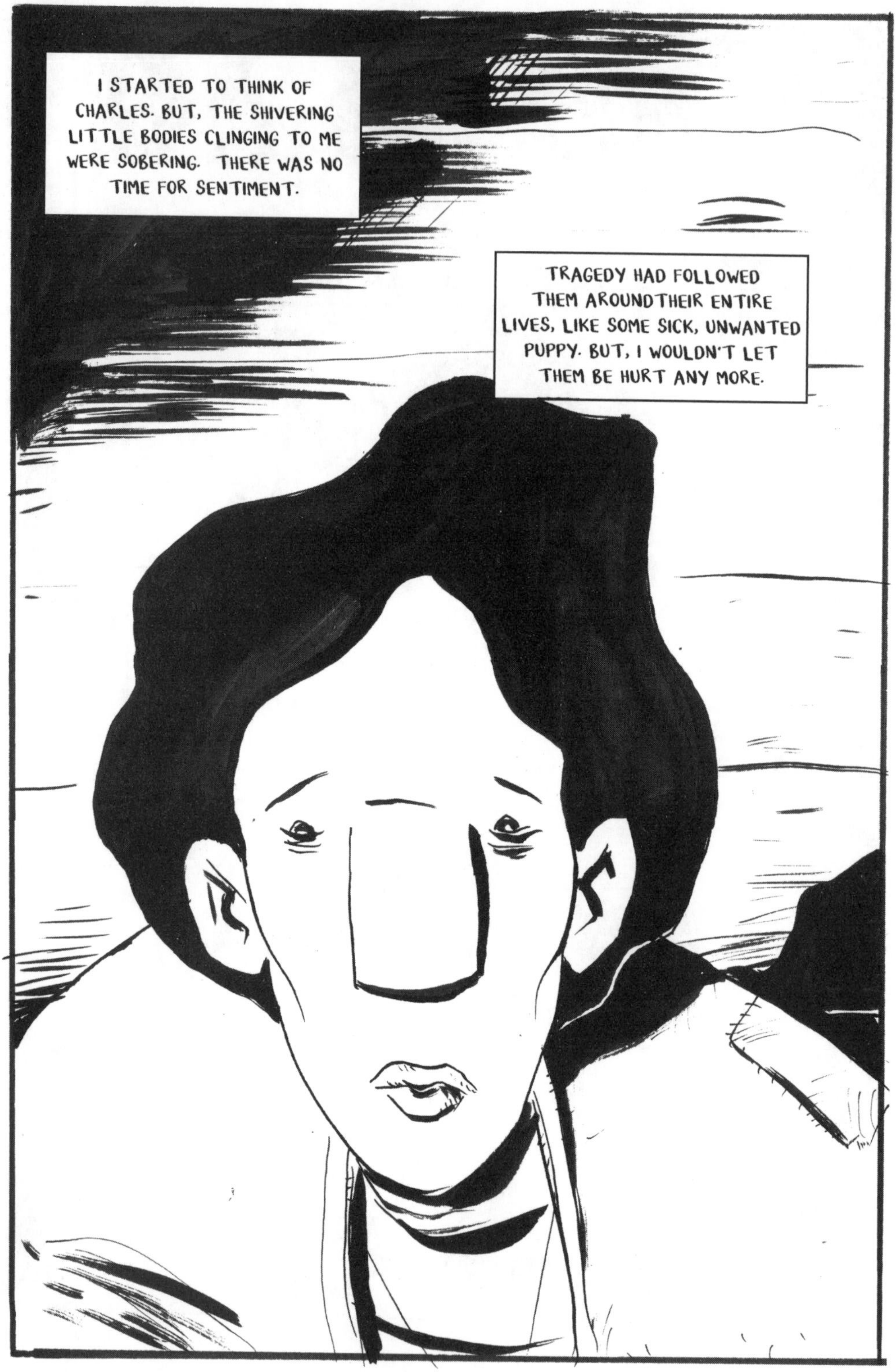
I STARTED TO THINK OF CHARLES. BUT, THE SHIVERING LITTLE BODIES CLINGING TO ME WERE SOBERING. THERE WAS NO TIME FOR SENTIMENT.
TRAGEDY HAD FOLLOWED THEM AROUND THEIR ENTIRE LIVES, LIKE SOME SICK, UNWANTED PUPPY. BUT, I WOULDN'T LET THEM BE HURT ANY MORE.

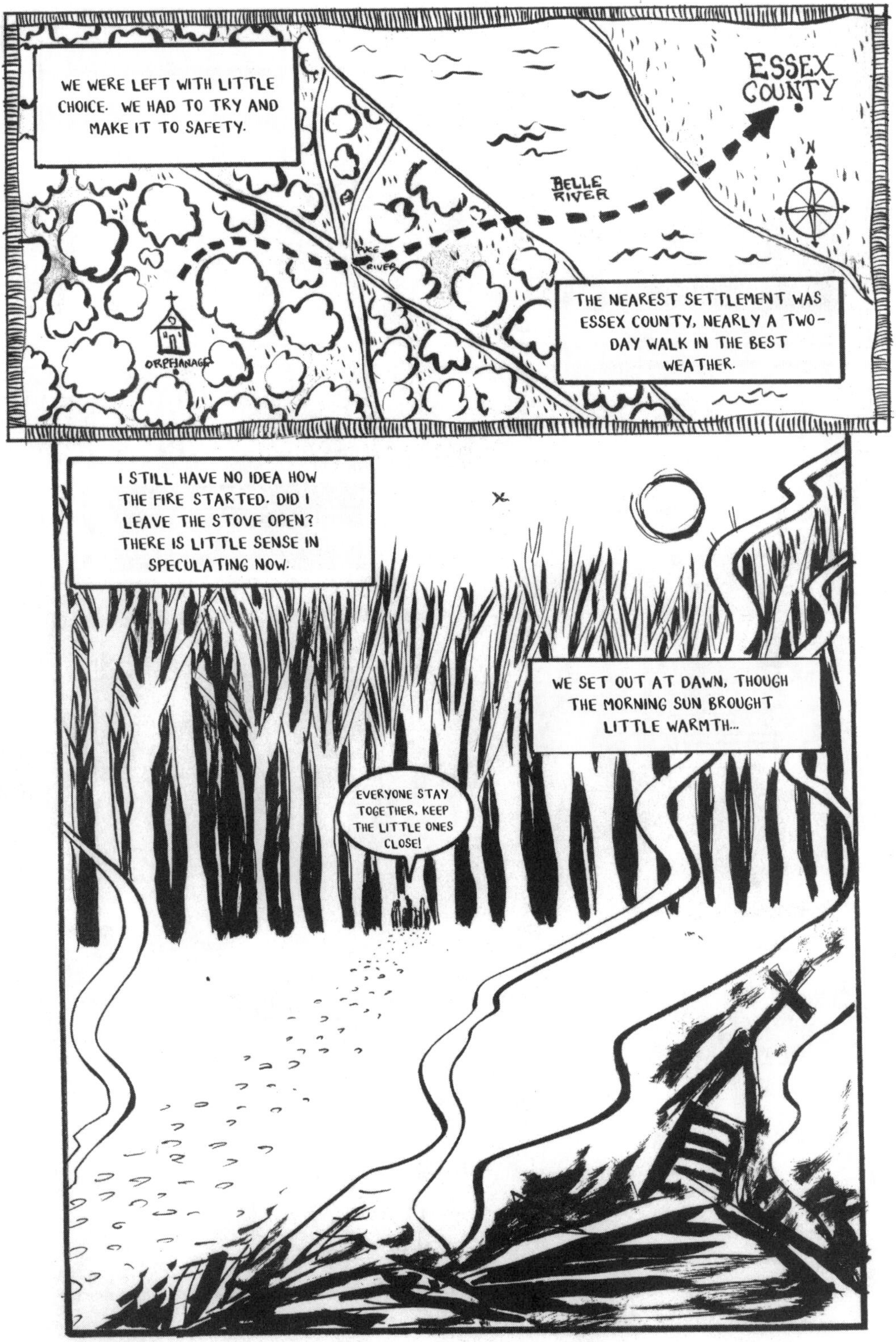
WE WERE LEFT WITH LITTLE CHOICE. WE HAD TO TRY AND MAKE IT TO SAFETY.
ESSEX COUNTY
N
BELLE RIVER
ORPHANAGE
THE NEAREST SETTLEMENT WAS ESSEX COUNTY, NEARLY A TWO-DAY WALK IN THE BEST WEATHER.
I STILL HAVE NO IDEA HOW THE FIRE STARTED. DID I LEAVE THE STOVE OPEN? THERE IS LITTLE SENSE IN SPECULATING NOW.
WE SET OUT AT DAWN, THOUGH THE MORNING SUN BROUGHT LITTLE WARMTH...
EVERYONE STAY TOGETHER, KEEP THE LITTLE ONES CLOSE!

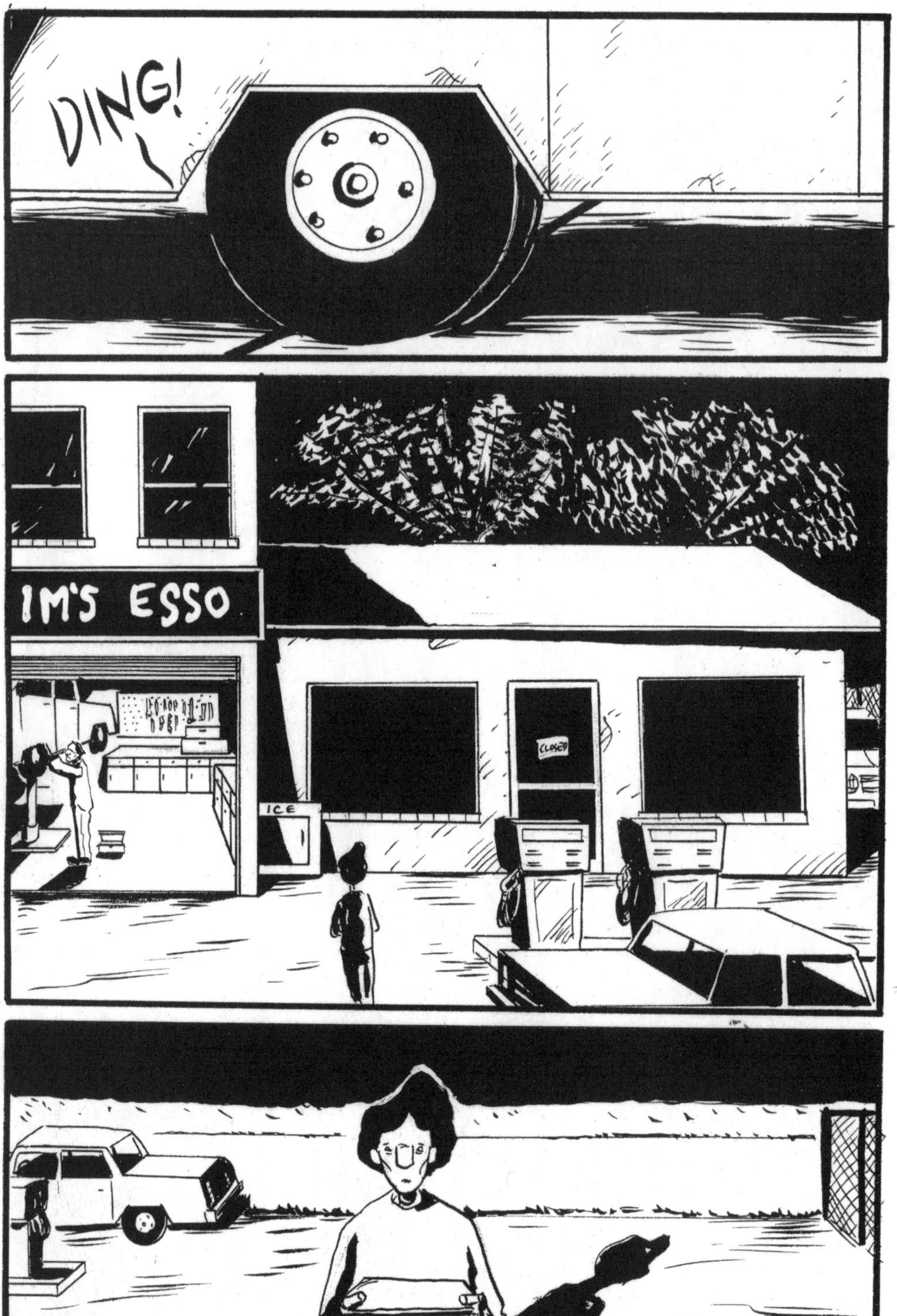
DING!
IM'S ESSO
ICE
CLOSED

JIMMY...

MRS. Q? YOUR CAR ACTING UP AGAIN?

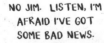

NO JIM. LISTEN, I'M AFRAID I'VE GOT SOME BAD NEWS.

IT'S YOUR UNCLE LOU, I'M AFRAID HE PASSED AWAY LAST NIGHT.

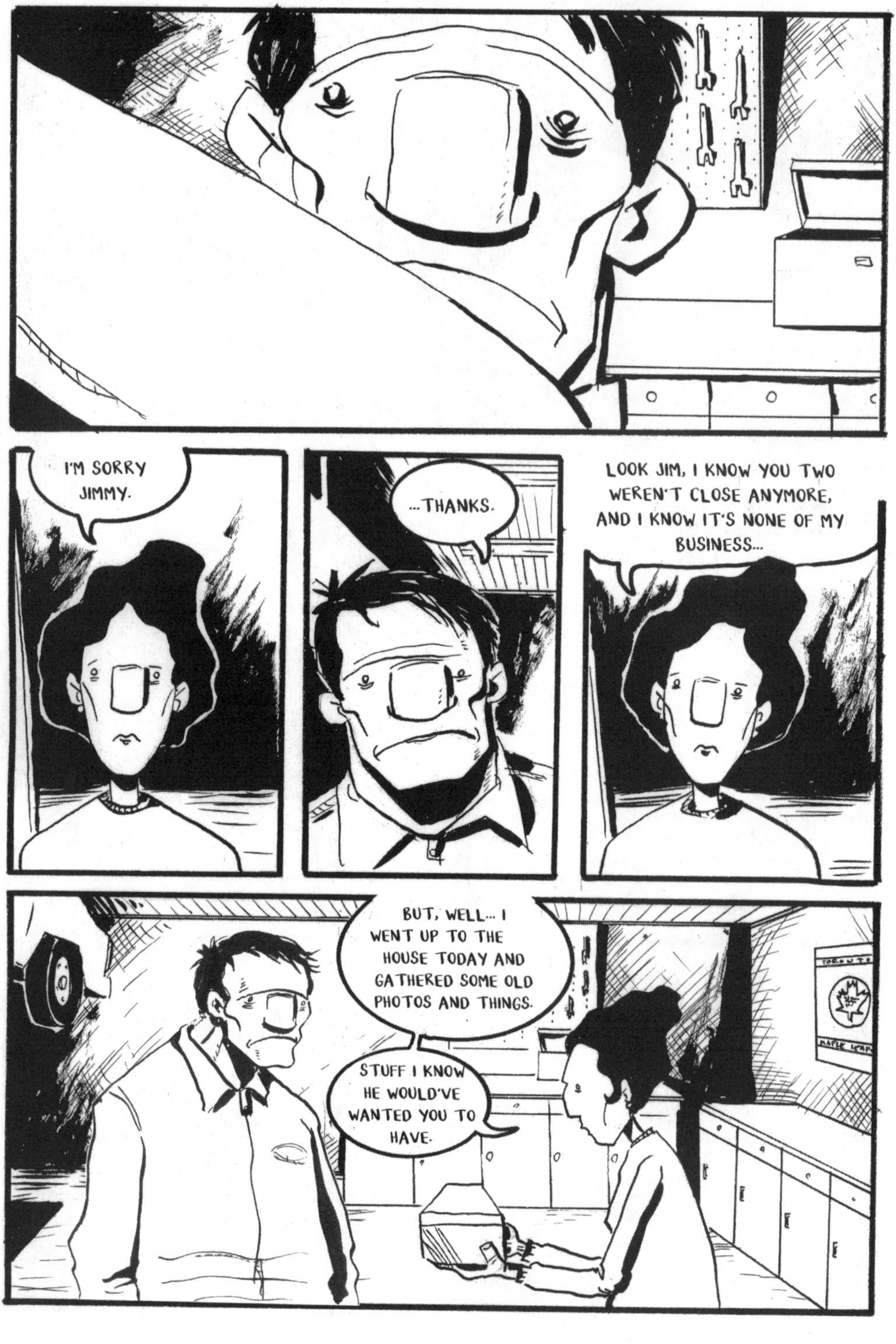
I'M SORRY JIMMY.
...THANKS.
LOOK JIM, I KNOW YOU TWO WEREN'T CLOSE ANYMORE, AND I KNOW IT'S NONE OF MY BUSINESS...
BUT, WELL... I WENT UP TO THE HOUSE TODAY AND GATHERED SOME OLD PHOTOS AND THINGS.
STUFF I KNOW HE WOULD'VE WANTED YOU TO HAVE.

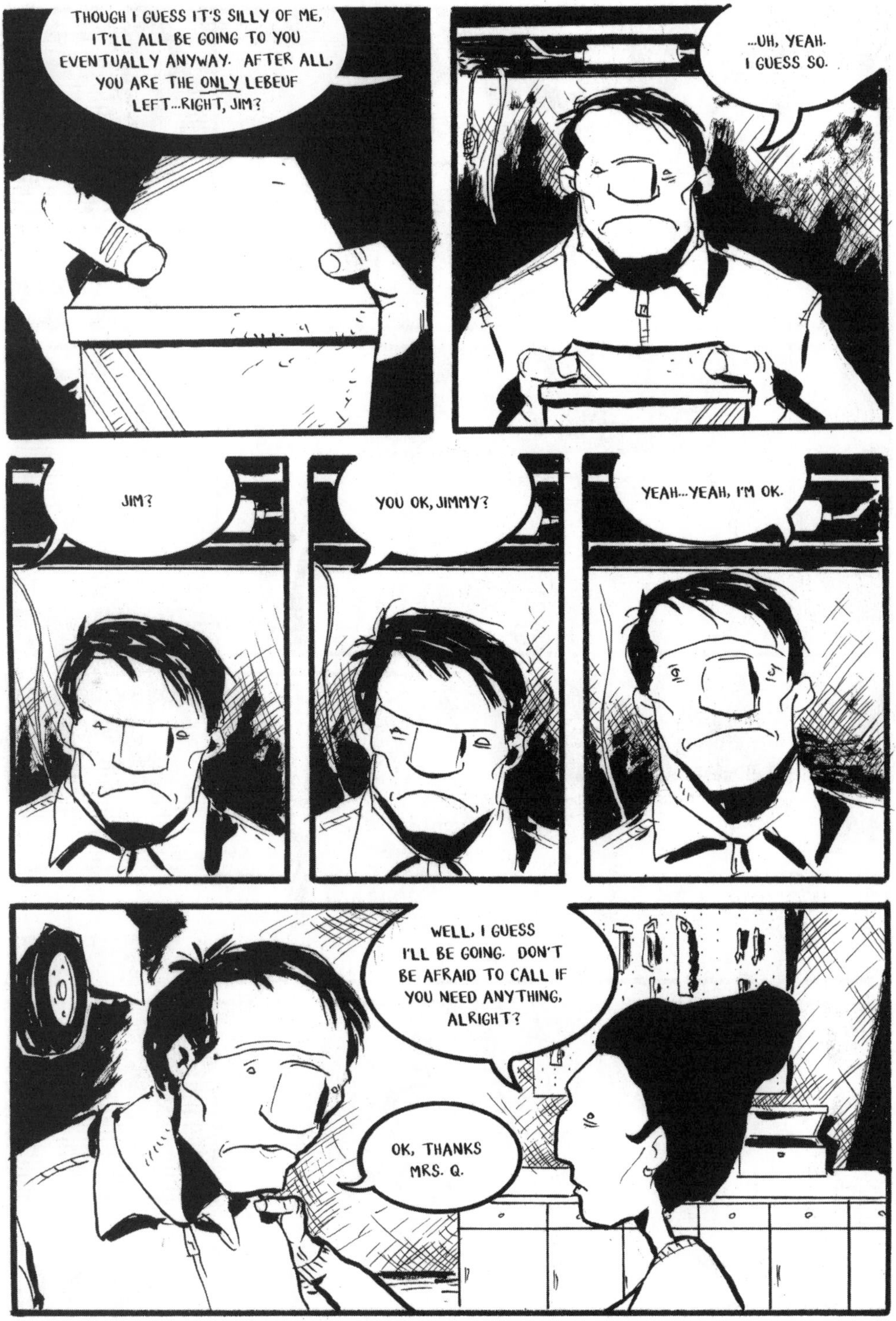
THOUGH I GUESS IT'S SILLY OF ME, IT'LL ALL BE GOING TO YOU EVENTUALLY ANYWAY. AFTER ALL, YOU ARE THE ONLY LEBEUF LEFT...RIGHT, JIM?
...UH, YEAH. I GUESS SO.
JIM?
YOU OK, JIMMY?
YEAH...YEAH, I'M OK.
WELL, I GUESS I'LL BE GOING. DON'T BE AFRAID TO CALL IF YOU NEED ANYTHING, ALRIGHT?
OK, THANKS MRS. Q.

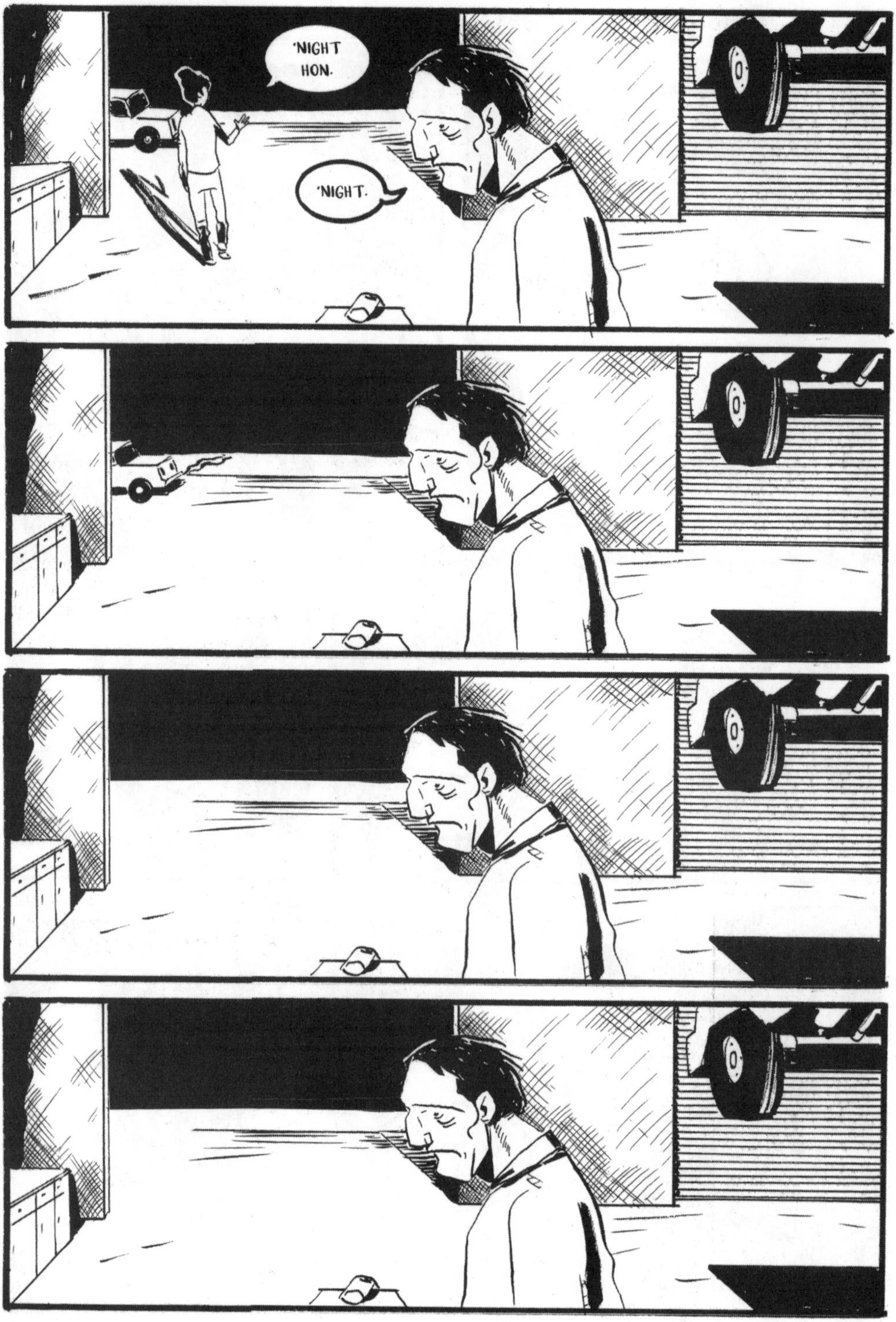
'NIGHT HON.
'NIGHT.

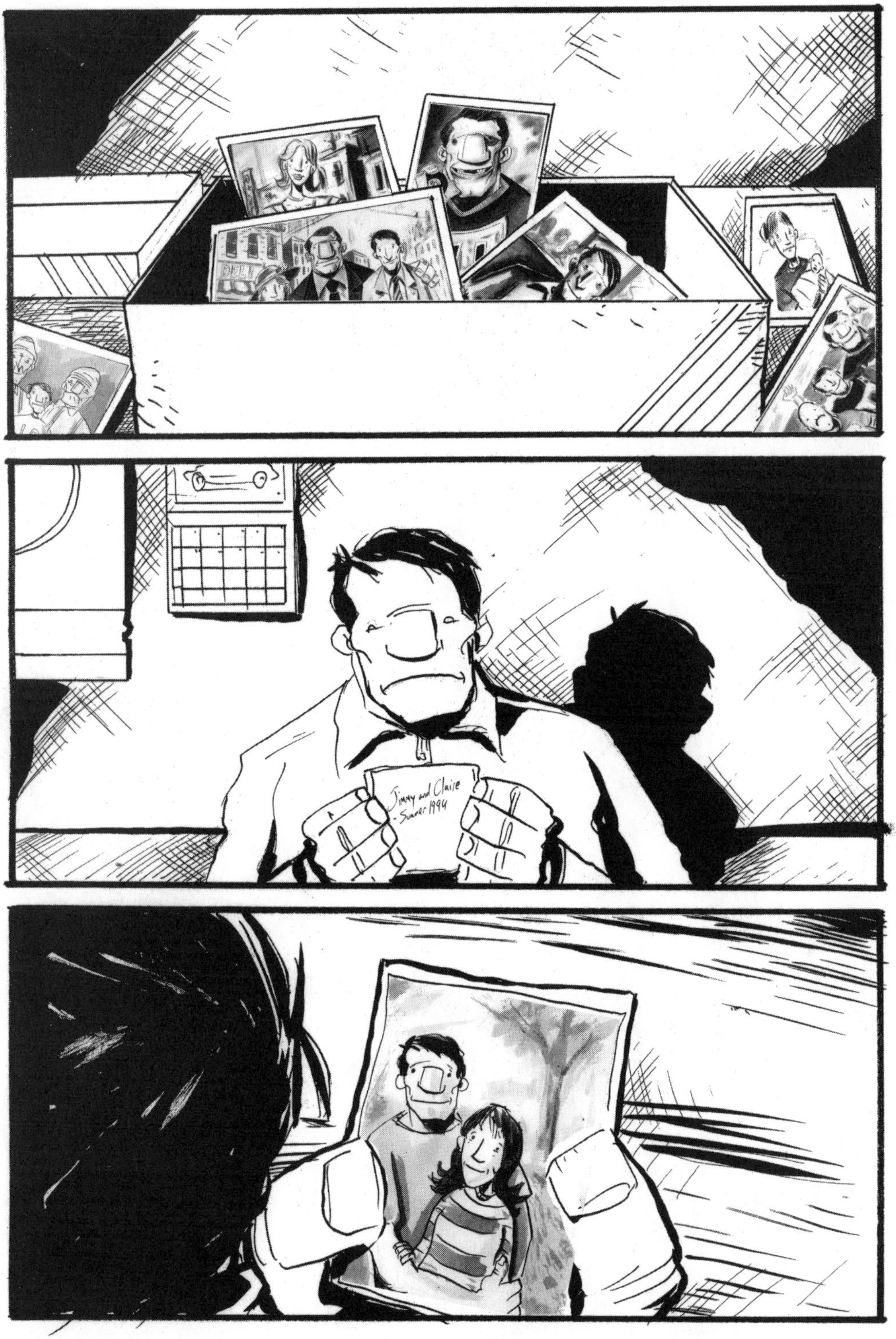
Jimmy and Claire - Summer 1994

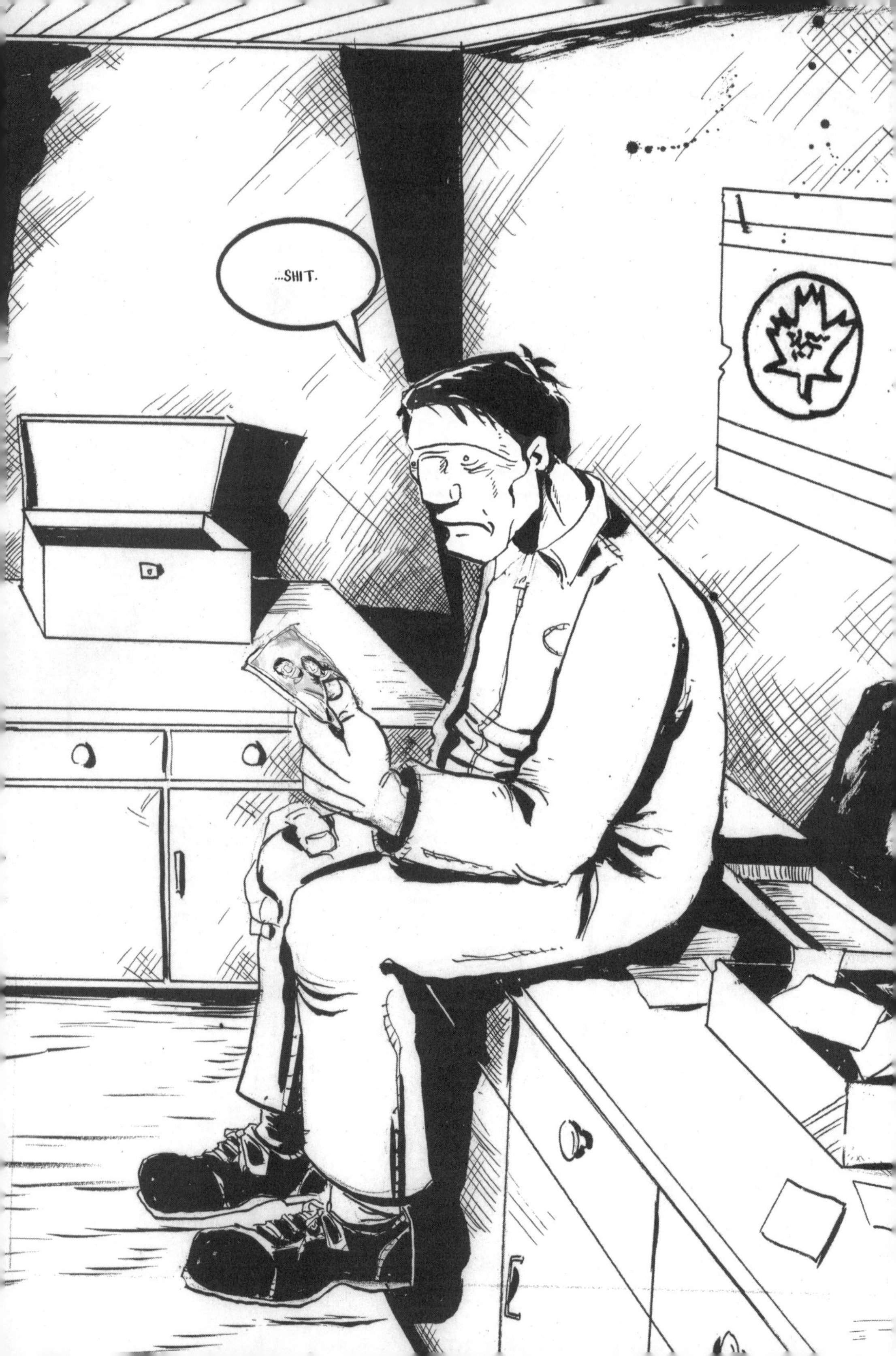
...SHIT.

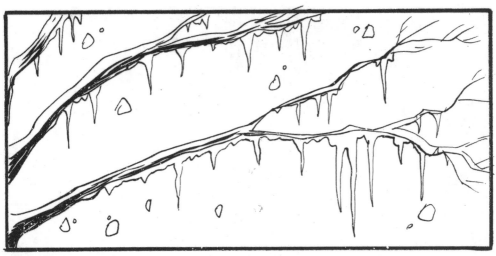

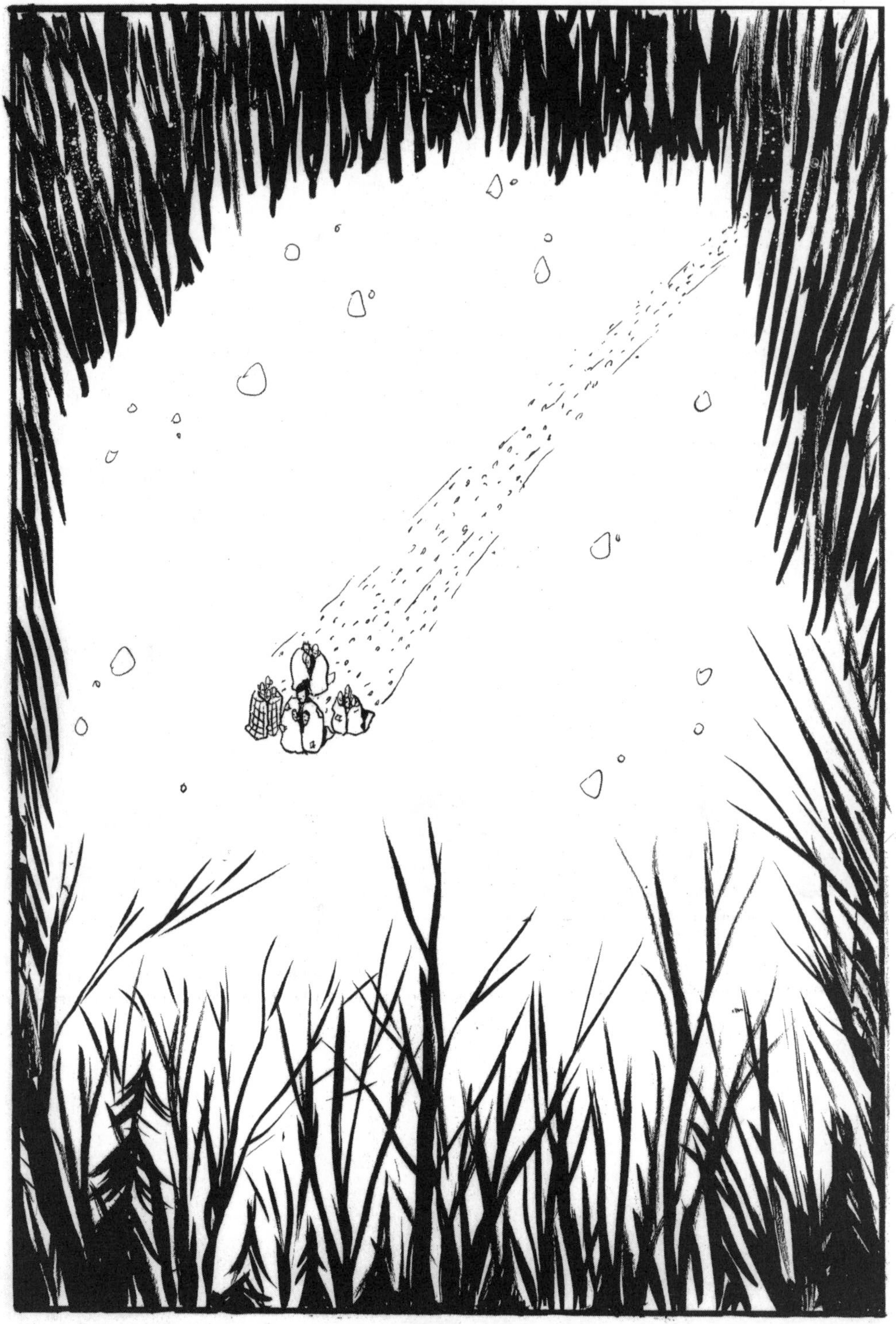

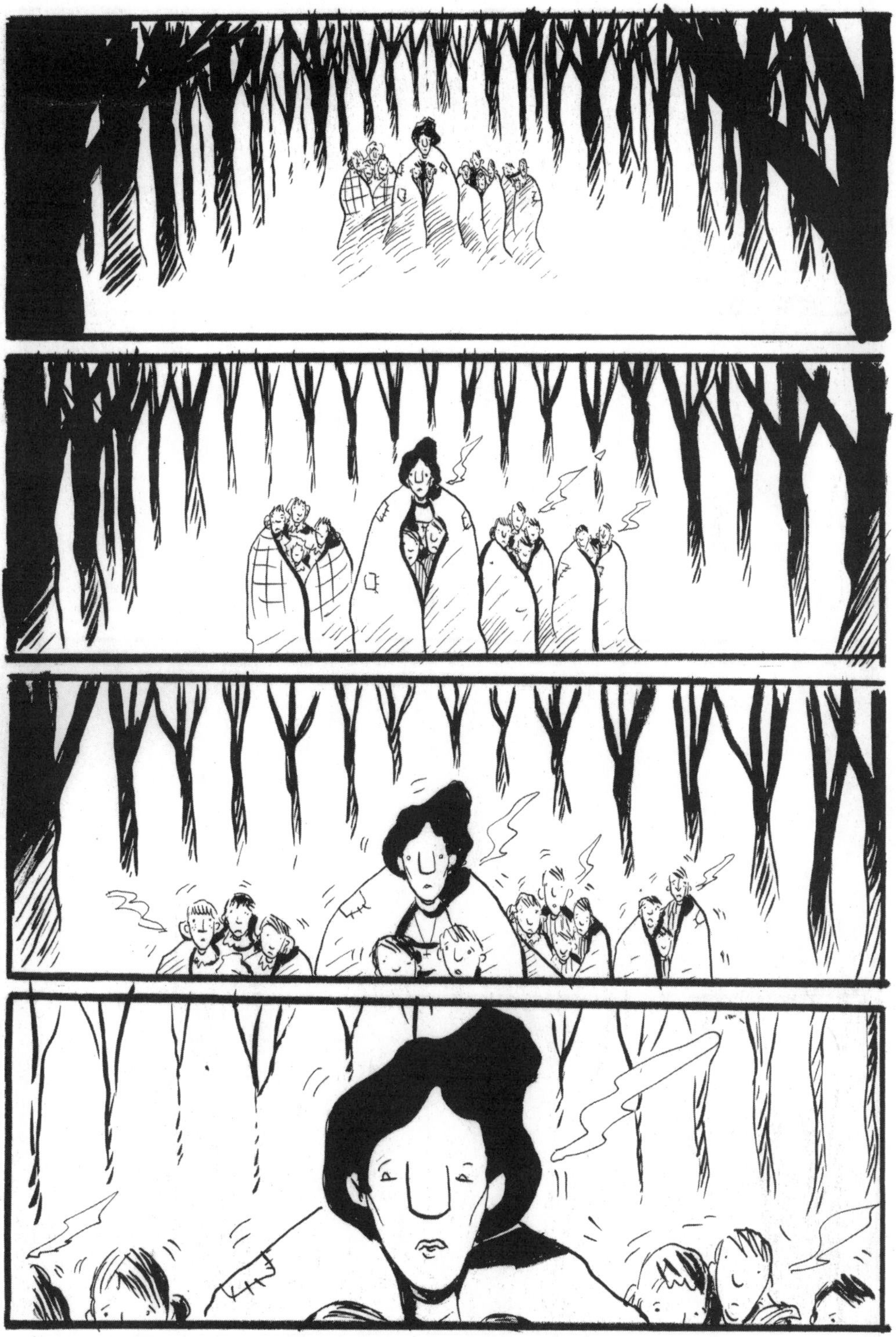

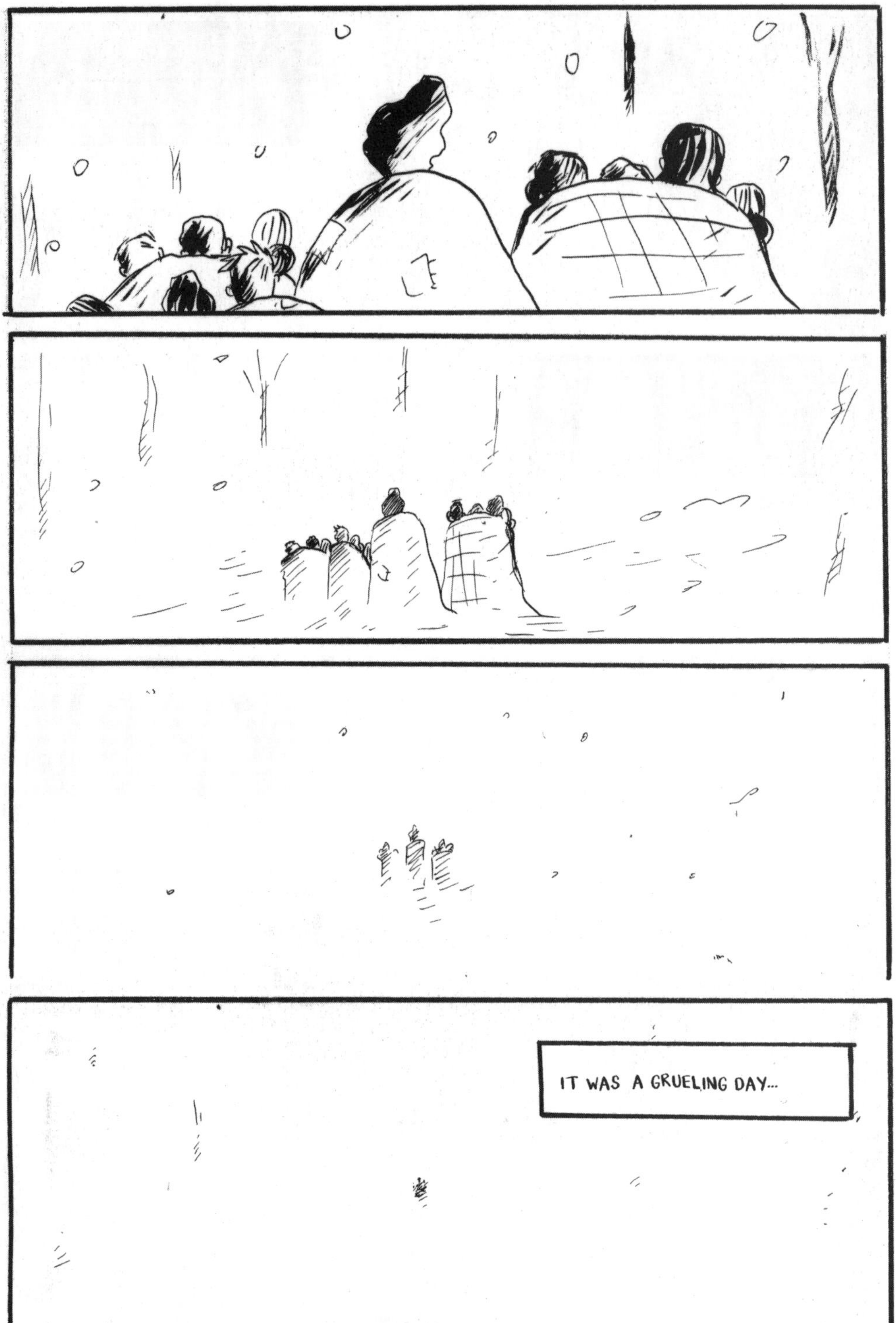
IT WAS A GRUELING DAY...

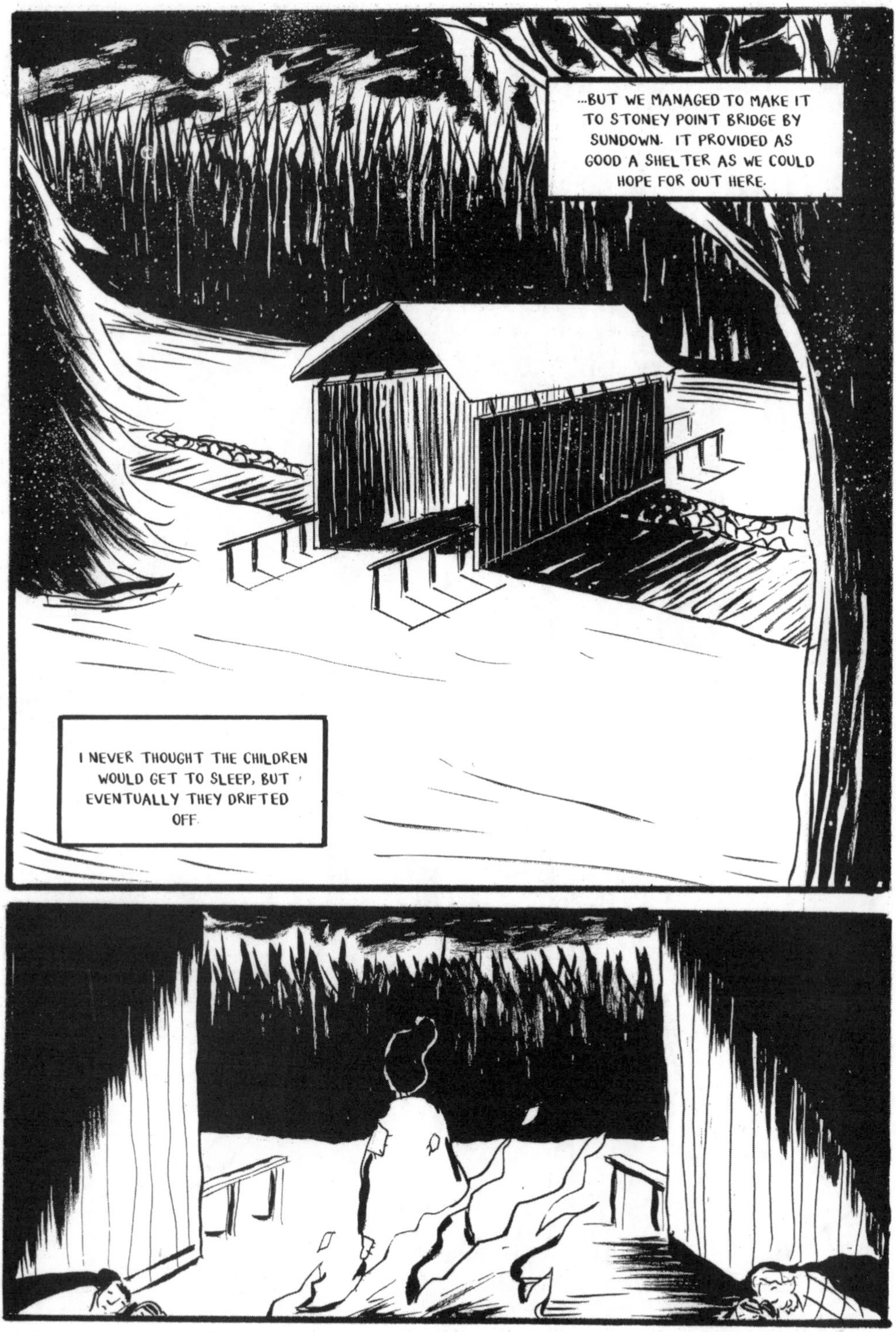
...BUT WE MANAGED TO MAKE IT TO STONEY POINT BRIDGE BY SUNDOWN. IT PROVIDED AS GOOD A SHELTER AS WE COULD HOPE FOR OUT HERE.
I NEVER THOUGHT THE CHILDREN WOULD GET TO SLEEP, BUT EVENTUALLY THEY DRIFTED OFF.

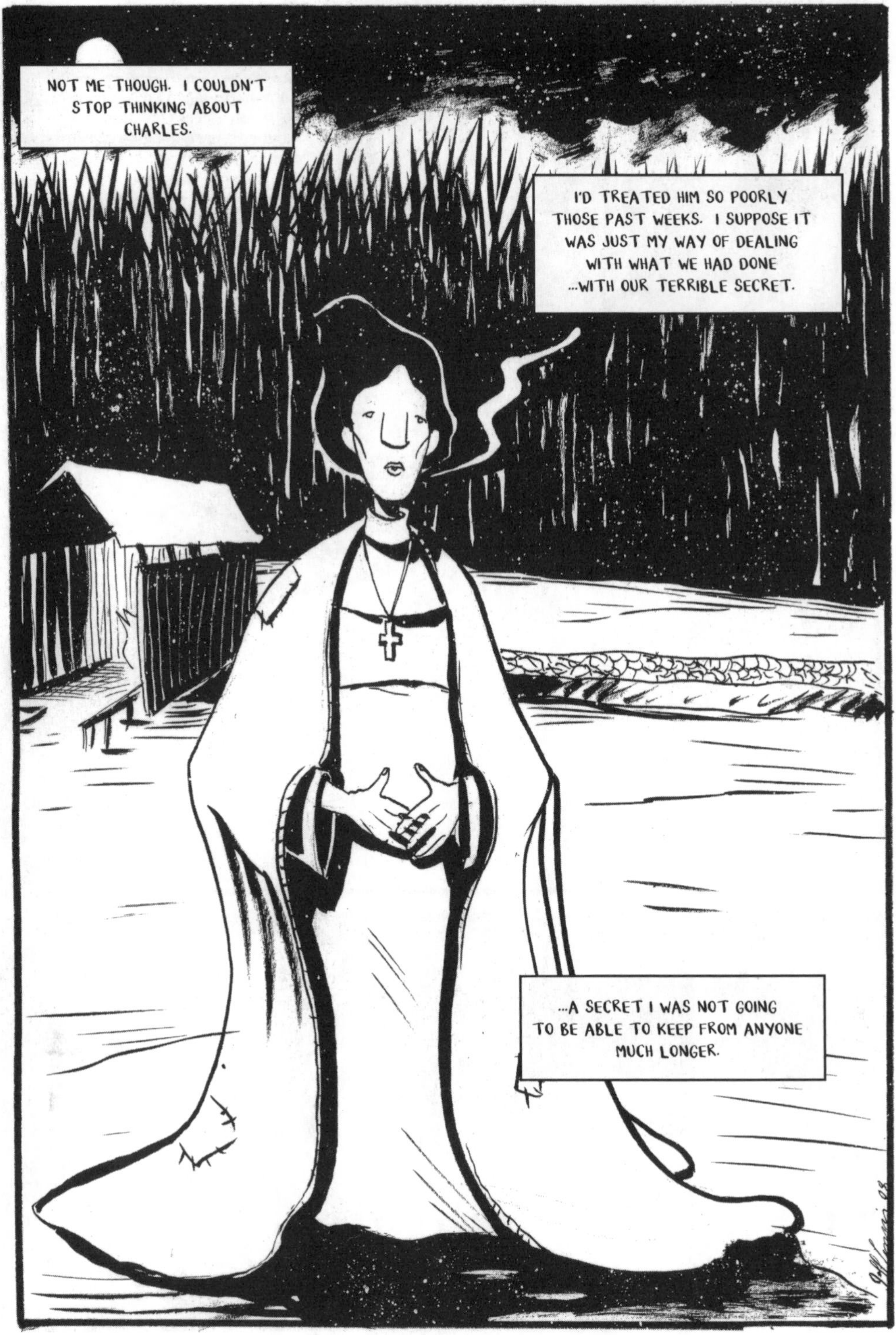
NOT ME THOUGH. I COULDN'T STOP THINKING ABOUT CHARLES.
I'D TREATED HIM SO POORLY THOSE PAST WEEKS. I SUPPOSE IT WAS JUST MY WAY OF DEALING WITH WHAT WE HAD DONE ...WITH OUR TERRIBLE SECRET.
...A SECRET I WAS NOT GOING TO BE ABLE TO KEEP FROM ANYONE MUCH LONGER.

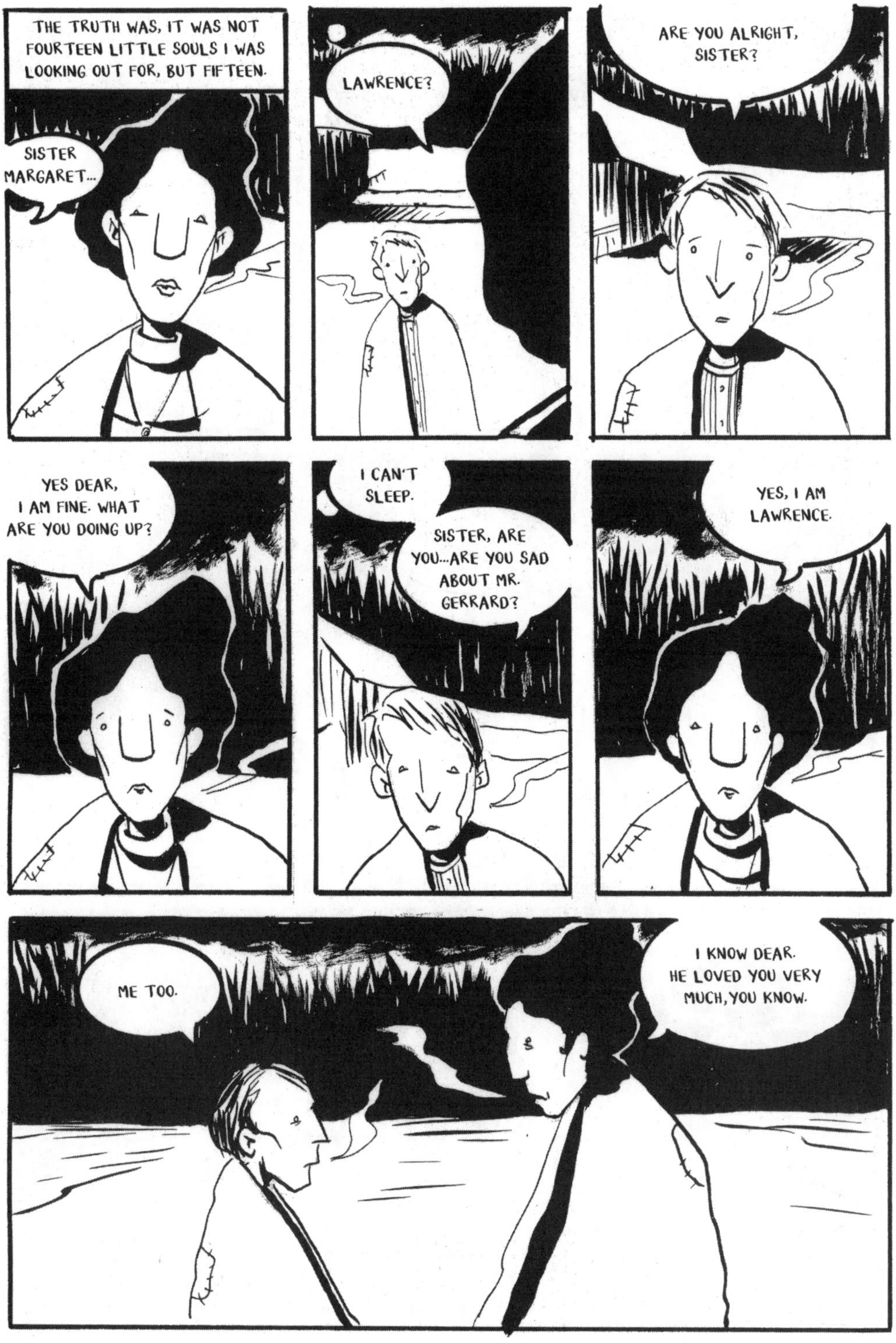
THE TRUTH WAS, IT WAS NOT FOURTEEN LITTLE SOULS I WAS LOOKING OUT FOR, BUT FIFTEEN.
SISTER MARGARET...
LAWRENCE?
ARE YOU ALRIGHT, SISTER?
YES DEAR, I AM FINE. WHAT ARE YOU DOING UP?
I CAN'T SLEEP.
SISTER, ARE YOU...ARE YOU SAD ABOUT MR. GERRARD?
YES, I AM LAWRENCE.
ME TOO.
I KNOW DEAR. HE LOVED YOU VERY MUCH, YOU KNOW.

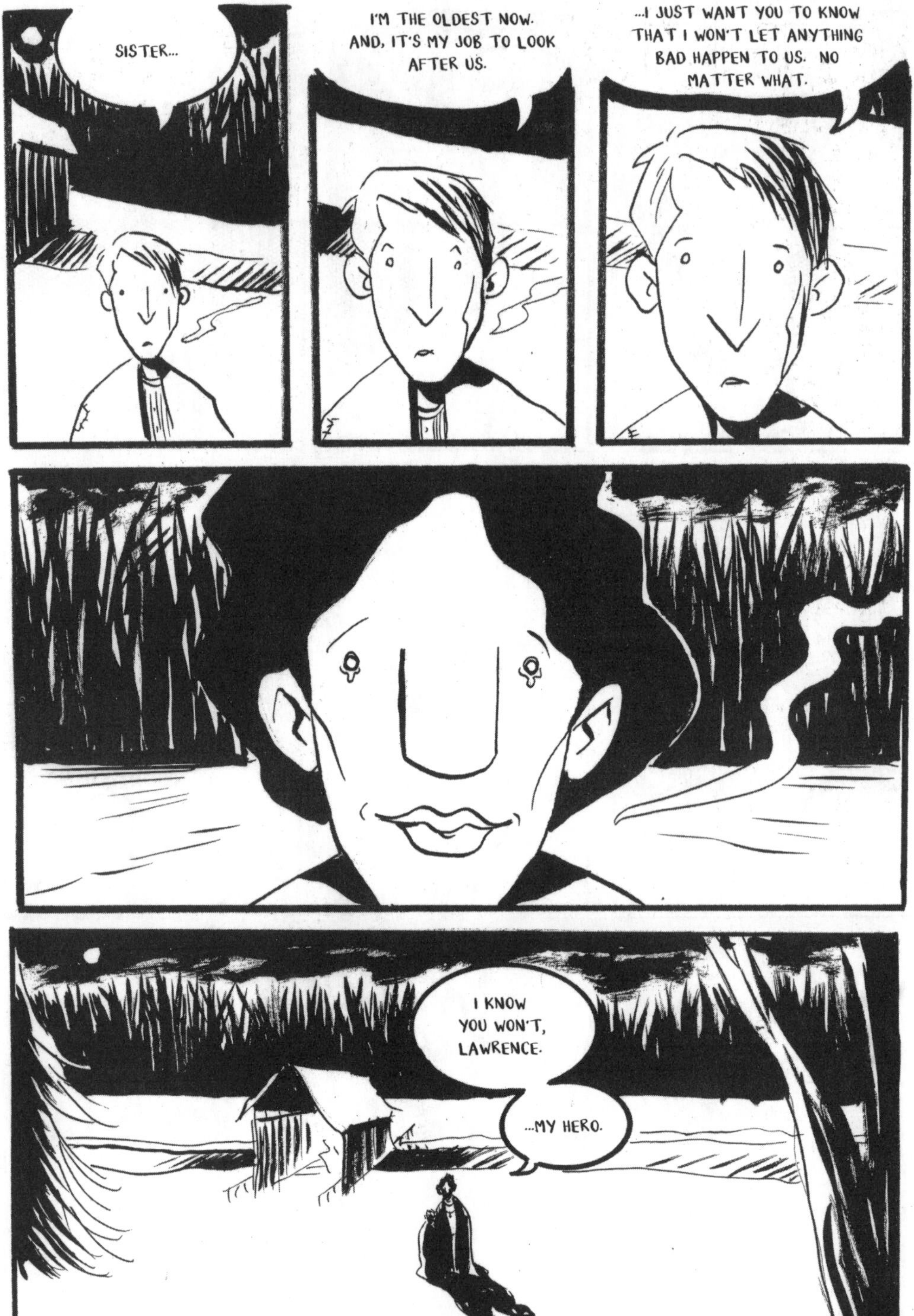
SISTER...
I'M THE OLDEST NOW. AND, IT'S MY JOB TO LOOK AFTER US.
...I JUST WANT YOU TO KNOW THAT I WON'T LET ANYTHING BAD HAPPEN TO US. NO MATTER WHAT.
I KNOW YOU WON'T, LAWRENCE.
...MY HERO.

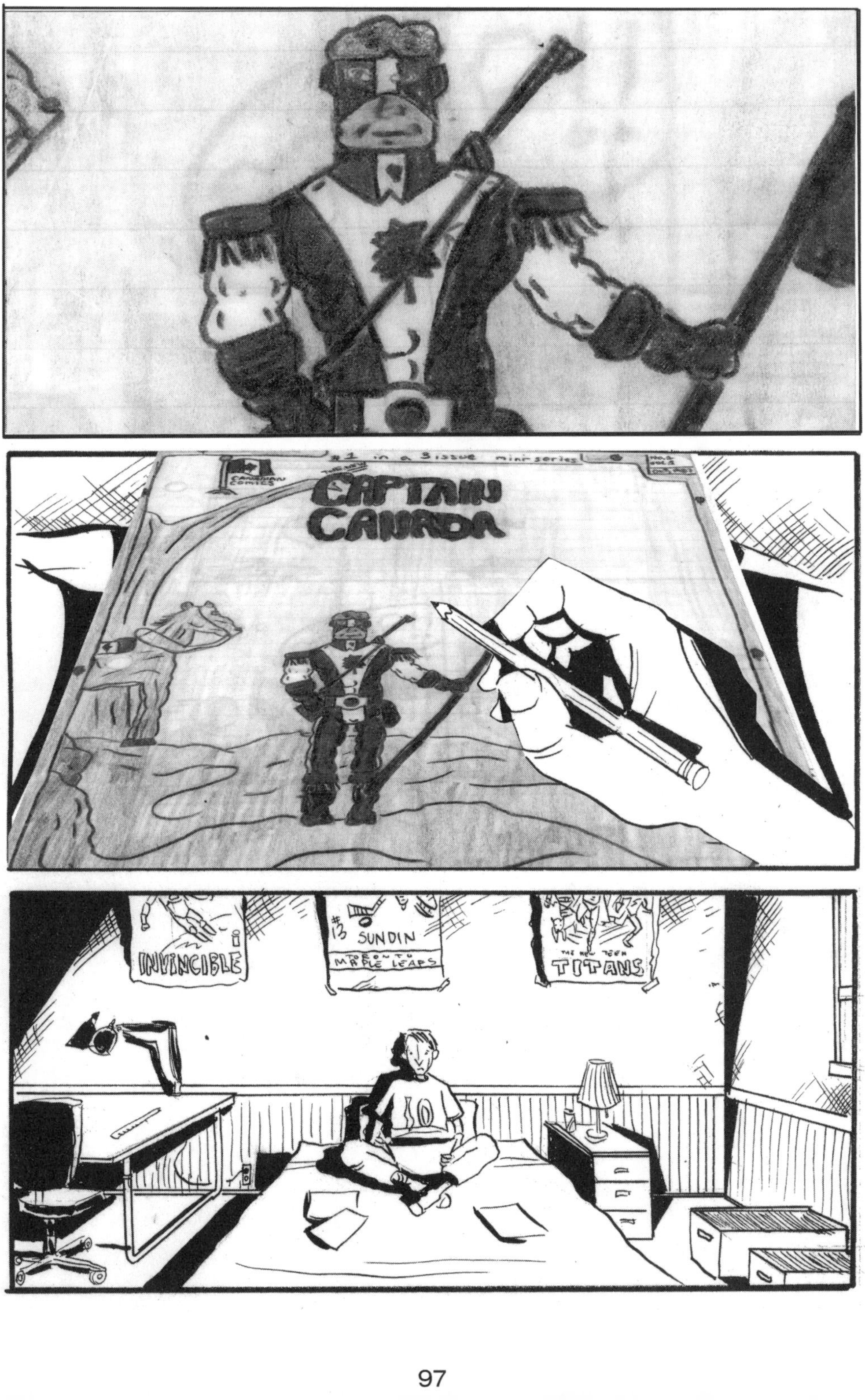
#1 in a 3 issue mini-series
CAPTAIN CANADA
INVINCIBLE
#13
SUNDIN
TORONTO MAPLE LEAFS
THE NEW TEEN TITANS
10

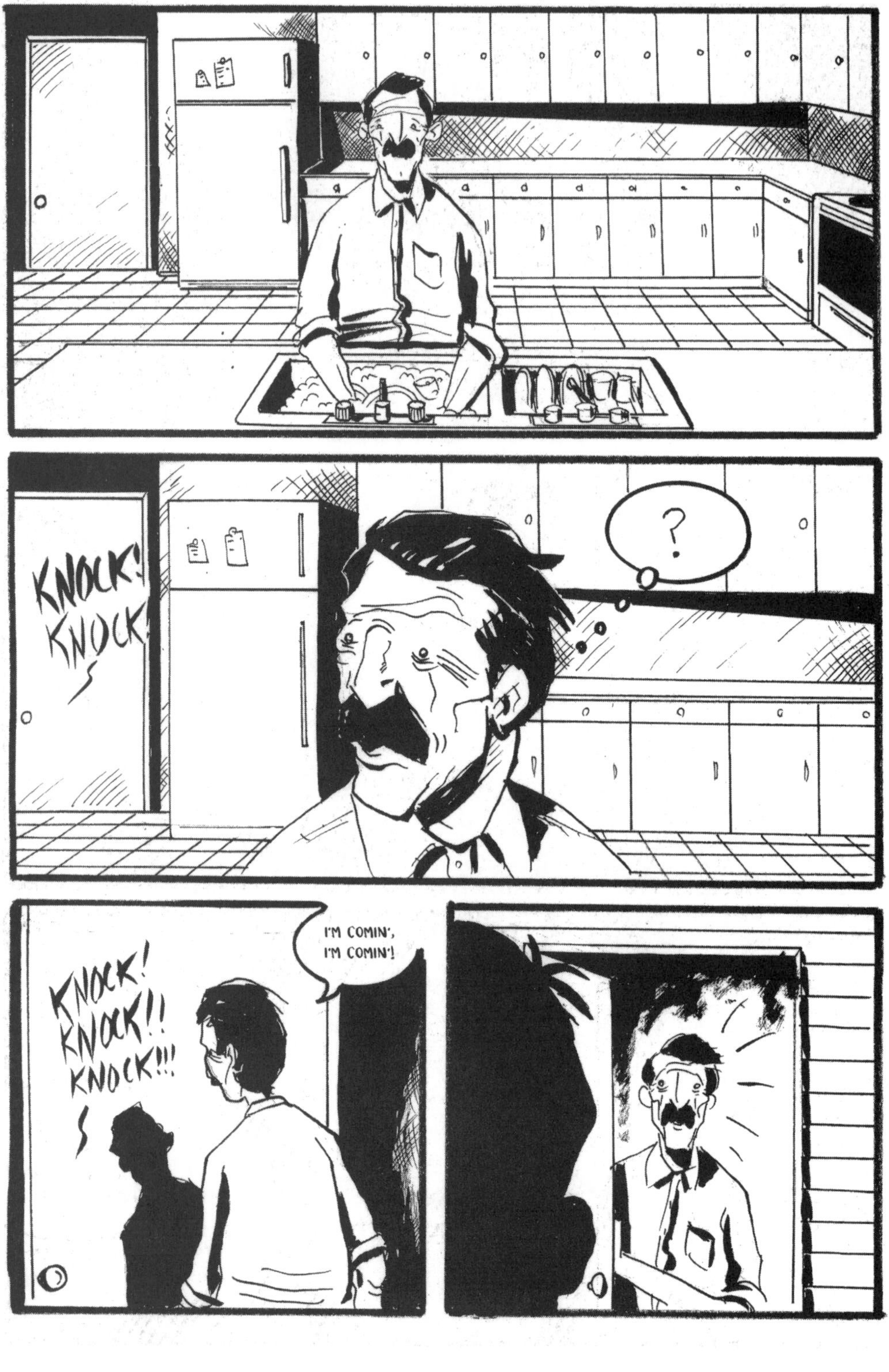
KNOCK!
KNOCK!
?
KNOCK!
KNOCK!!
KNOCK!!!
I'M COMIN',
I'M COMIN'!

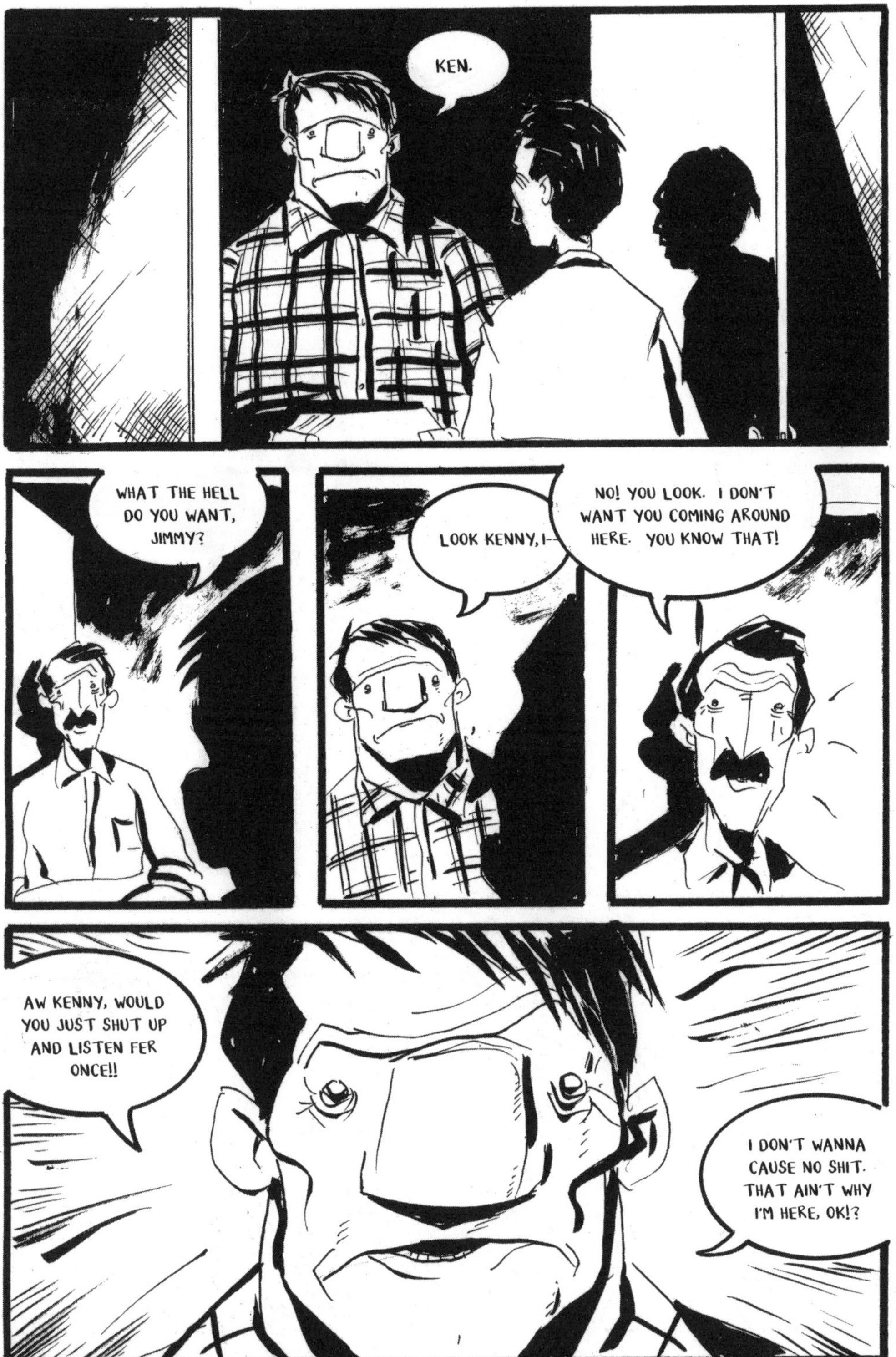
KEN.
WHAT THE HELL DO YOU WANT, JIMMY?
LOOK KENNY, I--
NO! YOU LOOK. I DON'T WANT YOU COMING AROUND HERE. YOU KNOW THAT!
AW KENNY, WOULD YOU JUST SHUT UP AND LISTEN FER ONCE!!
I DON'T WANNA CAUSE NO SHIT. THAT AIN'T WHY I'M HERE, OK!?

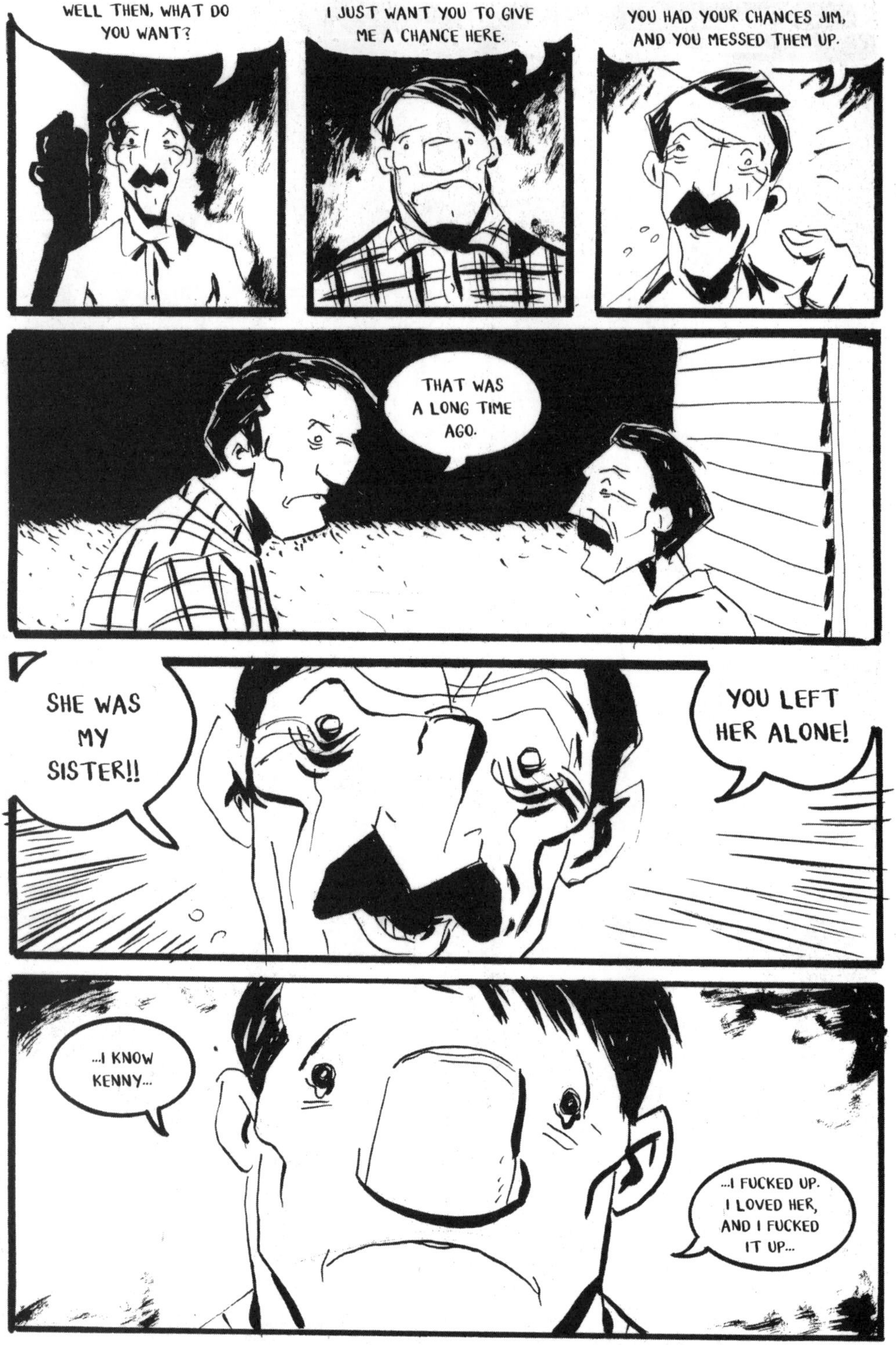
WELL THEN, WHAT DO YOU WANT?
I JUST WANT YOU TO GIVE ME A CHANCE HERE.
YOU HAD YOUR CHANCES JIM, AND YOU MESSED THEM UP.
THAT WAS A LONG TIME AGO.
SHE WAS MY SISTER!!
YOU LEFT HER ALONE!
...I KNOW KENNY...
...I FUCKED UP. I LOVED HER, AND I FUCKED IT UP...

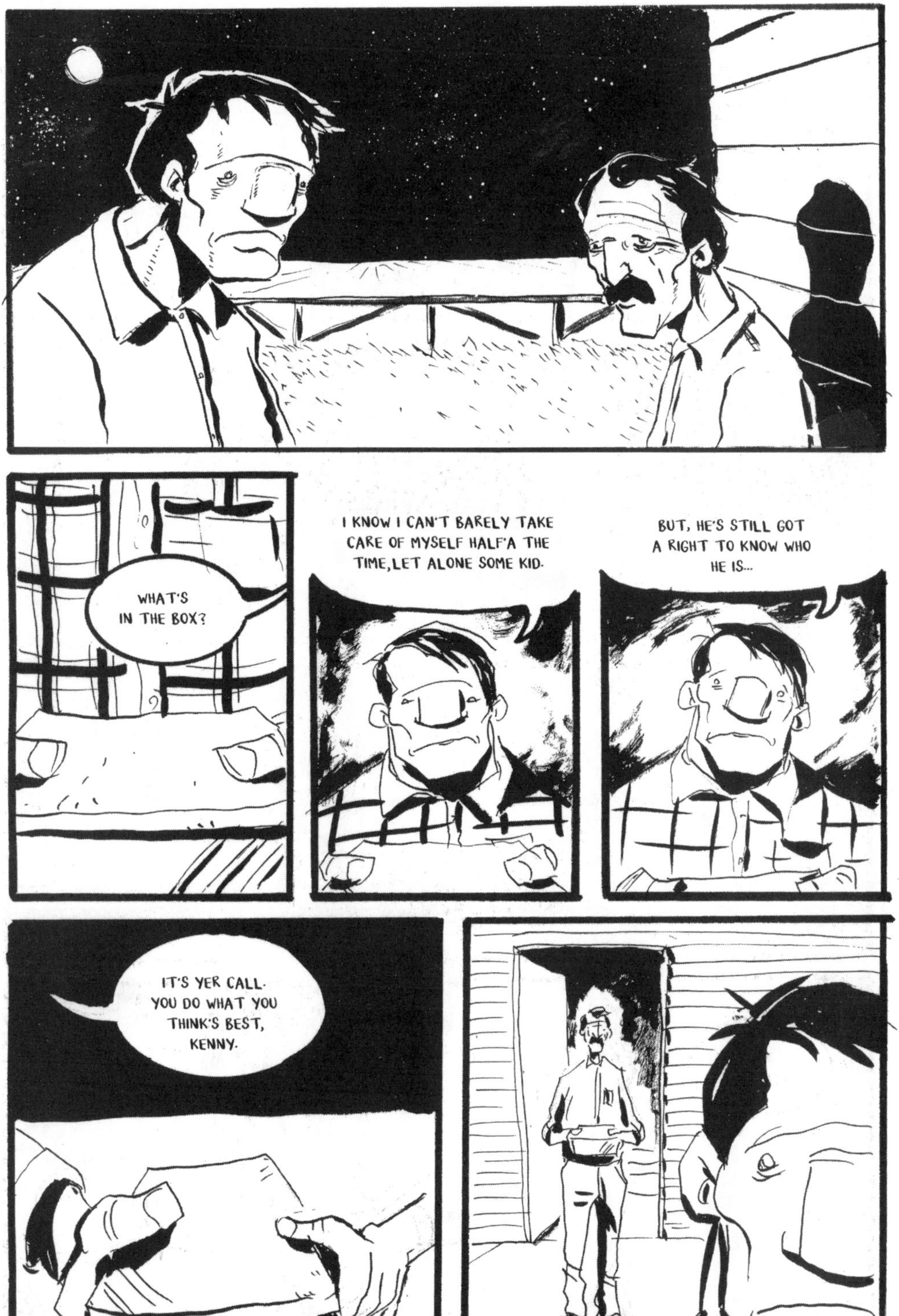
WHAT'S IN THE BOX?
I KNOW I CAN'T BARELY TAKE CARE OF MYSELF HALF'A THE TIME, LET ALONE SOME KID.
BUT, HE'S STILL GOT A RIGHT TO KNOW WHO HE IS...
IT'S YER CALL. YOU DO WHAT YOU THINK'S BEST, KENNY.

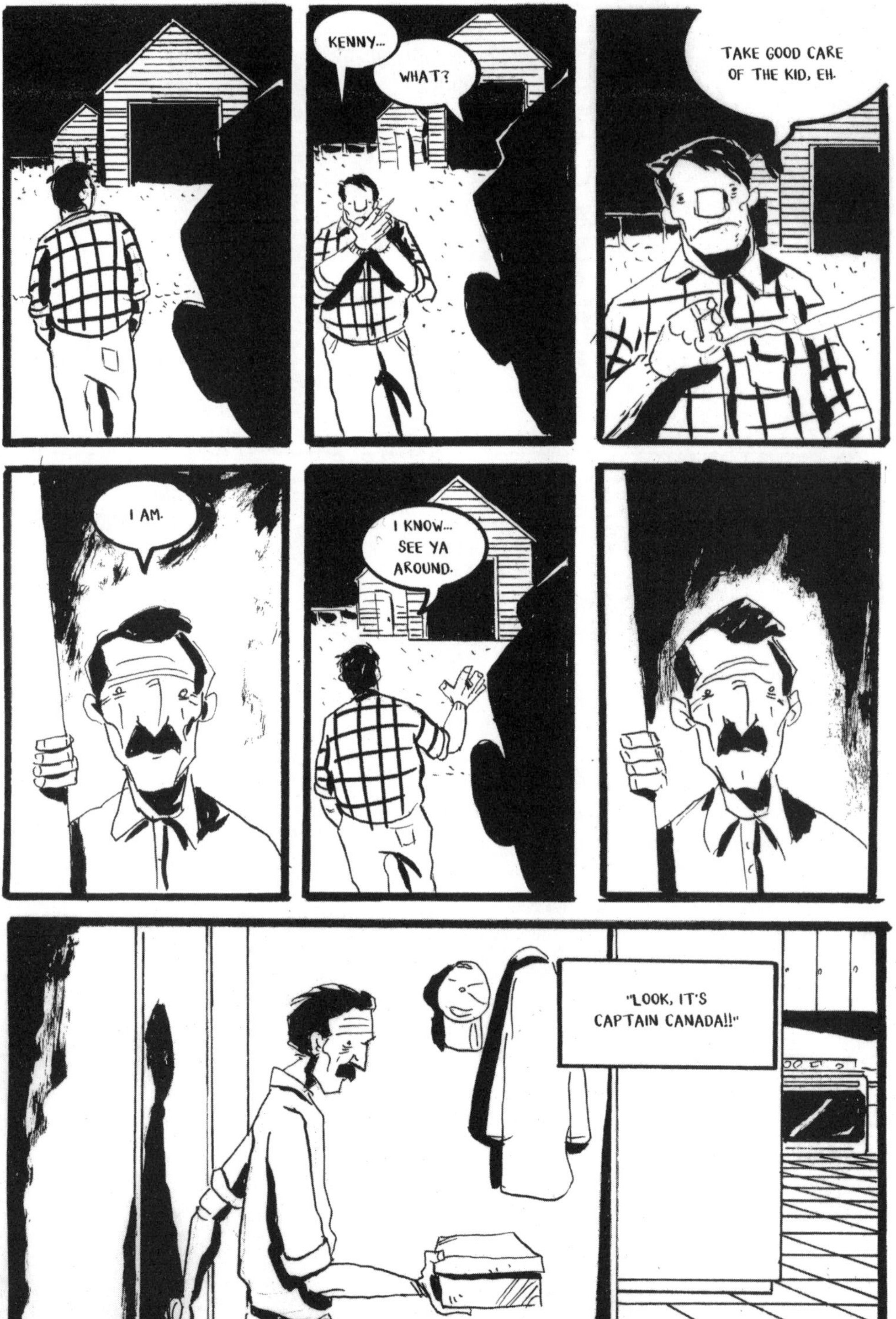
KENNY...
WHAT?
TAKE GOOD CARE OF THE KID, EH.
I AM.
I KNOW... SEE YA AROUND.
"LOOK, IT'S CAPTAIN CANADA!!"

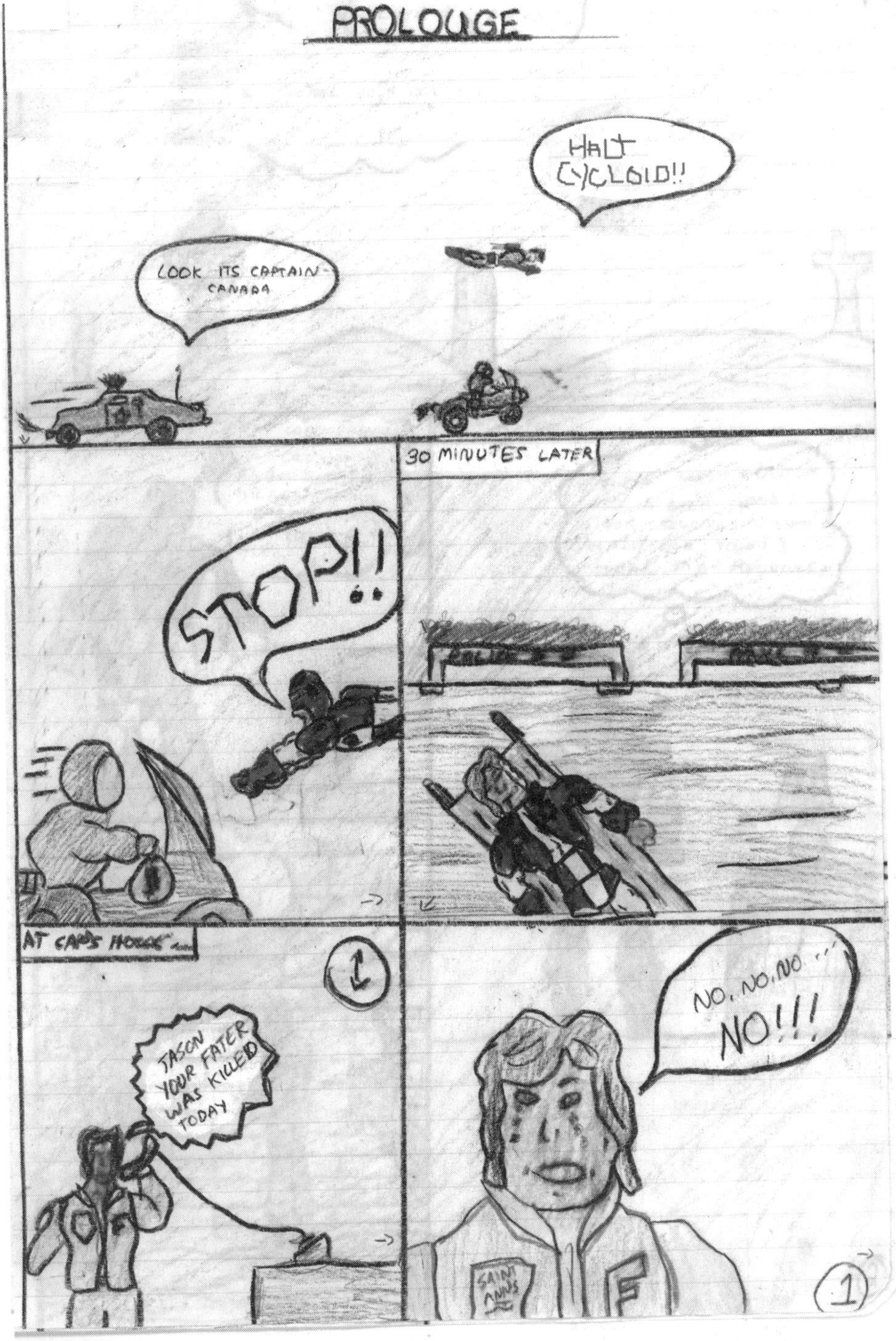
PROLOUGE
HALT CYCLOID!!
LOOK ITS CAPTAIN CANADA
STOP!!
30 MINUTES LATER
AT CAP'S HOUSE
JASON YOUR FATER WAS KILLED TODAY
NO, NO, NO ...
NO!!!
SAINT ANNS
1

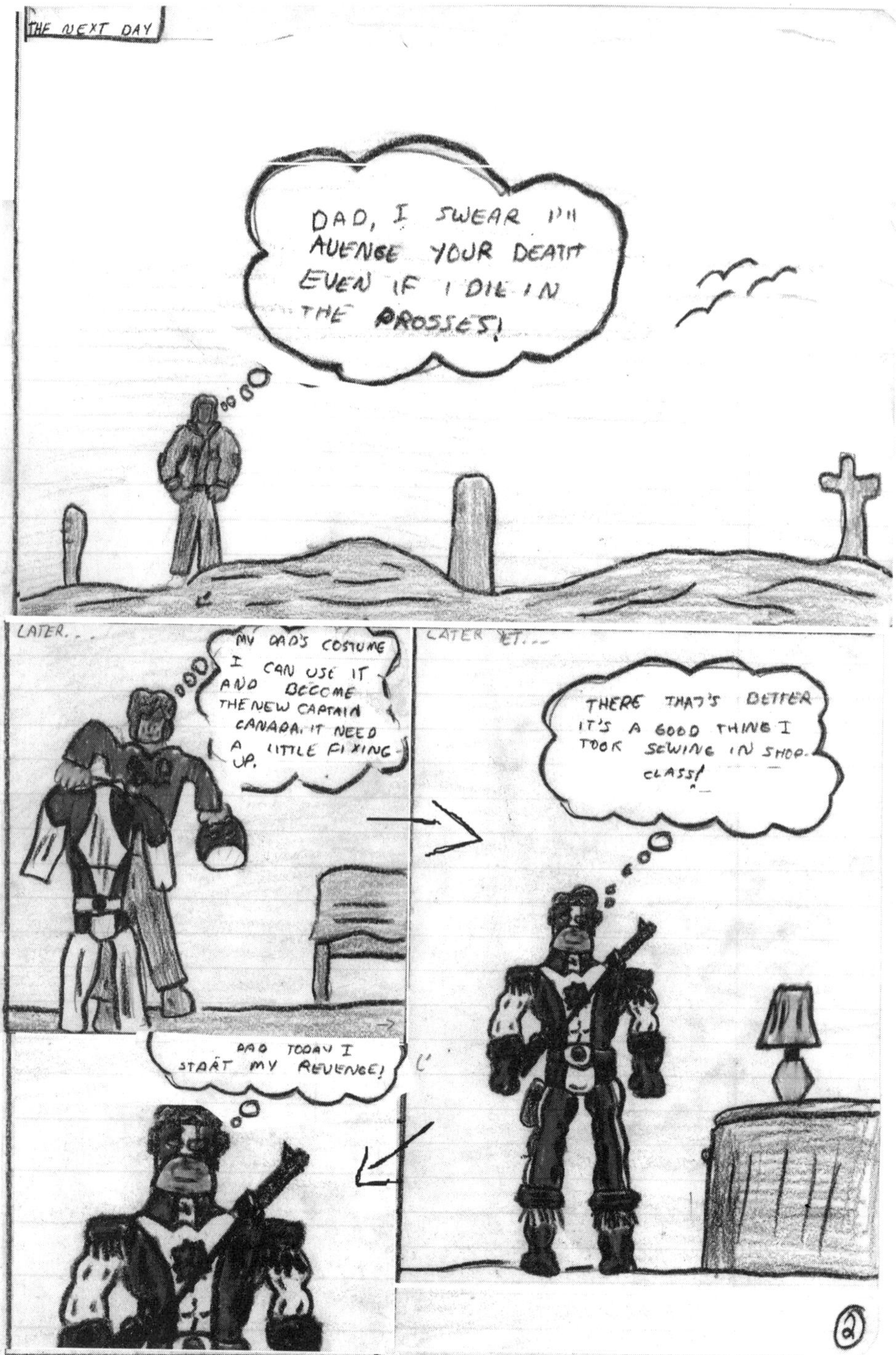
THE NEXT DAY
DAD, I SWEAR I'll AVENGE YOUR DEATH EVEN IF I DIE IN THE PROSSES!
LATER...
MY DAD'S COSTUME I CAN USE IT AND BECOME THE NEW CAPTAIN CANADA. IT NEED A LITTLE FIXING UP.
LATER YET...
THERE THAT'S BETTER IT'S A GOOD THING I TOOK SEWING IN SHOP-CLASS!
DAD TODAY I START MY REVENGE!
2

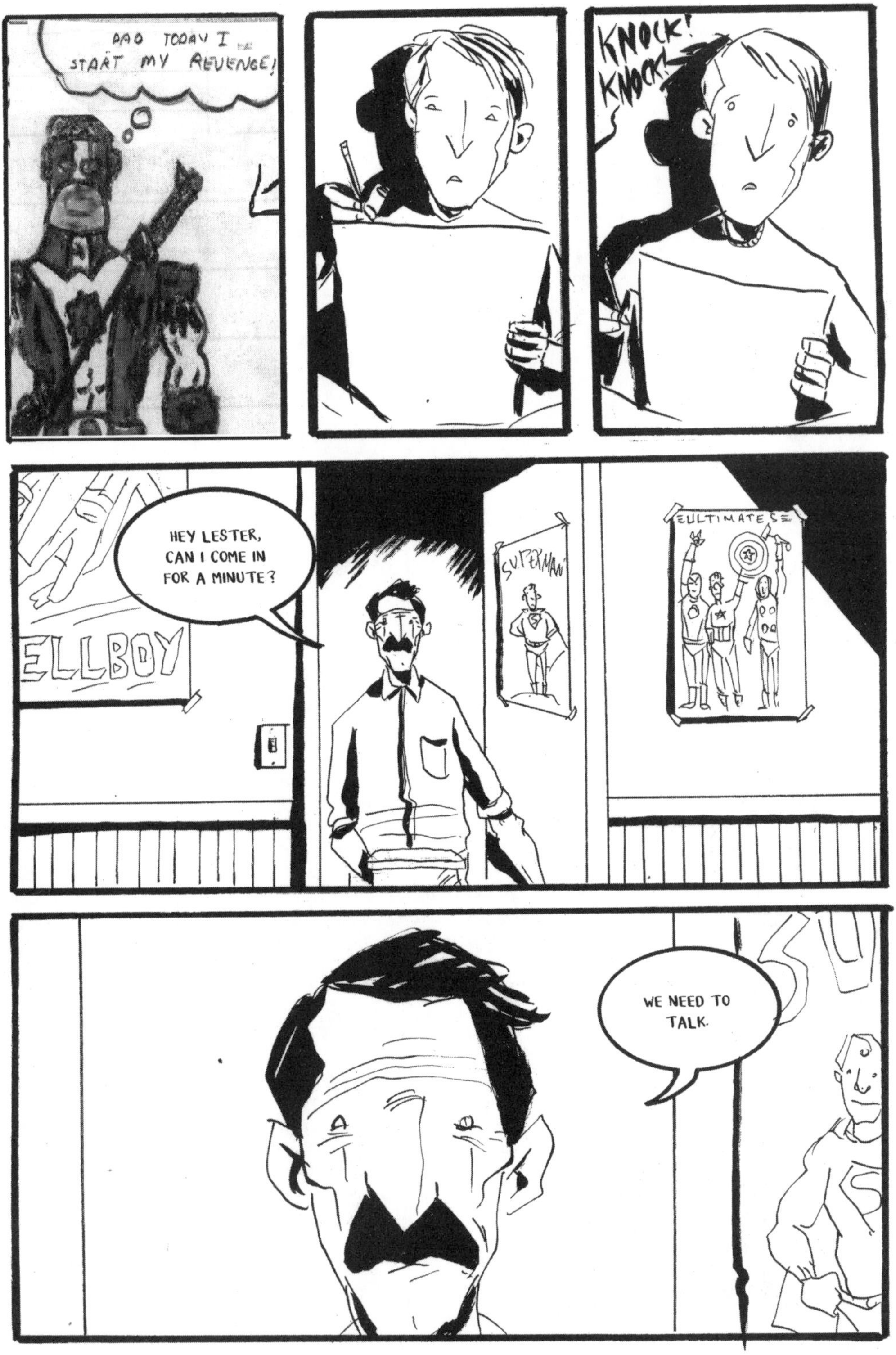
DAD TODAY I START MY REVENGE!
KNOCK! KNOCK!
ELLBOY
HEY LESTER, CAN I COME IN FOR A MINUTE?
SUPERMAN
ULTIMATES
WE NEED TO TALK.

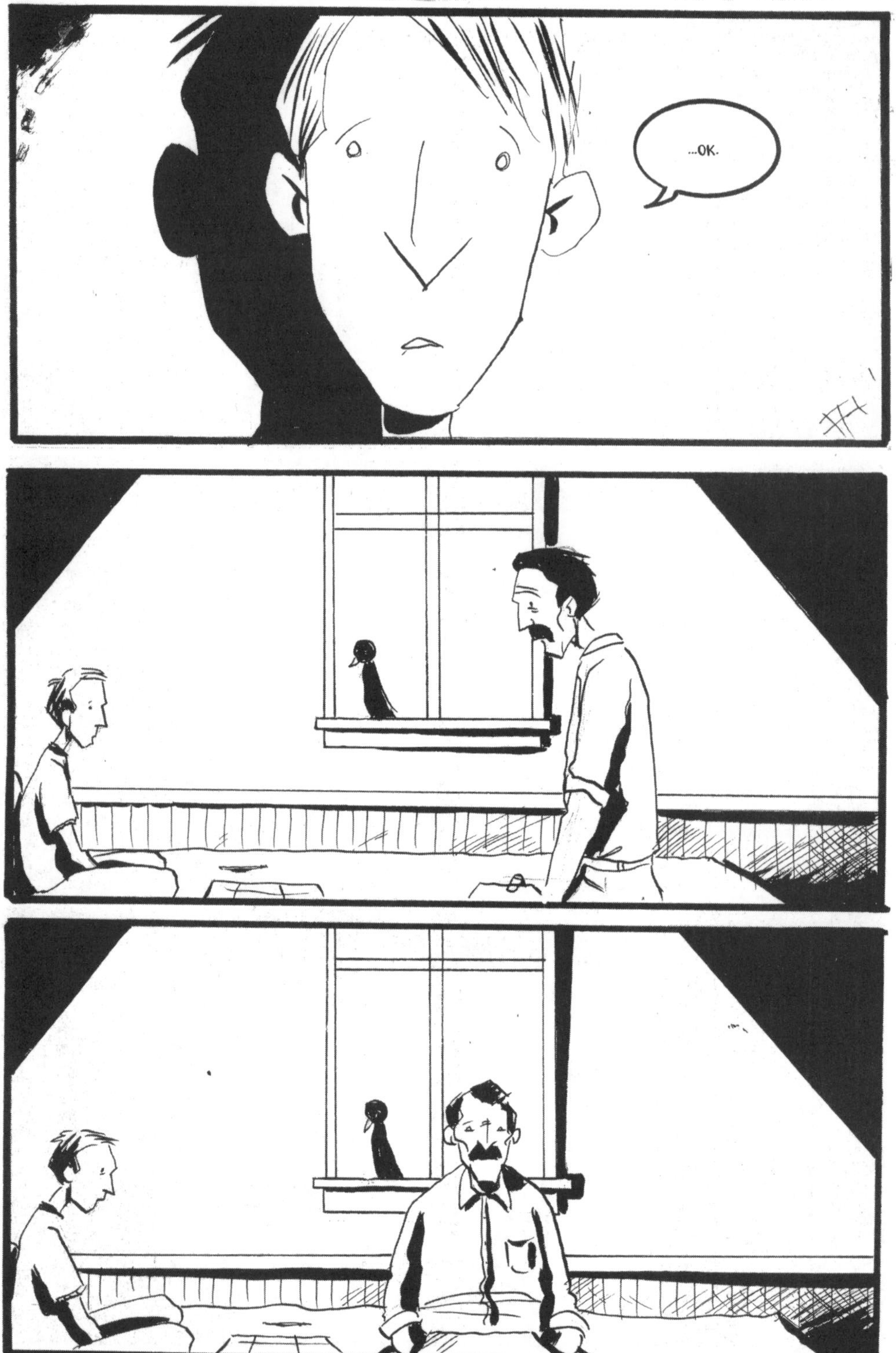
...OK.

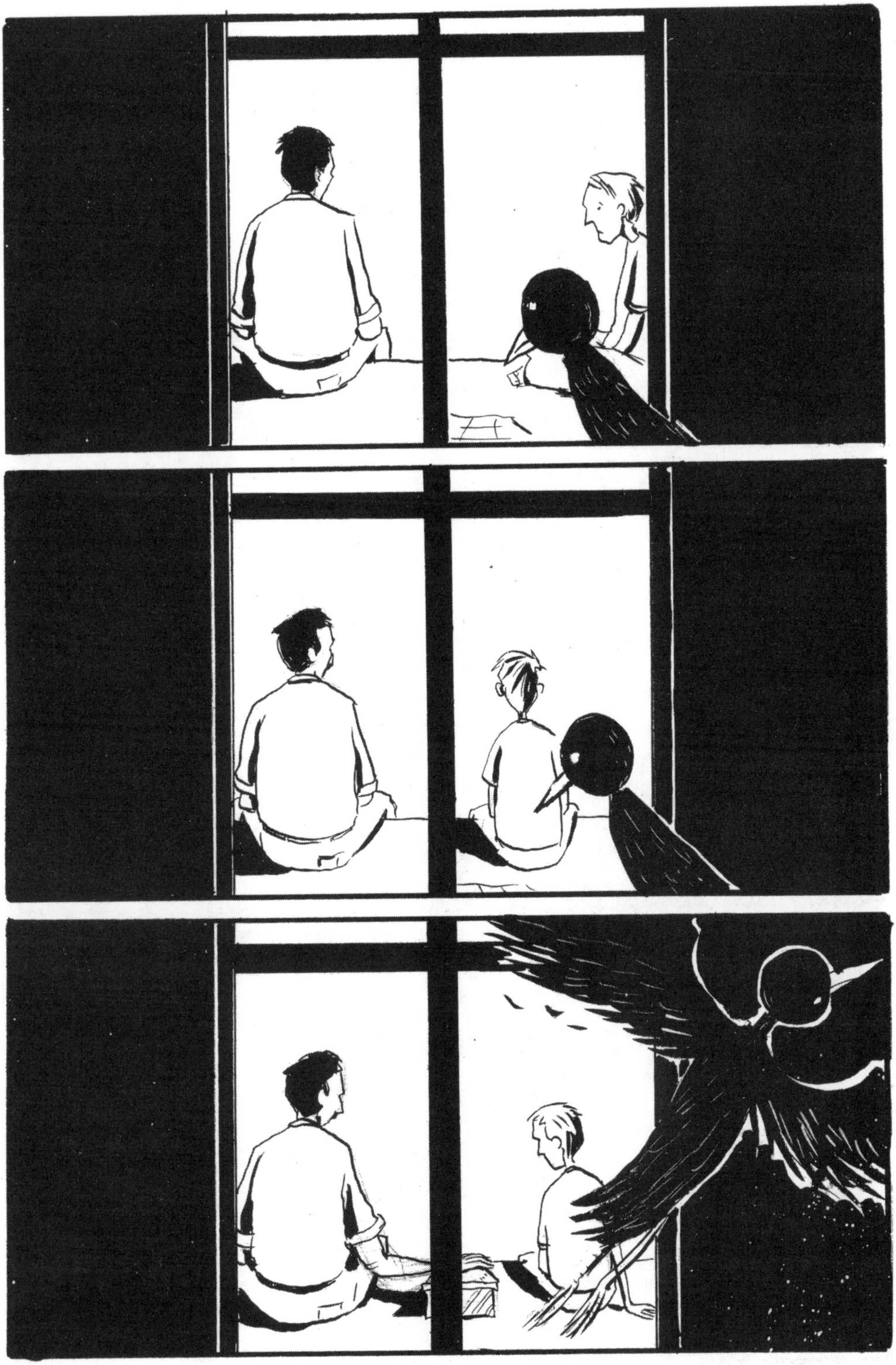

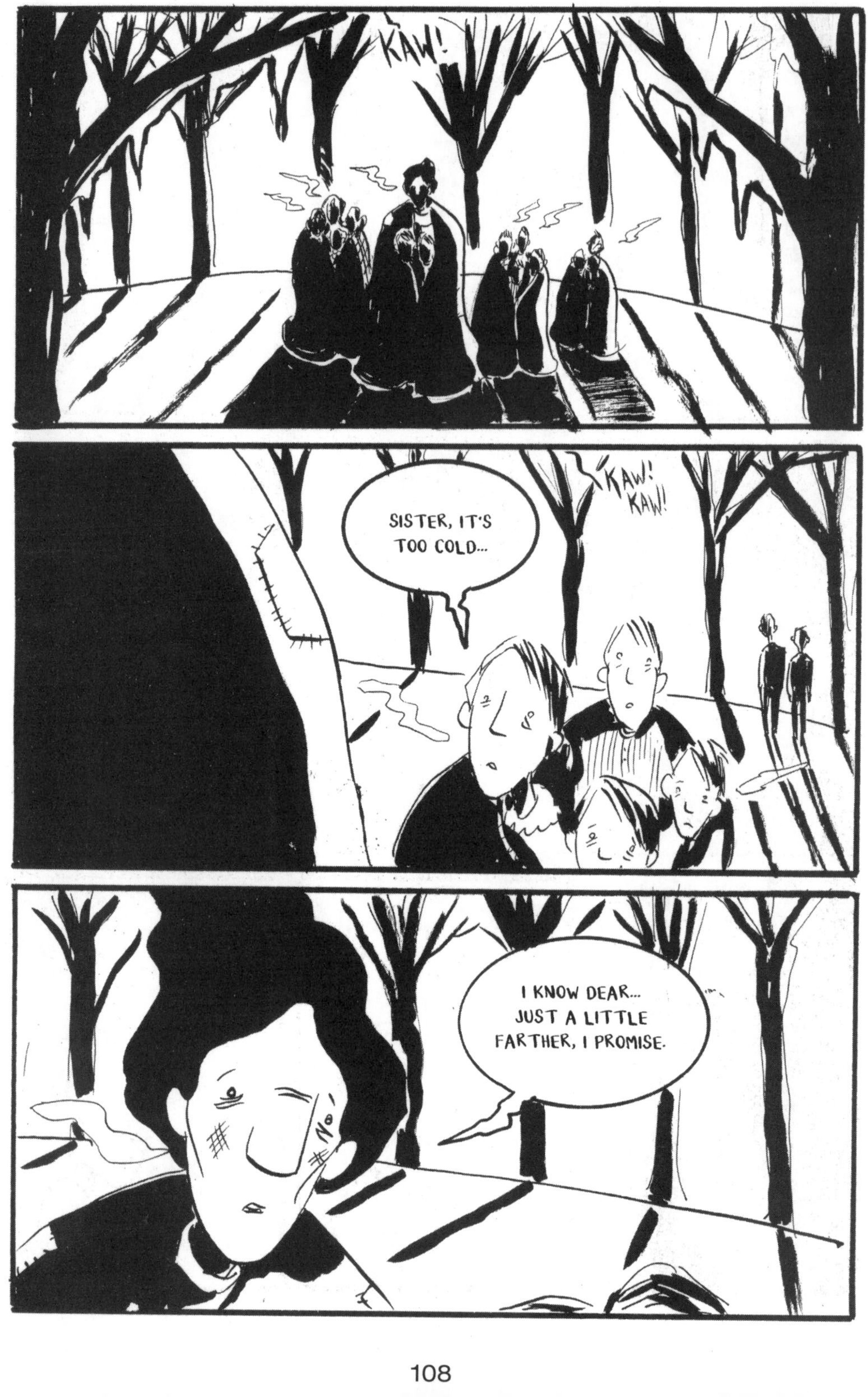
KAW!
KAW! KAW!
SISTER, IT'S TOO COLD...
I KNOW DEAR... JUST A LITTLE FARTHER, I PROMISE.

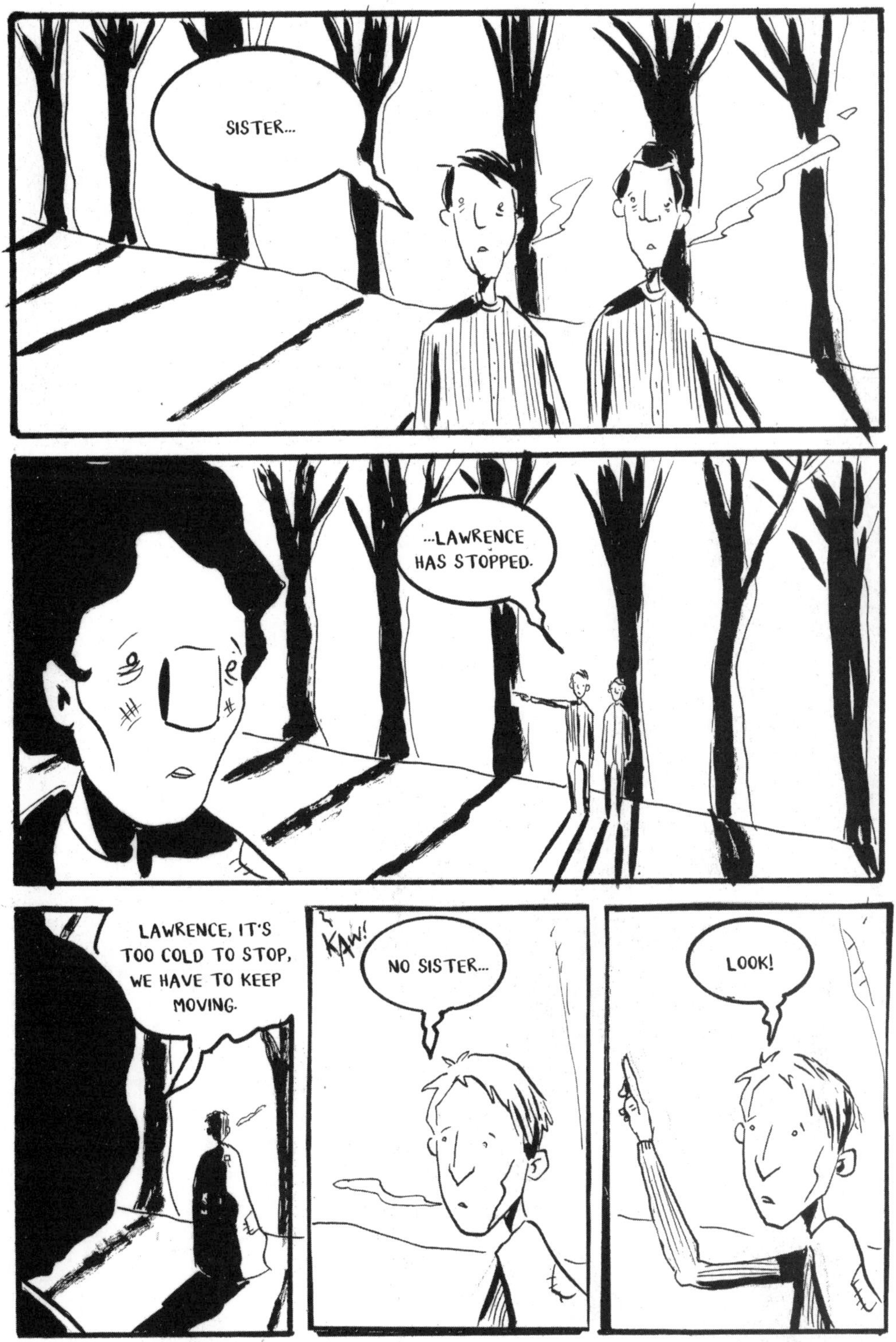
SISTER...
...LAWRENCE HAS STOPPED.
LAWRENCE, IT'S TOO COLD TO STOP, WE HAVE TO KEEP MOVING.
KAW!
NO SISTER...
LOOK!

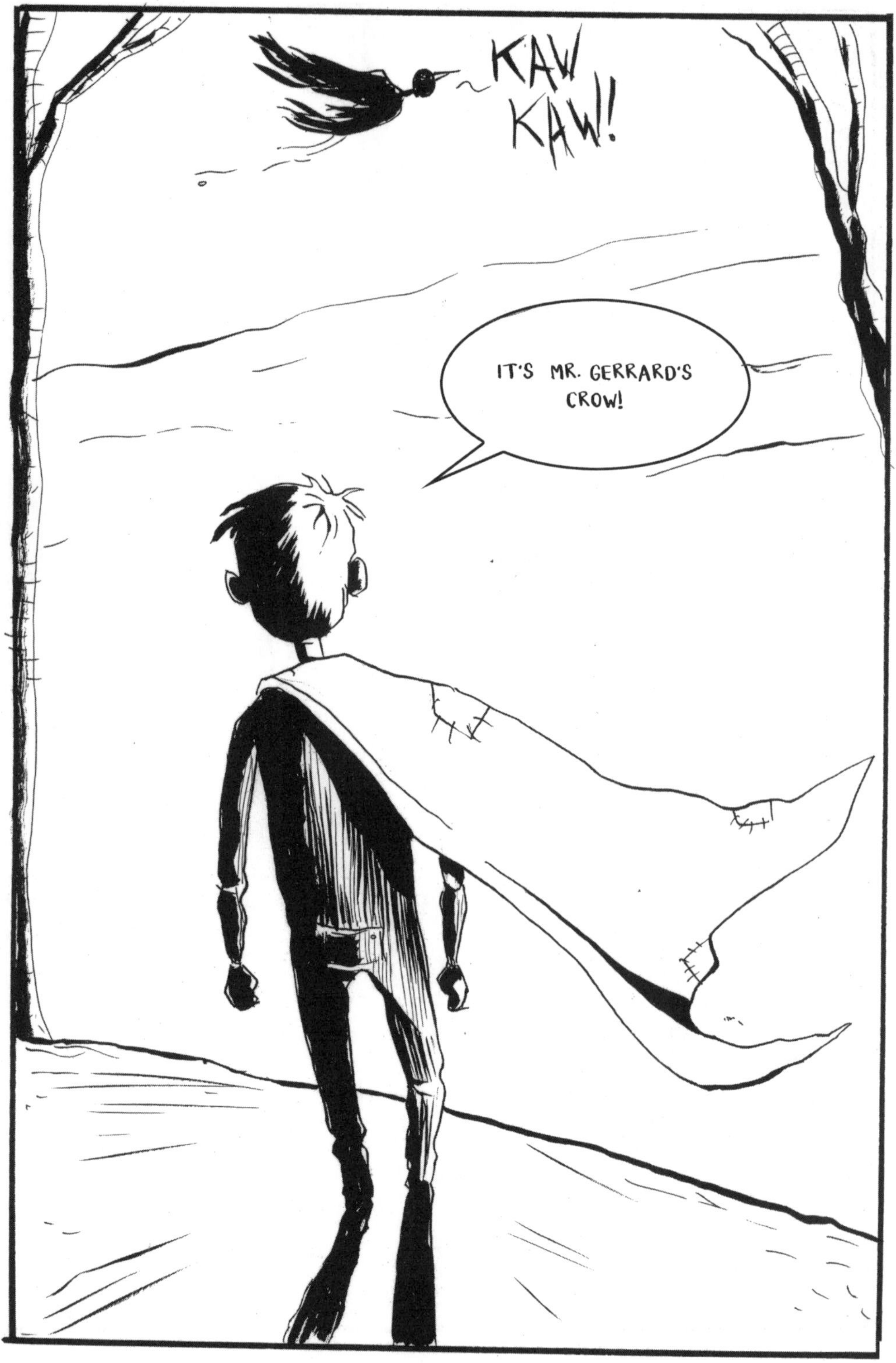
KAW KAW!
IT'S MR. GERRARD'S CROW!

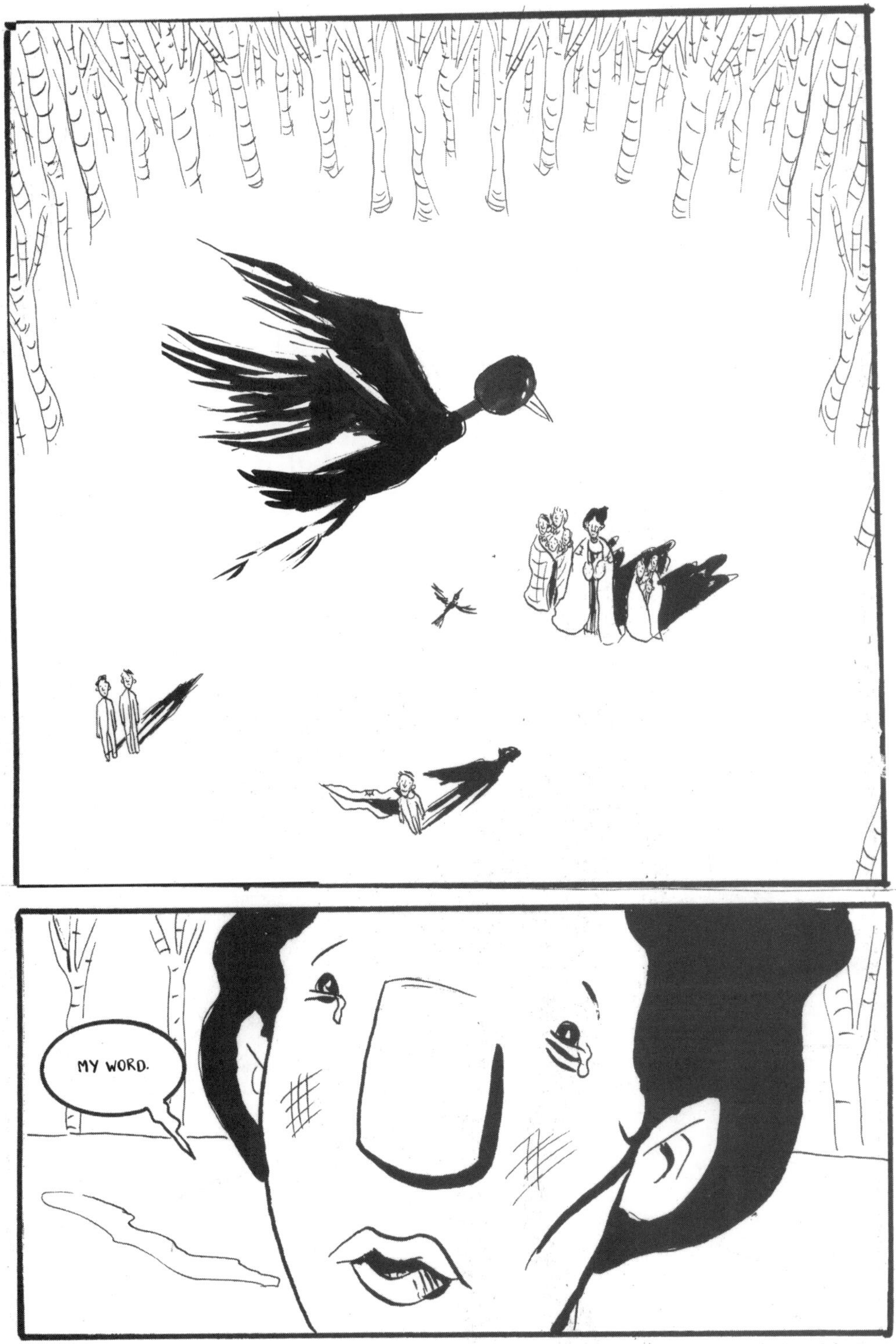
MY WORD.

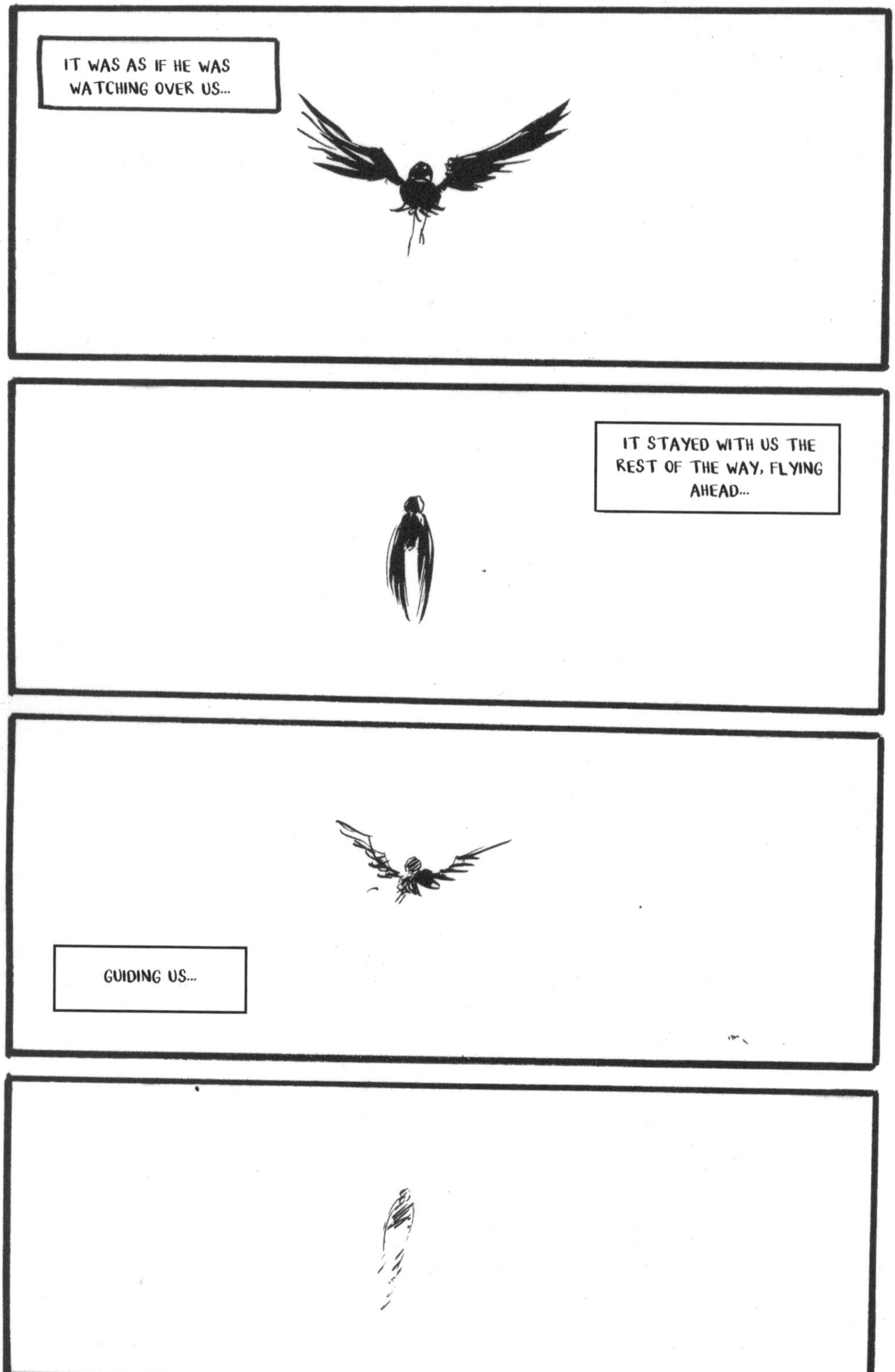
IT WAS AS IF HE WAS WATCHING OVER US...
IT STAYED WITH US THE REST OF THE WAY, FLYING AHEAD...
GUIDING US...

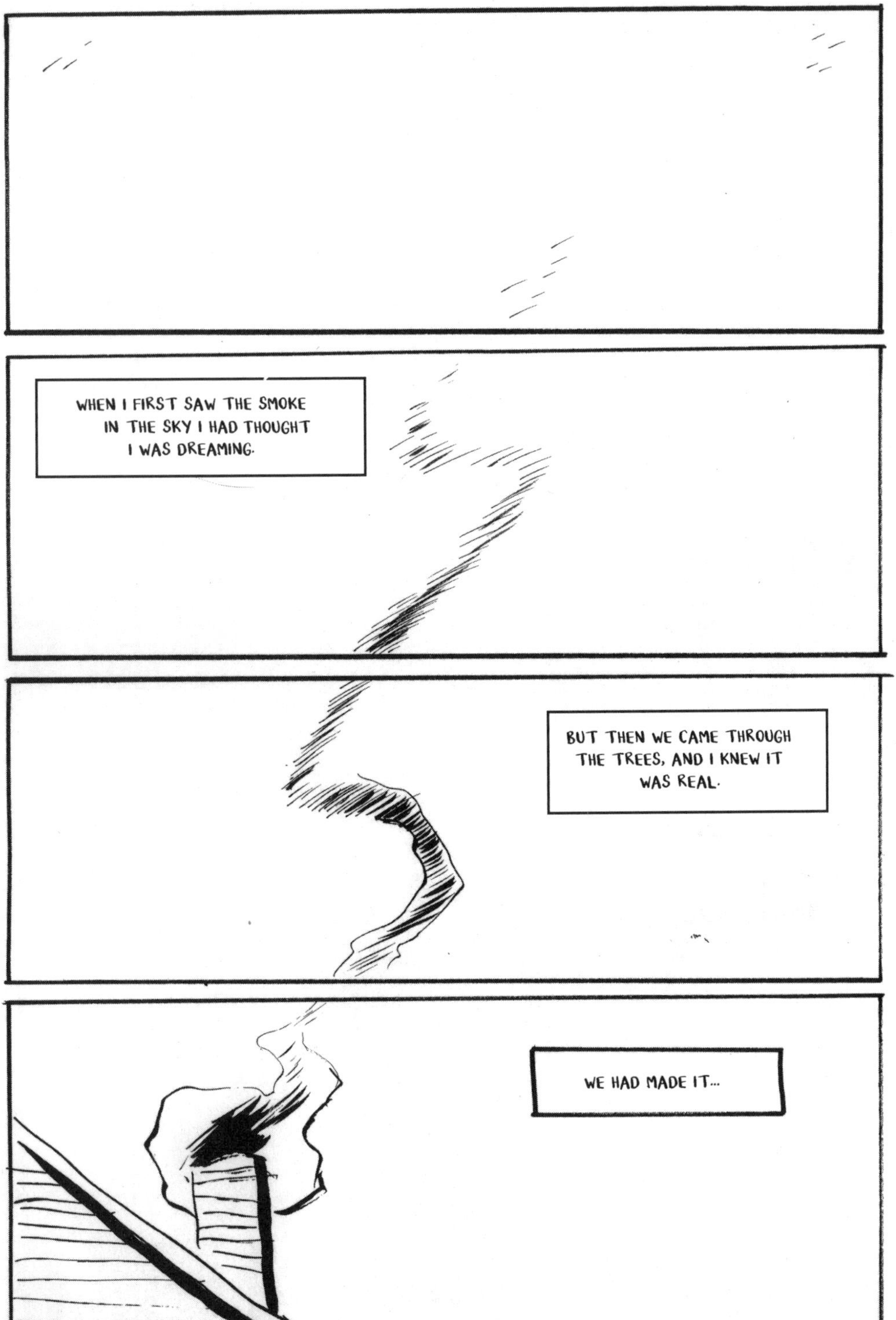
WHEN I FIRST SAW THE SMOKE IN THE SKY I HAD THOUGHT I WAS DREAMING.
BUT THEN WE CAME THROUGH THE TREES, AND I KNEW IT WAS REAL.
WE HAD MADE IT...

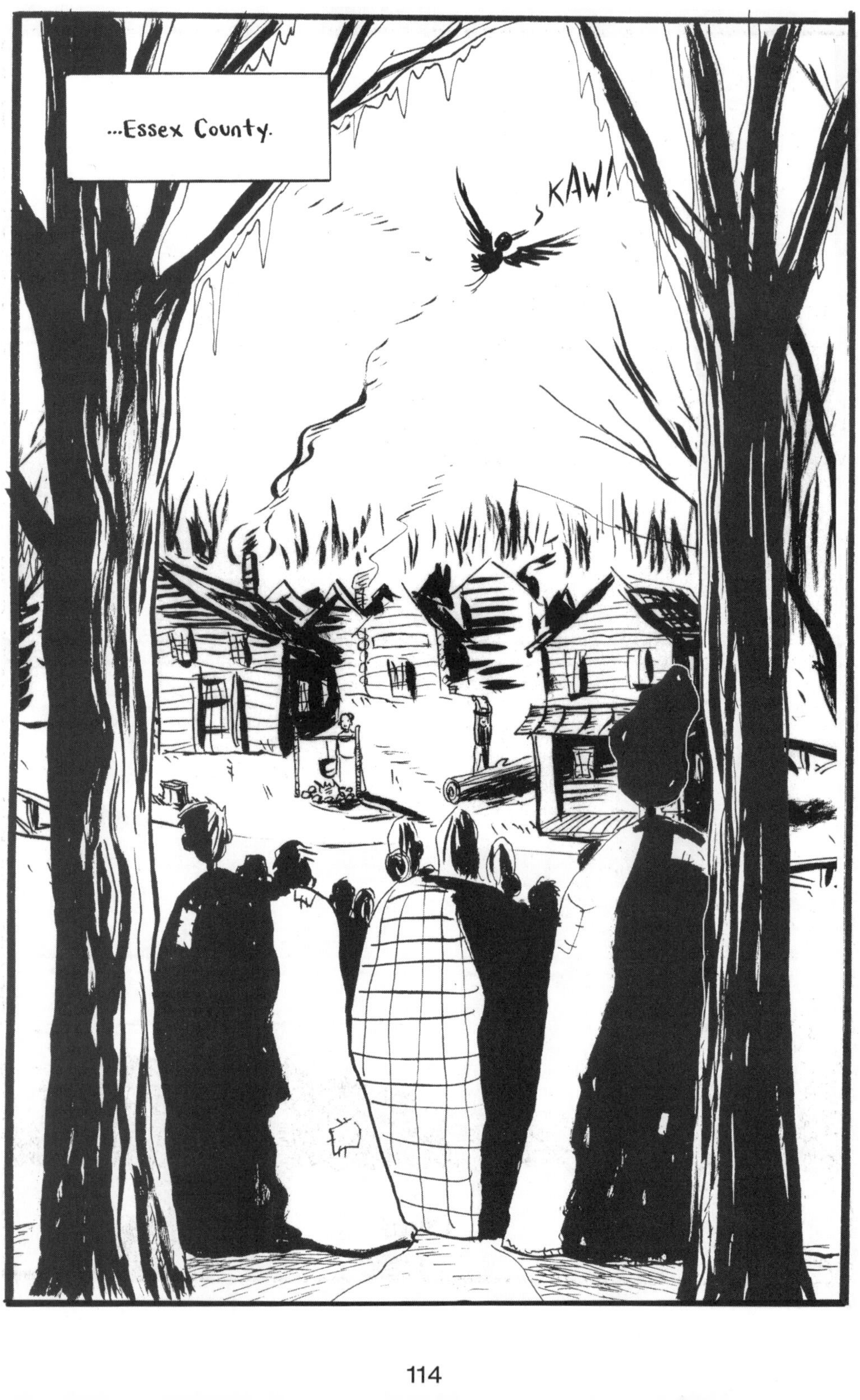
...Essex County.
KAW!

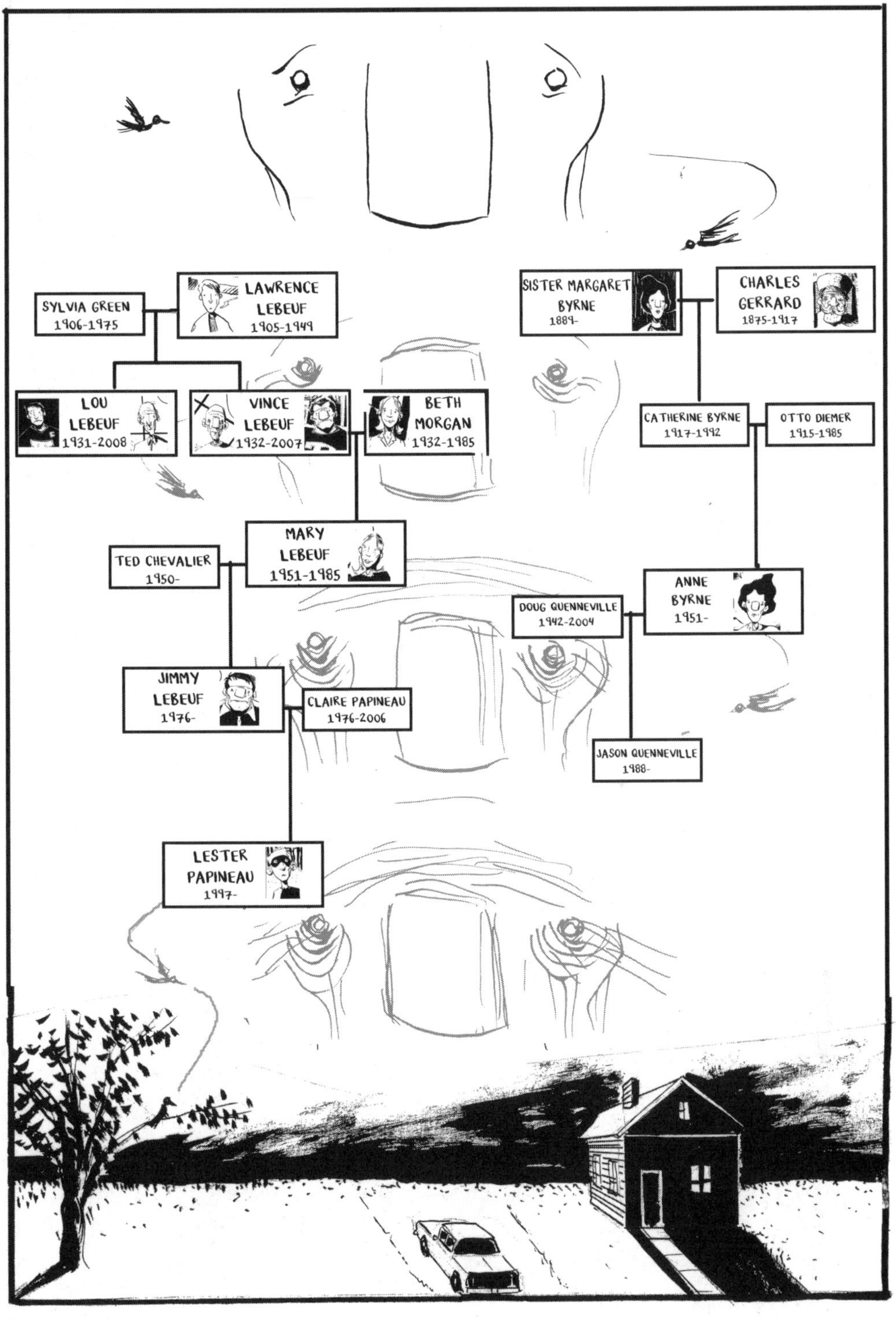
SYLVIA GREEN 1906-1975
LAWRENCE LEBEUF 1905-1949
SISTER MARGARET BYRNE 1889-
CHARLES GERRARD 1875-1917
LOU LEBEUF 1931-2008
VINCE LEBEUF 1932-2007
BETH MORGAN 1932-1985
CATHERINE BYRNE 1917-1992
OTTO DIEMER 1915-1985
TED CHEVALIER 1950-
MARY LEBEUF 1951-1985
DOUG QUENNEVILLE 1942-2004
ANNE BYRNE 1951-
JIMMY LEBEUF 1976-
CLAIRE PAPINEAU 1976-2006
JASON QUENNEVILLE 1988-
LESTER PAPINEAU 1997-

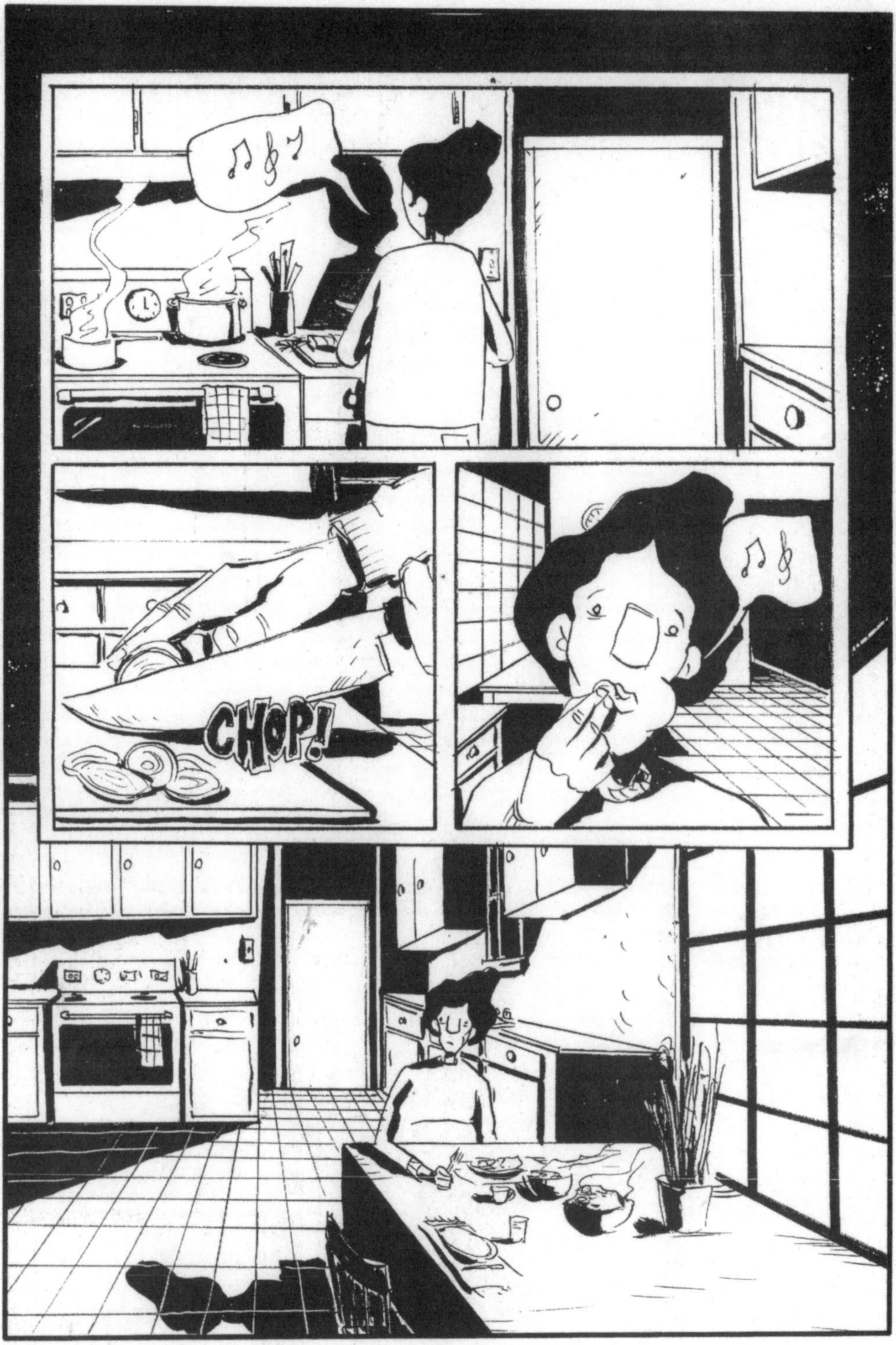
CHOP!

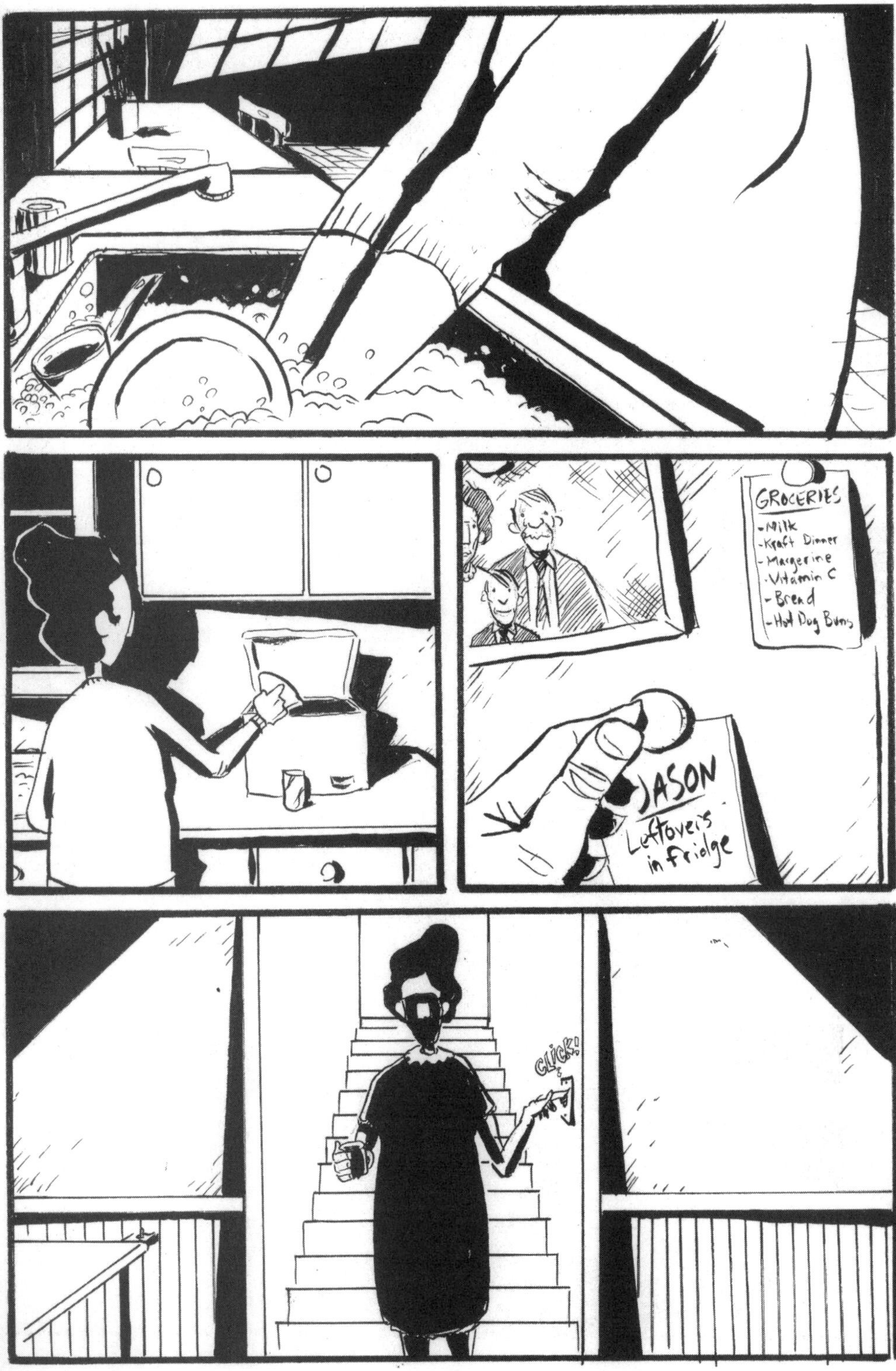
GROCERIES
-Milk
-Kraft Dinner
-Margerine
-Vitamin C
-Bread
-Hot Dog Buns
JASON
Leftovers in Fridge
CLICK!

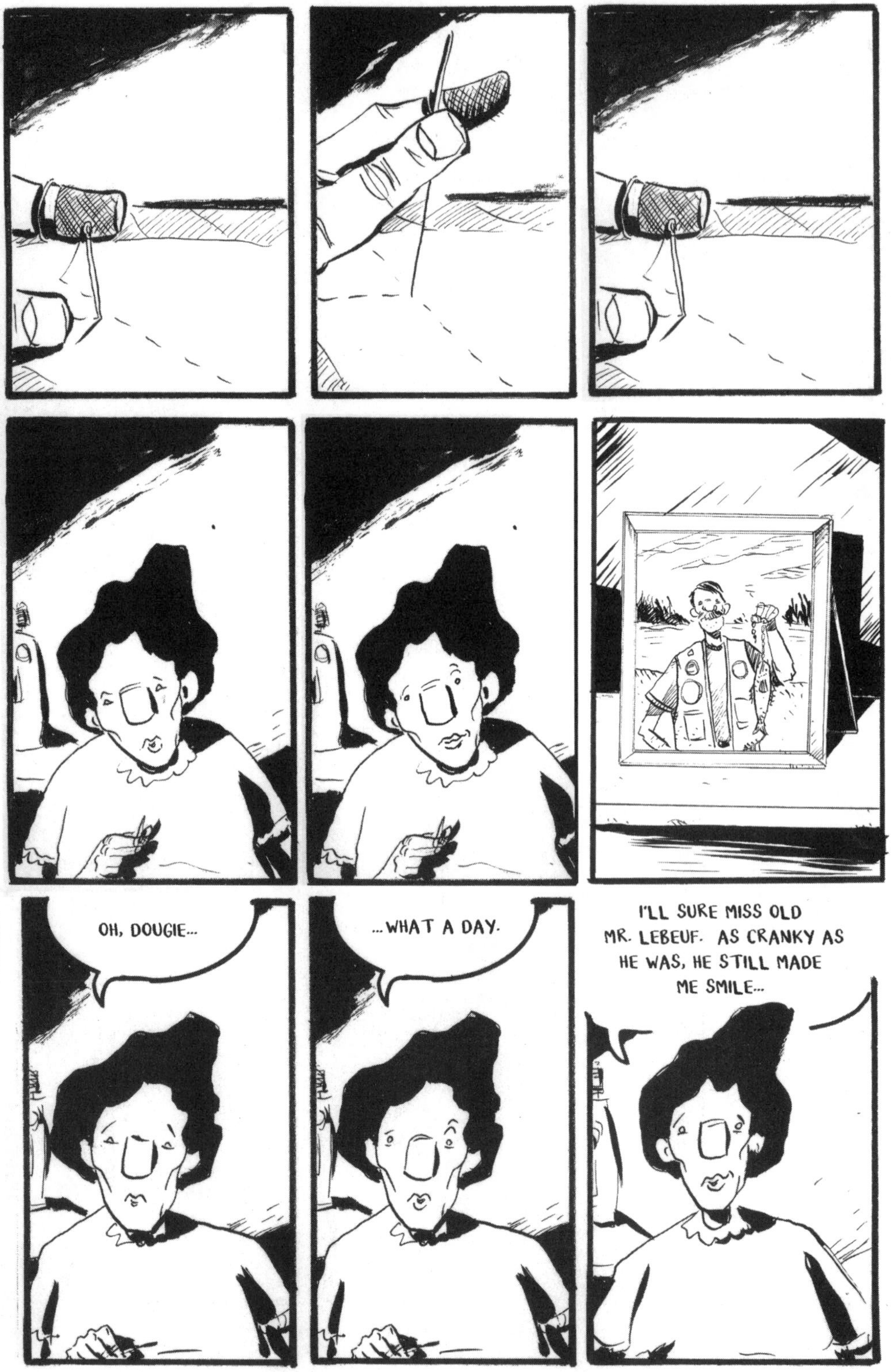
OH, DOUGIE...
...WHAT A DAY.
I'LL SURE MISS OLD MR. LEBEUF. AS CRANKY AS HE WAS, HE STILL MADE ME SMILE...

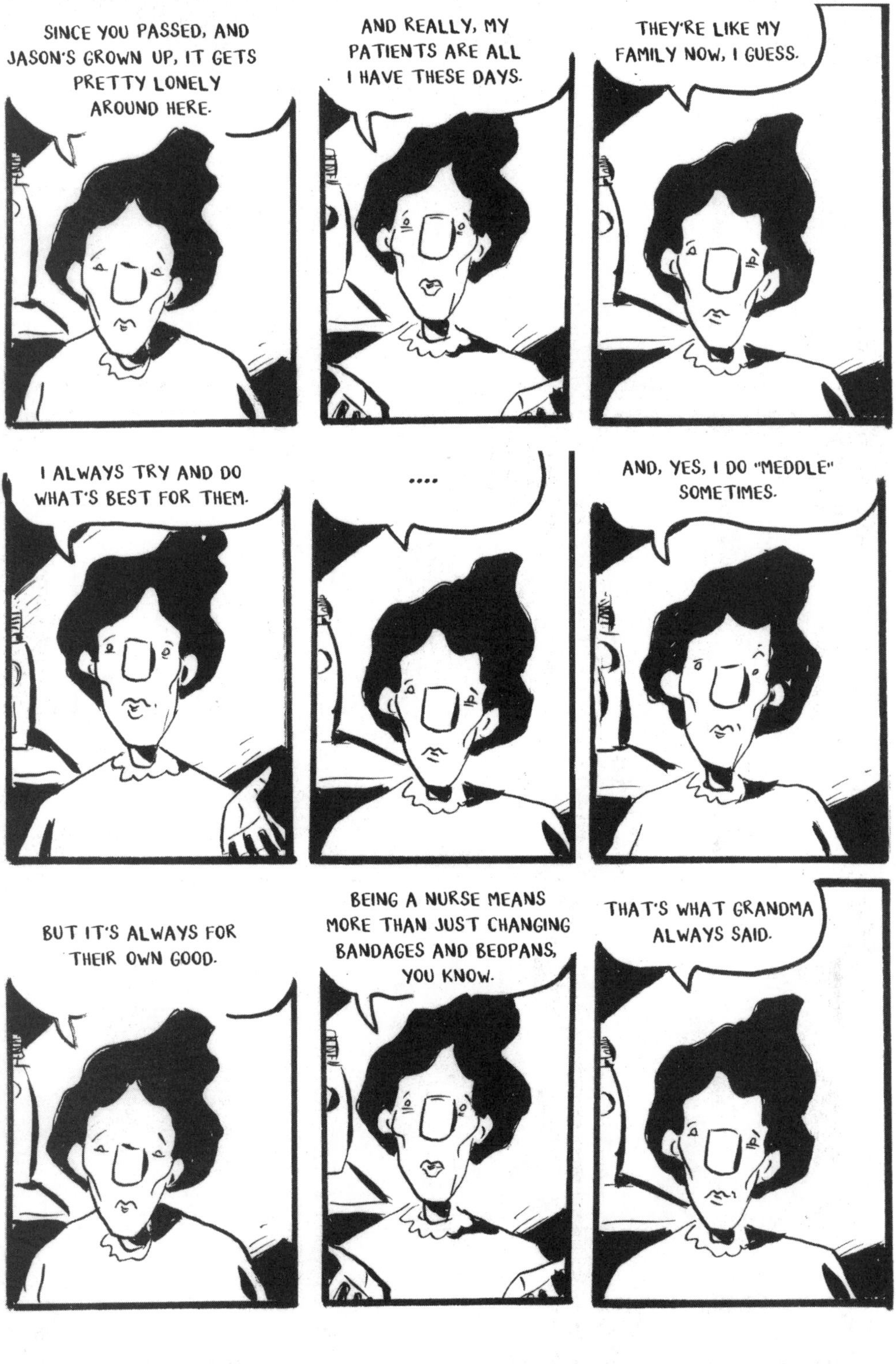
SINCE YOU PASSED, AND JASON'S GROWN UP, IT GETS PRETTY LONELY AROUND HERE.
AND REALLY, MY PATIENTS ARE ALL I HAVE THESE DAYS.
THEY'RE LIKE MY FAMILY NOW, I GUESS.
I ALWAYS TRY AND DO WHAT'S BEST FOR THEM.
....
AND, YES, I DO "MEDDLE" SOMETIMES.
BUT IT'S ALWAYS FOR THEIR OWN GOOD.
BEING A NURSE MEANS MORE THAN JUST CHANGING BANDAGES AND BEDPANS, YOU KNOW.
THAT'S WHAT GRANDMA ALWAYS SAID.

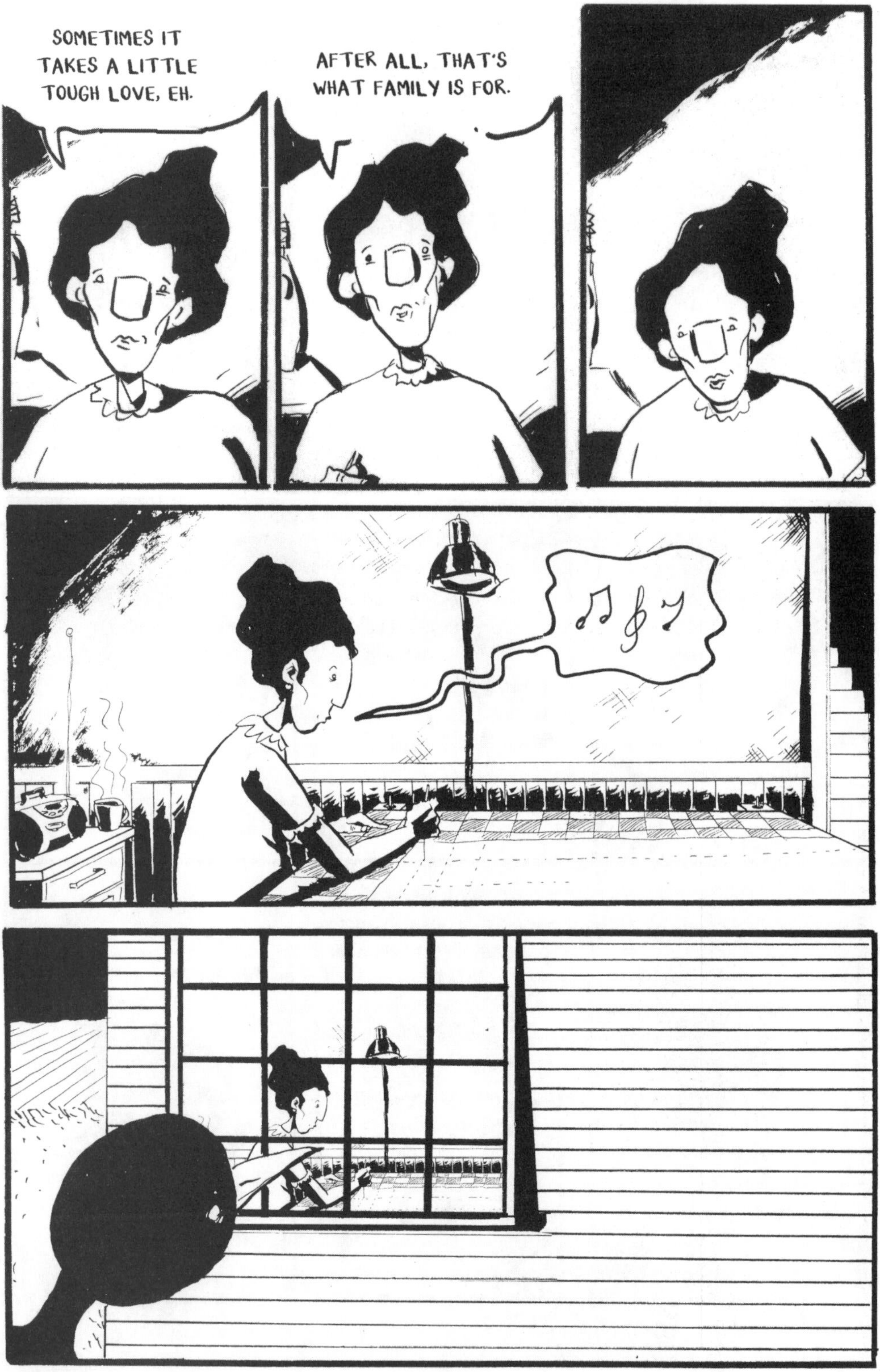
SOMETIMES IT TAKES A LITTLE TOUGH LOVE, EH.
AFTER ALL, THAT'S WHAT FAMILY IS FOR.

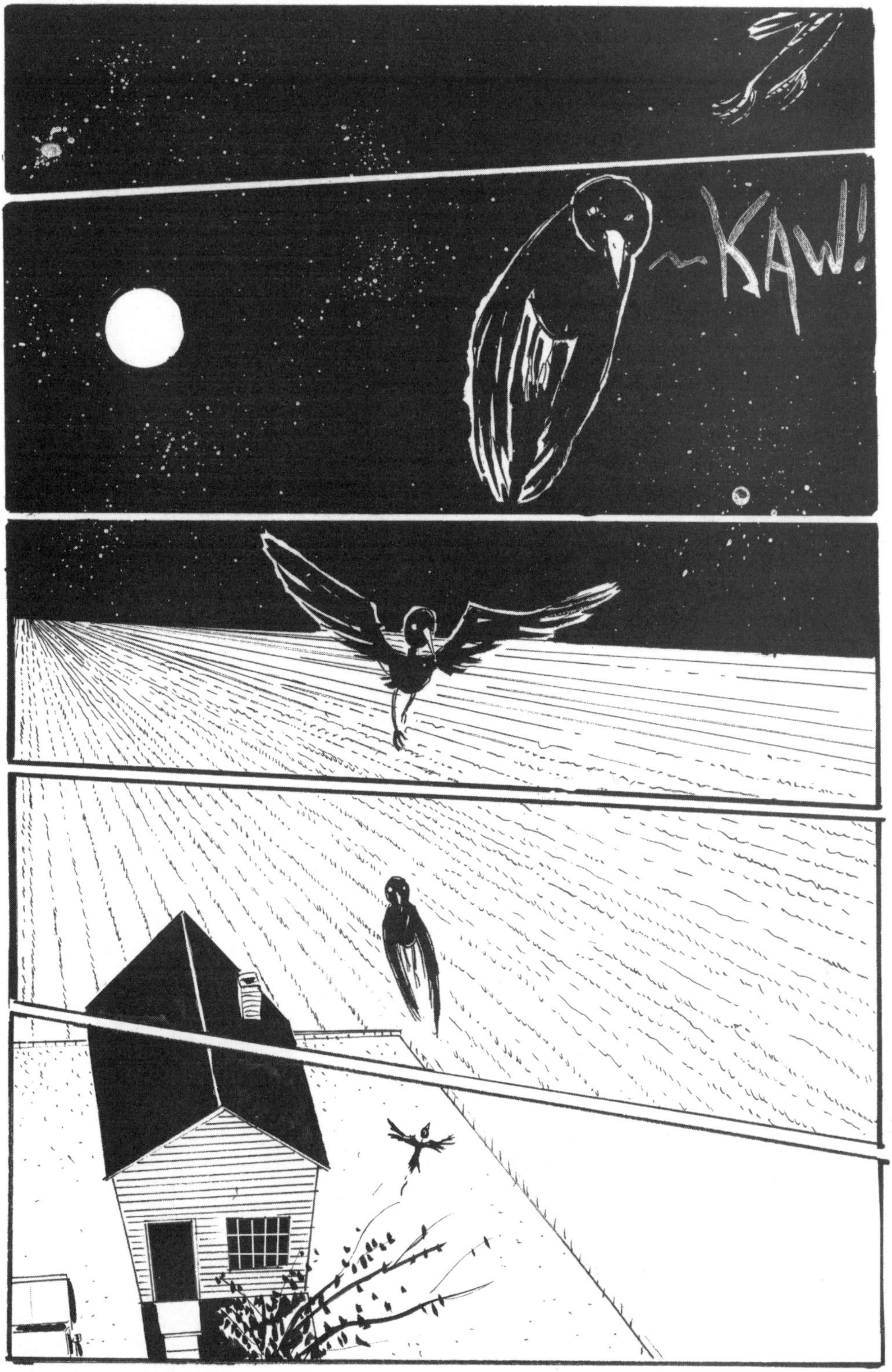
KAW!

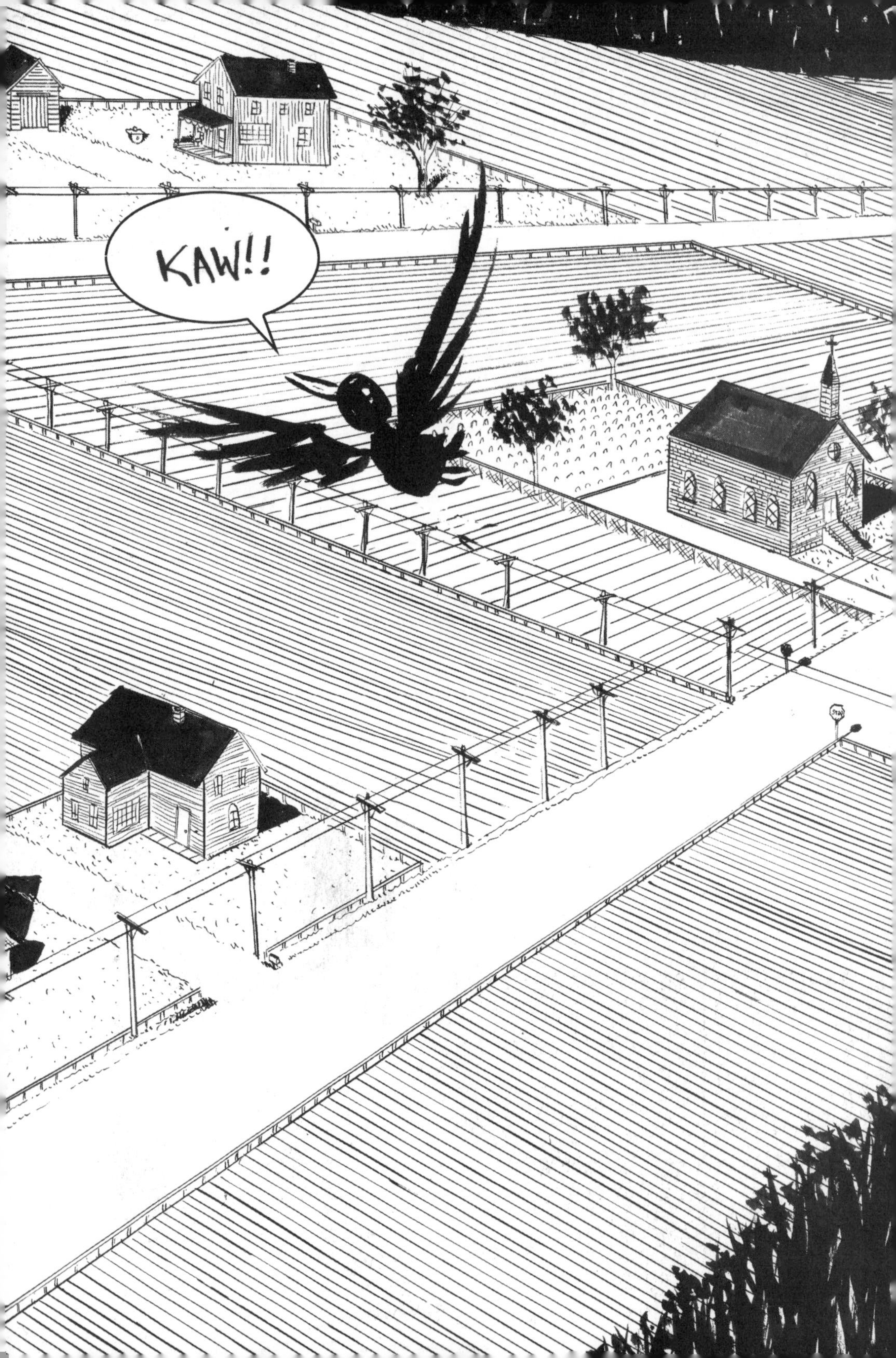
KAW!!

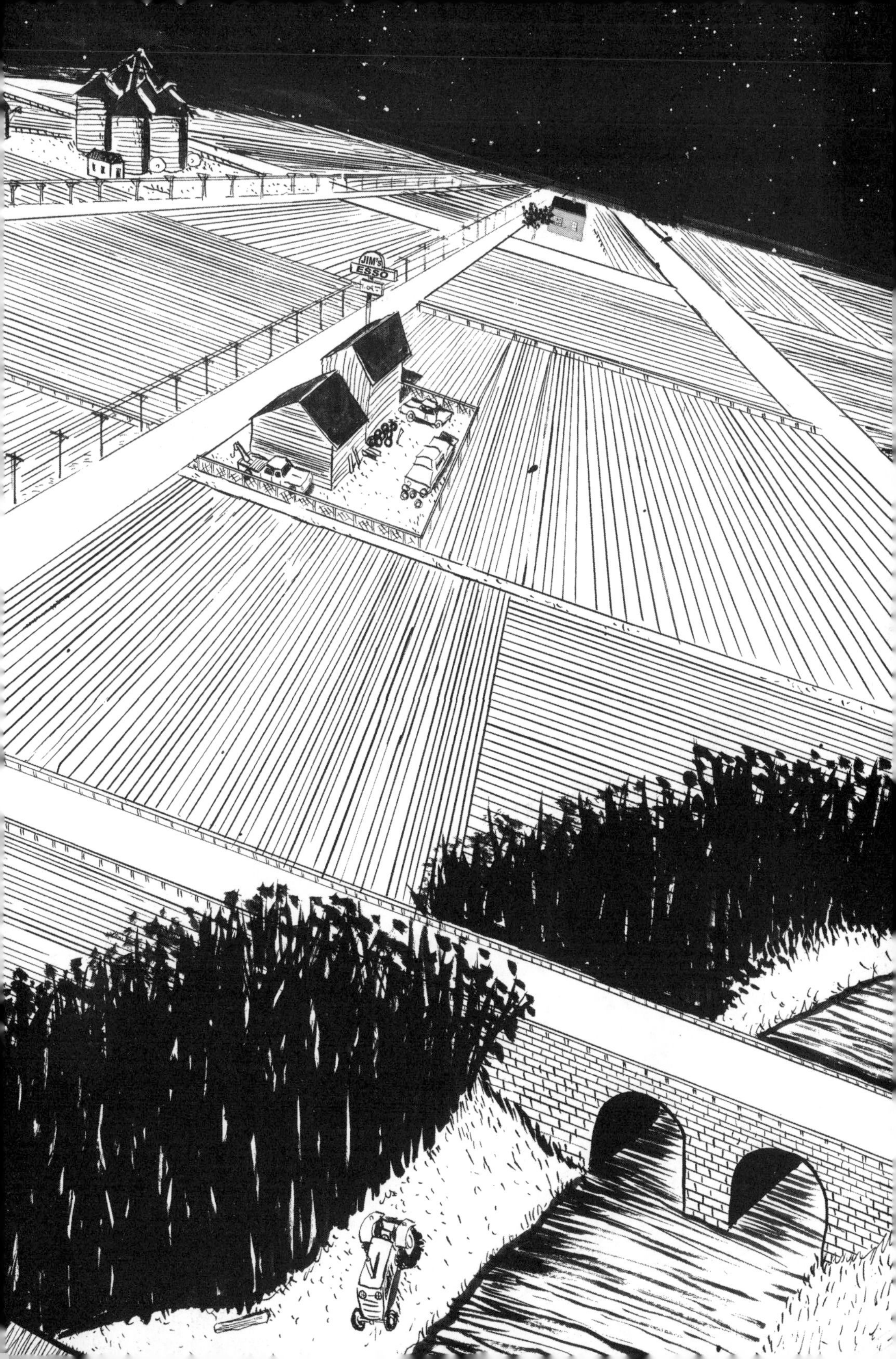
JIM's
ESSO

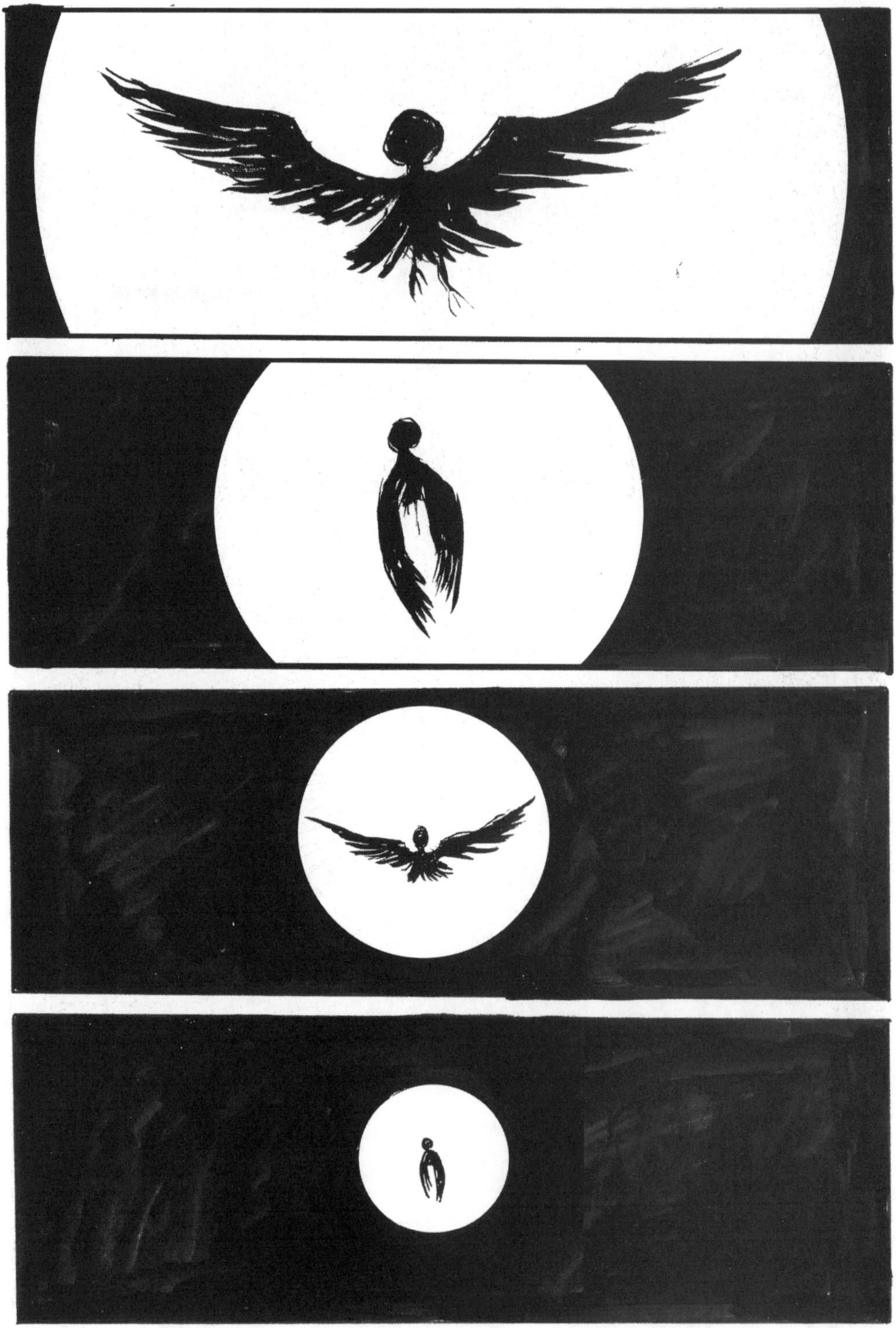

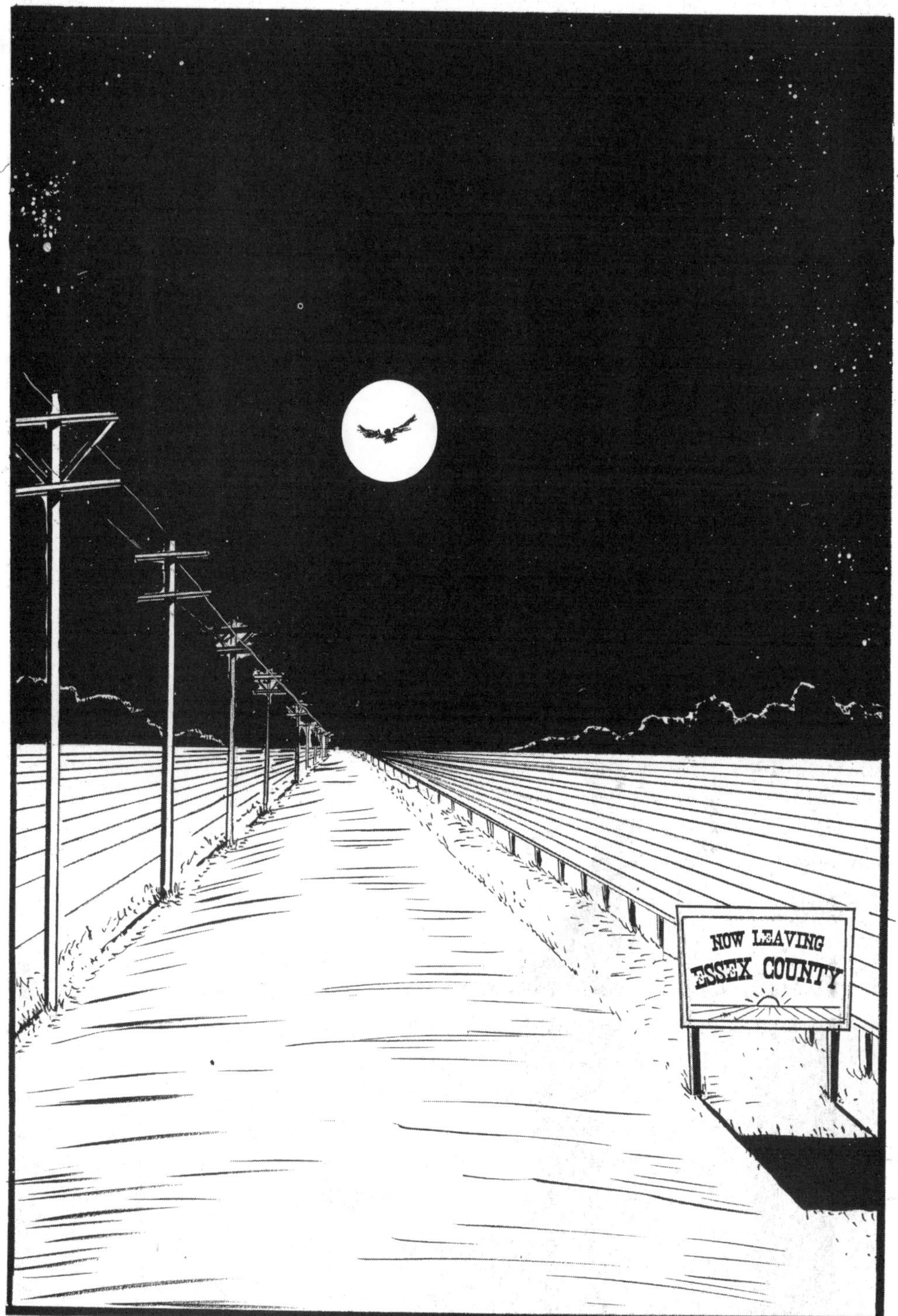
NOW LEAVING
ESSEX COUNTY

J. Lemire 2005-2008

Dedicated to my favorite superheroes, Chris and Brett.

-J

Thanks to: Chris Staros and Brett Warnock, Christopher Butcher and Peter Birkemoe at the Beguiling, John King and the guys at Dragon Lady Comics, George and Sean at Rogues Gallery Comics, Rob Venditti, Jeffrey Brown, Matt Kindt, Andy Hartzell, Andy Runton, Noel Tuazon, Leigh Walton, Mark Askwith, Zach Warton, The Flying Burritos Hockey Club, Janusz, Anna, John and everyone at La Hacienda Restaurant, and to all my friends and family.

Special thanks to Leslie-Anne Green.

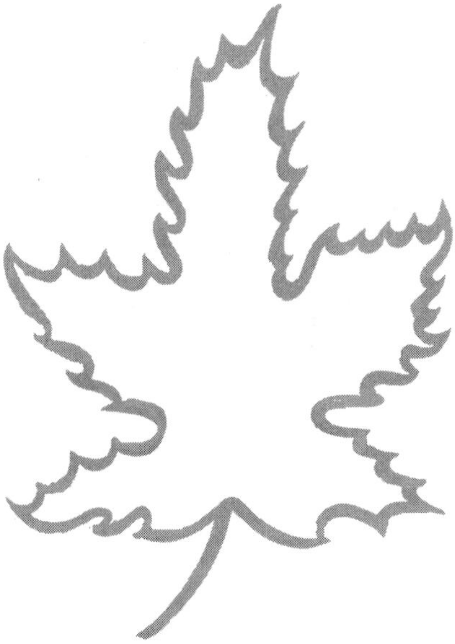